Leadership and Command
in the American Civil War

edited by

Steven E. Woodworth

Manufactured in the United States of America

Leadership and Command in the American Civil War
edited by Steven E. Woodworth

© 1996 Savas Woodbury Publishers
1475 S. Bascom Avenue, Suite 204,
Campbell, California 95008 (800) 848-6585

Includes bibliographic references and index

Printing Number
10 9 8 7 6 5 4 3 2

ISBN 1-882810-00-7

This book is printed on fifty-five pound
Glatfelter acid-free paper

The paper in this book meets or exceeds the guidelines for permanence
and durability of the Committee on Production Guidelines for Book
Longevity of the Council on Library Resources

TABLE OF CONTENTS

LIST OF MAPS AND ILLUSTRATIONS

Ole Joe in Virginia
Joseph E. Johnston's 1861-1862 Period of Command in the East

The Detachment of Longstreet Considered
Braxton Bragg, James Longstreet, and the Chattanooga Campaign

A Failure of Command?
A Reassessment of the Generalship of Edwin V. Sumner and the Federal II Corps at the Battle of Antietam

continued

LIST OF MAPS AND ILLUSTRATIONS (continued)

The Seeds of Disaster
The Generalship of George E. Pickett After Gettysburg

On Smaller Fields
Gen. P. G. T. Beauregard and the Bermuda Hundred Campaign

Introduction

The exercise of command has always fascinated students of the history of warfare. From Thucydides' critique of the generalship of Nicias to modern assessments of the actions of H. Norman Schwartzkopf in the 1991 Gulf War, historians have asked what shaped the thinking and informed the decisions of the men who bore the lonely responsibility of command. The American Civil War, as the central event and most cataclysmic struggle in United States history, has also attracted deep interest both from scholars and interested laymen. It follows, therefore, that Civil War commanders have received a considerable amount of attention. Why, then, another book about them?

In part, the reason for this book is that the exercise of command is in itself a process so complex as to defy simple analysis. The myriad facets of command in even a single battle, and the multitude of considerations lying behind each such decision, demand long, thorough, and painstaking consideration before yielding their full cargo of insights and lessons.

Civil War command is a subject much more complex than comparable studies in almost any other war. The Civil War occurred in a unique period of transition between the traditional and the modern. It was, in at least some sense, a modern war. Military technology and associated tactics had changed little in a century and a half. Then, in the decade before the guns of Fort Sumter in April 1861, technology was revolutionized to the extent that Civil War officers had to face a battlefield in many ways more similar to that of the Somme or Verdun of World War I than the Mexican War battlefields on which many of them had first practiced the art of war.

Aside from technological changes, the Civil War was different from anything in American experience simply because of its sheer mass. A single example will illustrate this fact. When the opposing armies of Ulysses S. Grant and Albert Sidney Johnston clashed at Shiloh early in the war, they suffered and inflicted in two days more casualties than United States forces had suffered in the American Revolution, the War of 1812, and the Mexican War combined.

And the Civil War was a people's war, peculiarly so as it related to its corps of officers. The total number of trained officers in the United States in 1860 was an insignificant fraction of the number of officers that would be needed to lead the mass armies of the Civil War. This meant that, of necessity, common men—the most un-military of civilians but a few months or even weeks before—were to become the leaders of combat troops in America's bloodiest armed struggle. College professors, lawyers, businessmen, and planters faced the life-and-death decisions of the battlefield. They did so with remarkably little training and few standard doctrines or procedures—a fact that makes their exercise of command fascinatingly idiosyncratic. The common man had always formed the cannon fodder of mass armies. Now for one of the first times in history, the common man filled the role normally taken by the privileged classes in Europe; he was to lead those armies. Even the West Point-trained professionals had dealt with nothing on this scale before, and they too would be cast largely upon their own good sense and native intelligence to find the methods necessary for success.

All of this means that while the victors have been celebrated and the vanquished excoriated several hundred times over, the real study of the complexities of Civil War command is still in its infancy. Much more can be learned, both about the nature of the war, and about what it meant to be an American in the 1860s.

To gain such insight, historians must begin to ask new questions and pursue new lines of inquiry. Rather than simply judging that successful actions were wise and that failed actions foolish, questions about the bases for those actions must be asked. Was a successful operation favored by apparent chance, or did a residue of good planning lie behind it? Was a failed endeavor based on a flawed plan or might that plan have succeeded under the normal conditions of war? What options did the commanders have before them? A battlefield is no chessboard, and its participants are not immune to illness, fatigue, emotional stress, and human failings. What factors beyond the sterile calculus of strategic treatises and sand-table exercises entered into the decisions of these men? What did the officers hope to accomplish? And what did their contemporaries expect of them? In short, in what ways have the telling and re-telling of Civil War "history" worked to obscure the real story—and the living, breathing, individuals who were part of it? This volume and its successors will address such questions.

Noted Civil War historian Richard M. McMurry opens this volume of essays with "Ole Joe in Virginia: Joseph E. Johnston's 1861-1862 Period of Command in the East." Few Civil War commanders have generated more controversy than Confederate Joe Johnston. Much ink has been spilled on the questions of whether Johnston's performance as Western Theater commander and, subsequently, as the leader of the Army of Tennessee, was brilliant or pathetic. McMurry's monograph addresses instead the issue of how Johnston's Civil War service during the war's first year in Virginia both foreshadowed and helped to determine the course of his later commands in other theaters of the war. His article possesses all of the historical insight, sagacity, and graceful writing that we have come to expect from McMurry's pen.

While Johnston may be controversial, the same cannot be said of Braxton Bragg. Bragg is beyond controversy. Since disgruntled subordinates turned their considerable political and public relations influence against him less than six months after his accession to command of the Confederate Army of Tennessee, it has been an article of faith among students of the war that Bragg was a perfectly atrocious general in virtually every sense of the word. Edward Carr Franks, an economics Ph.D and long-time student of the Civil War, dares to question this monolithic orthodoxy, at least in connection with one of Bragg's most harshly—and perhaps unfairly—criticized actions: the detachment of James Longstreet's Confederate divisions to East Tennessee during the late fall of 1863, and its impact on the battles for Chattanooga. The title of Franks' article, "The Detachment of Longstreet Considered: Braxton Bragg, James Longstreet and the Chattanooga Campaign," is meant to suggest that this important episode has not been carefully considered on its own merits. Thus, it cannot be "reconsidered" until it is first "considered." Franks' essay will certainly convince some anti-Bragg students that his detachment of Longstreet was reasonable and perhaps a necessary strategic move. It will give all thoughtful students of the war in the West cause for serious reflection.

Edwin Vose Sumner, a Federal corps commander during the war's early years, has been less vilified than simply dismissed into obscurity as an aged mediocrity. Sumner has been harshly criticized for his leadership (or lack thereof) of the II Corps at Antietam on September 17, 1862. He has been particularly chastised for launching John Sedgwick's division headlong into the West Woods, where it was slaughtered by the Rebels. Marion Vince Armstrong, a former United States army officer and professionally-trained historian, questions the conventional wisdom in his in-depth, revisionistic study entitled "A Failure of Command? A Reassessment of the Generalship of Maj. Gen. Edwin V. Sumner and the Federal II Corps at the Battle of Antietam." In what will surely be recognized as the definitive account of this general's actions on America's bloodiest day, Armstrong provides a careful and detailed analysis of the ever-changing battlefield situation and the information actually available to Sumner as the fighting unfolded. His rich knowledge of Civil War tactical procedures, coupled with a keen appreciation of the undulating terrain surrounding Sharpsburg, brings to life the battlefield dilemmas faced by an officer long dismissed as incompetent. The "fog of war" perspective employed by Armstrong effectively places the readers in Sumner's boots as his divisions march across Antietam Creek and into the smoky East Woods.

Far from forgotten, George E. Pickett has been frozen in memory at a particular time and place. Pickett of the perfumed ringlets remains, as if etched in stone as durable as any granite monument, sending his doomed division to its glorious destruction at Gettysburg on the afternoon of July 3, 1863. For Civil War history, Pickett is the creature of a day. But who was this man? What sort of subordinate and commanding officer was he? And what Civil War career lay ahead of him as his broken brigades reeled back from Cemetery Ridge? University of Georgia historian Lesley J. Gordon explores these and other issues in "The Seeds of Disaster: The Generalship of George E. Pickett After Gettysburg." Here, finally, is a thoughtful presentation of Pickett the person, an active participant in multiple facets of the Civil War rather than merely the historical equivalent of the mute statuary of the southern Pennsylvania field his men helped to make famous. The fascinating and little-known episodes of Pickett's service after the Gettysburg Campaign, as detailed within Gordon's article, will enlighten all students of the Civil War, especially those who focus on the Army of Northern Virginia and its cadre of general officers.

Bringing up the rear in this compendium of essays is my own contribution, "On Smaller Fields: Gen. P. G. T. Beauregard and the Bermuda Hundred Campaign," which addresses the performance of that flamboyant Confederate commander during the critical early phases of the May 1864 fighting south of Richmond, Virginia. In particular, this essay attempts to assess the degree to which Beauregard contributed to the Confederate success in that campaign.

Steven E. Woodworth
Toccoa Falls College, Toccoa Falls, Georgia

Richard M. McMurry

Historian Richard McMurry is the author of several notable studies, including *John Bell Hood and the War for Southern Independence* (Lexington, 1982), winner of the Simon Baruch University Award of the United Daughters of the Confederacy, and *Two Great Rebel Armies: An Essay in Confederate Military History* (Chapel Hill, 1989). He regularly contributes book reviews and articles to a variety of publications, and is a frequent leader of Civil War battlefield tours. McMurry makes his home in Americus, GA.

Ole Joe in Virginia

Joseph E. Johnston's 1861-1862
Period of Command in the East

The main Confederate military force that operated in the Eastern Theater of the Civil War is so closely identified with its most renowned commander that it is often referred to simply as "Lee's army," "Lee's force," "Lee's men," or—on more formal occasions—"Lee's Army of Northern Virginia." Another variation is "Lee's starving and ill-equipped Army of Northern Virginia."[1]

In the spring of 1861, Robert E. Lee did play an important role in the organization first of the "Provisional Army of [the state of] Virginia," the nucleus of the Rebels' main eastern army, and then of the Confederate forces that evolved into the Army of Northern Virginia.[2] Lee, however, did not assume actual command of the secessionists' major eastern army until June 1, 1862. Once he took command, Lee seized the soul of that army and made it uniquely his. Its organization,

---

1

For examples of this near-universal practice, see Craig L. Symonds, *Joseph E. Johnston: A Civil War Biography* (New York, 1992), pp. 244, 339, 343; Jeffrey N. Lash, *Destroyer of the Iron Horse: General Joseph E. Johnston and Confederate Rail Transport, 1861-1865* (Kent, 1991), pp. 111, 158, 199, note 7; and Peter Cozzens, *This Terrible Sound: The Battle of Chickamauga* (Urbana, 1992), p. 203.

2

For Robert E. Lee's role in the spring and summer of 1861, see Douglas Southall Freeman, *R. E. Lee: A Biography*, 4 vols. (New York, 1934-1935), vol. 1, pp. 472-540; and Clifford Dowdey, *Lee* (Boston, 1965), pp. 139-163.

administration, discipline, esprit, elan, and its confidence were but reflections of Lee's personality, intelligence, dedication, self-discipline, competence, and character. Just before the end of the war one of Lee's generals told him: "There is no country. There has been no country, general, for a year or more. You are the country to these men. They have fought for you. Without pay or clothes, or care of any sort, their devotion to you and faith in you have been the only things which have held this army together. If you demand the sacrifice, there are still left thousands of us who will die for you."[3]

The association of Lee with the Army of Northern Virginia is so close that it often obscures the fact that for the first one-fourth of its existence "Lee's army" was, in fact, commanded by other officers.

The force that was to become "Lee's army" began to gather around Manassas Junction in north-central Virginia soon after the Old Dominion seceded on April 17, 1861. On May 31, President Jefferson Davis, recently arrived in Richmond from the Confederacy's first capital in Montgomery, Alabama, assigned Brig. Gen. Pierre Gustave Toutant Beauregard to command at Manassas and directed him to organize the troops assembling there into a field army. Beauregard scurried north to his new post, formally took command on June 3, and plunged enthusiastically into his new assignment.[4]

While Beauregard busied himself at Manassas, troops were also gathering at other points across the state. The most important of these

3
    John Sergeant Wise, *The End of an Era*, ed. Curtis Carroll Davis (New York, 1965), pp. 434-435. Thomas Lawrence Connelly has argued that Lee's exalted reputation is the product of a post-1865 "Lee cult" which glorified its hero at the expense of other former Rebels and thereby elevated him to an heroic position that he did not hold during the war. Albert Castel answered Connelly, pointing out that while Lee's status was enhanced after the war, there is overwhelming contemporary evidence that Lee—while not a lesser god or even a saint—was, almost from the first, a man who enjoyed wide respect and even adulation. My research supports Castel. Connelly, "Robert E. Lee and the Western Confederacy: A Criticism of Lee's Strategic Ability," *Civil War History*, vol. 15 (1969), pp. 116-132, and *The Marble Man: Robert E. Lee and His Image in American Society* (New York, 1977); Castel, "The Historian and the General: Thomas L. Connelly versus Robert E. Lee," *Civil War History*, vol. 16 (1970), pp. 50-63.

4
    Colonel Philip St. George Cocke, of the Virginia state army, and Brig. Gen. Milledge L. Bonham, of the Confederate army, had successively commanded in the Manassas area prior to Beauregard's arrival. For Beauregard's work at Manassas, see T. Harry Williams, *P. G. T. Beauregard: Napoleon in Gray* (Baton Rouge, 1955), pp. 67-77; and Douglas Southall Freeman, *Lee's Lieutenants: A Study in Command*, 3 vols. (New York, 1942-1944), vol. 1, pp. 1-13.

satellite aggregations was concentrated at Harpers Ferry in the lower Shenandoah Valley, some fifty miles northwest of Manassas. Even before he left Montgomery for Richmond, Davis had dispatched Brig. Gen. Joseph E. Johnston to command at Harpers Ferry. Johnston assumed his new post on May 24, and was soon hard at work organizing his men into a field army.[5]

In mid-July separate Union forces advanced against both Beauregard and Johnston. Each Federal army outnumbered the Rebels in its front, and the secessionists' only hope was to combine their strength against one of the invading columns. To that end Johnston, who had evacuated Harpers Ferry on June 15 and shifted to a position near Winchester, hastened eastward with most of his army. He hoped to win a victory at Manassas before the Yankees there were reinforced by their men from the Valley. Owing to the timid conduct of the Federal commander in the Valley—who did not realize that Johnston had gone—the Confederates were able to unite their forces at Manassas and triumph there on July 21.[6]

The merger of Johnston's troops with those of Beauregard created the largest field force yet assembled by the Confederacy. Johnston, as the senior officer, took command of the combined armies in the Manassas area. From the time of his arrival at Manassas on the afternoon of July 20 until he toppled, wounded, from his horse at Seven Pines some ten months later, Joseph E. Johnston commanded the embryonic Army of Northern Virginia.[7]

---

[5]
For Johnston's activities at Harpers Ferry and in the lower Valley, see Symonds, *Johnston*, pp. 101-111; and Gilbert E. Govan and James W. Livingood, *A Different Valor: The Story of General Joseph E. Johnston, C. S. A.* (Indianapolis, 1956), pp. 34-44.

[6]
For the campaign and battle, see William C. Davis, *Battle at Bull Run: A History of the First Major Campaign of the Civil War* (New York, 1977).

[7]
For Johnston's wounding, see Symonds, *Johnston*, p. 172; Govan and Livingood, *A Different Valor*, p. 156; and Freeman, *Lee's Lieutenants*, 1, p. 262. Beauregard's army at Manassas was usually called the Army of the Potomac; Johnston's Valley force was often designated the Army of the Shenandoah. When the latter was absorbed into the former, the name Army of the Potomac was usually used to refer to the combined force, although the designation "Army of Northern Virginia" occasionally appears in the records from the winter of 1861-1862, especially after November when the Department of Northern Virginia was created. What had been Beauregard's old command was

When Johnston was disabled on May 31, 1862, the command devolved onto his ranking subordinate Maj. Gen. Gustavus Woodson Smith. Almost immediately, however, Smith suffered some sort of nervous breakdown that rendered him even more completely unfit to command the army than he already was. Realizing that Johnston would be incapacitated for a long, indefinite period, Davis tapped his military adviser, Gen. Robert E. Lee, to take over the army, which was then backed up to the gates of Richmond. The Army of Northern Virginia never had another commander.

Johnston was unable to return to duty until November 1862. By then Lee had proved so successful that there simply was no possibility of his being removed so that Johnston could resume his old post. Davis, therefore, gave Johnston a new and even more important assignment in the West. For the remainder of the war Johnston served in Tennessee, Mississippi, Georgia, and North Carolina.[8]

Three men, Beauregard, Johnston, and Smith, successively directed the army before it passed into Lee's hands. Smith's fleeting moment of command made no impact on the army or the Confederacy. Beauregard's short period at the top came in the hectic early weeks of the war when everything was fluid and therefore left but slight imprint on the army and the country. Johnston's ten months of command in Virginia, however, did have a lasting effect—not on the army but on him and the nation. In many ways the events of those ten months were significant harbingers of the Confederacy's ultimate fate.

The Joseph E. Johnston who arrived at Harpers Ferry in late May 1861 was widely regarded as one of the more promising military men in America. He had graduated from the United States Military Academy in the Class of 1829 and had spent virtually his entire adult life in the army. He had compiled a distinguished record in operations against the Florida Indians and the Mexicans, and had suffered several wounds while

then designated the District of the Potomac. After Lee took command in June 1862, the name Army of Northern Virginia was used (except as noted above). I have used the army's most famous name throughout for simplicity's sake.

8
For Johnston's assignment to the West and his unhappy months there, see Symonds, *Johnston*, pp. 187-335 and 344-357; and Govan and Livingood, *A Different Valor*, pp. 162-376.

accumulating honors and promotions. In April 1861, when he resigned to follow his native Virginia into the Confederacy, he was the Quartermaster General of the United States Army.

Two significant, and in some ways consuming, themes ran through Joseph E. Johnston's military career. One was a long, partially subconscious, rivalry with Robert E. Lee. Craig Symonds, Johnston's most recent biographer, calls it "his latent jealousy of his old friend and rival." The second was a burning, and in the end self-immolating, absorption with his "rank." Overt "ambition [for promotion] drove Johnston almost relentlessly," writes historian Steven Newton.

These two themes merged during Johnston's 1861-1862 service in Virginia and affected his attitude and actions for the rest of the war. The result was what Symonds labels "the one great tragedy of. . .[Johnston's] life. . .his feud with President Jefferson Davis." "His failure to achieve the whole-hearted support of Davis," write two of the general's other biographers, "was responsible for the major part of his difficulties."[9]

Johnston and Lee had known each other since at least their days as West Point classmates, and their families' connections went back at least another generation. During the War for Independence Johnston's father had served in a unit commanded by General Henry "Light-Horse Harry" Lee, the father of Robert E. Lee. At the Military Academy Robert E. Lee ("clearly the superior of the two," notes Symonds) eclipsed Joseph E. Johnston both academically and militarily. In their senior year Lee served as adjutant, the highest post in the Corps of Cadets. Johnston, after a brief stint as a cadet lieutenant, was reduced to private (possibly for reasons of health). During his Academy career, Johnston received a total of fifty-five demerits; Lee received none. Lee graduated second among the forty-six men in the class; Johnston a respectable thirteenth.

---

[9]
Symonds, *Johnston,* pp. 126, 169, 199, 343; Steven Harvey Newton, "Joseph E. Johnston and the Defense of Richmond," dissertation, William and Mary, 1989, pp. 250-254; Govan and Livingood, *A Different Valor,* pp. 66, 159, 170. The crucial question, of course, is why Johnston failed to receive Davis' wholehearted support.

Lee was commissioned into the elite Corps of Engineers; Johnston into the less prestigious artillery.[10]

Over the following three decades Lee and Johnston moved upward through the army's hierarchy on parallel courses. Lee was usually a jump or two ahead, especially after 1836, when Johnston left the army for two years to try his luck as a civilian. Lee, for example, made captain in 1838; Johnston not until 1846.[11]

The Mexican War (1846-1848) brought distinction and promotion to both Lee and Johnston. In that conflict both served on the staff of Maj. Gen. Winfield Scott. For his outstanding service in Mexico, Lee won three brevet promotions, and after September 13, 1847, he was entitled to style himself "Brevet Colonel Lee." Johnston's heroism won for him a temporary appointment as lieutenant colonel of a regiment of light infantry, and he also received two brevet promotions. There was, however, some question over just which two brevets he had been awarded. Johnston was convinced that his two wartime brevets had jumped him three grades from captain to colonel. The War Department asserted that, in reality, his first brevet promotion had been to major and, therefore, the second had been to lieutenant colonel. Some of this confusion may have stemmed from Johnston's temporary lieutenant colonelcy. Johnston, who admitted in 1851 that he wanted promotion "more than [did] any man in the army," appealed the department's ruling. Two Secretaries of War (one of whom was Jefferson Davis) and the United States Senate all rejected his claim. In 1855 both Lee and Johnston were appointed lieutenant colonels in newly-organized cavalry regiments.[12]

10
    For the Academy career of the two men, see Freeman, *Lee*, 1, pp. 48-85; Dowdey, *Lee*, pp. 43-47; Symonds, *Johnston*, pp. 10-21; and Govan and Livingood, *A Different Valor*, pp. 14-15. Thanks to Suzanne Christoff, archivist at the Military Academy, for information on the West Point careers of the two men.

11
    The antebellum military careers of the two are covered in Freeman, *Lee*, 1, 86-447; Dowdey, *Lee*, pp. 53-133; Symonds, *Johnston*, pp. 22-98; and Govan and Livingood, *A Different Valor*, pp. 15-28.

12
    For Johnston's Mexican War brevets, see Symonds, *Johnston*, pp. 88-90. Davis' role in the matter is noted briefly in Lynda L. Crist and Mary S. Dix, eds., *The Papers of Jefferson Davis*, 8 vols. (Baton Rouge, 1985), vol. 5, pp. 440-441.

A few years later Johnston was finally able to vault ahead of Lee, but the manner in which he did so tainted his reputation and provoked unfavorable comments among some of his contemporaries. In 1860 Secretary of War John B. Floyd, who hailed from Johnston's home town of Abingdon, Virginia, and who was related to Johnston through a series of marriages and adoptions ("a kind of cousin-by-adoption," notes Symonds) came to his aid. Floyd, who has been called Johnston's "patron," overturned his predecessors' decisions and decreed that Johnston was indeed a brevet colonel as of April 12, 1847. A few months later Johnston's "patron" selected him to be the Army's new Quartermaster General. Occupation of that coveted post carried with it the "staff grade" of brigadier general. After both of these decisions, mutterings of favoritism rippled through the Army.[13]

When Johnston resigned in April 1861, he traveled to Richmond, where he found Lee a major general commanding the Virginia state forces. At Lee's suggestion, Johnston was also named a major general in the state army and placed in charge of the Virginia troops in the Richmond area. State authorities soon decided that only one major general was necessary and that that officer should be Lee. Declining an appointment as brigadier general in the state forces, Johnston hastened to Montgomery. There he was named a Confederate brigadier general (then the highest grade in the Rebel army) and ordered to Harpers Ferry.[14]

During the weeks prior to the Battle of Manassas there were some early manifestations of the tragic drama that was soon to engulf Johnston, Davis, and the Confederacy. The general had scarcely taken up his new duties at Harpers Ferry before he began to complain about his situation. He had too few troops, and the reinforcements he did receive were not trained and disciplined. His men did not have enough ammunition. He did not understand what the government wanted him to do. On the day after he assumed command he concluded that his new

---

[13]
For Johnston's selection as Quartermaster General, see Symonds, *Johnston*, pp. 81, 91; and Govan and Livingood, *A Different Valor,* pp. 25-26.

[14]
Symonds, *Johnston,* pp. 96-98; and Govan and Livingood, *A Different Valor*, pp. 29-34.

post could not be defended. "I regard Harper's [sic] Ferry as untenable by us at present against a strong enemy," he wrote. The message proved to be but the first in a long series of discouraging reports that he would send to Richmond over the next four years.[15]

Most of Johnston's requests were simply vague demands for "more" of whatever was the subject of the message. When he tried to be specific, he often contradicted himself. For example, on February 8, 1864 he stated that he needed "about 400" horses for his artillery. On February 27, he reported that his artillery required "at least 1,000 fresh horses." On February 28, he put his need at "at least 600" artillery horses. Richmond bureaucrats must have pulled out their hair and whiskers upon reading such messages.

The weeks that Johnston commanded in the lower Shenandoah Valley also brought forth hints of another and far more serious flaw in the general's makeup. The man was very reluctant to assume responsibility and to make decisions that might result in criticism. What his biographer Symonds calls "the ambiguities of high command" seemed difficult for Johnston to handle. The specific issue in this case was whether the Confederates should evacuate Harpers Ferry. Although Johnston had pronounced the place untenable and, as commander, had the authority to decide the matter, he was reluctant to abandon the town without positive orders to do so lest he be subject to criticism. Johnston seemed to hope that his pessimistic assessments of the situation in the lower Valley would lead the authorities to order him to act. Eventually,

[15]
    Symonds, *Johnston*, pp. 103-107. "I am too late," Johnston telegraphed to Davis on May 13, 1863, just hours after he arrived in Jackson, Mississippi, in response to orders from the president to take charge of the effort to save Vicksburg. Ibid., p. 205. "I consider saving Vicksburg hopeless," he informed Davis on June 15, 1863. Joseph E. Johnston, *Narrative of Military Operations Directed During the Late War Between the States* (Bloomington, 1959), p. 511. On December 28, 1863, one day after he had taken command of the Army of Tennessee, Johnston informed Davis, "This army is now far from ready to resume the offensive. It is deficient in numbers, arms, subsistence stores, and field transportation." He immediately began to bombard Richmond with requests for small arms, new general officers, permission to reorganize the army into three corps, permission to restore the divisional organization that had existed prior to the fall of 1863, food, shoes, bayonets, reinforcements, wagons, bridge equipment, and horses. U. S. War Department, *The War of the Rebellion: Official Records of the Union and Confederate Armies* (Washington, 1880-1902), Series I, vol. 21, pt. 3, pp. 874, 882; 32, pt. 2, pp. 511. 537, 552, 559, 560, 563-564, 644, 808-809; pt. 3, p. 882. Hereinafter cited as *OR*. All references are to volumes in Series I. *OR*, 32, pt. 2, pp. 697-698, 809, 811.

on June 13, the War Department did send a message to Johnston: "As you seem to desire. . .that the responsibility of your retirement should be assumed here. . .you will consider yourself authorized, whenever the position of the enemy shall convince you that he is about to turn your position. . .to destroy everything at Harpers Ferry. . .and retire. . .towards Winchester."

Johnston had spent several weeks hoping for this message (pleading for "orders that would absolve him of the responsibility for ordering a retreat," wrote Symonds). Soon after receiving the telegram, Johnston sent a message to the War Department denying that he had done any such thing.[16]

As the afterglow of the Rebels' Manassas victory slowly faded, Johnston found himself burdened with the myriad administrative tasks of an army commander. Over the next six months, so it must have seemed, virtually every issue that arose became a cause of friction between the general at army headquarters and the president's government in Richmond. At the end of the winter of 1861-1862—"that long, dreary winter of discord and difficulty, in many ways the most critical [period] of Johnston's entire professional career"—the chief executive and the army commander were so at loggerheads that it was impossible for them even to communicate on any meaningful level.[17]

Davis and Johnston were both thin-skinned men, each all too aware of his position, overly conscious of his status, jealous of his prerogatives, possessed of far too much dignity for his own good, and constantly on guard against any effort to infringe upon his "rights." Despite their unseemly concern with status, however, they might have put their country above themselves, worked through their lesser differences, and

---

[16]
Symonds, *Johnston*, pp. 107-109. Pressure on Johnston's position became so great that he was finally compelled to evacuate Harpers Ferry a short time before he received the War Department telegram. The points that need stressing, however, are his anguish at having to make such a risky (to his reputation) decision, and the impression that his conduct obviously created among War Department officials.

[17]
Ibid., p. 125; Govan and Livingood, *A Different Valor*, p. 89.

built an effective partnership had not one of Davis' actions been perceived by the general as a cruel, unjust rebuke. The president denied Johnston the "rank" that the general believed to be rightfully his.

The problem arose from some fuzzy and incompletely-thought-out Confederate military legislation. By two different statutes approved on March 6 and 14, 1861, the Rebel Congress created a small "Regular Army" for the new nation and authorized the appointment of five brigadier generals as that army's highest-ranking officers. The second of these laws provided that officers who left the United States Army prior to September 15, 1861, to join the Confederacy and who were appointed to "original vacancies" in the Secessionist forces would hold their Confederate commissions as of "the same date, so that the relative rank of officers of each grade shall be determined by their former commissions in the U. S. Army." The obvious intent of the legislation was to ensure that a Confederate officer would outrank other Confederate officers of the same grade if he had outranked those men in the United States Army.

A third law, enacted on May 16, 1861, provided among other things for a new position in the Regular Army—that of "full general," the "highest military grade known to the Confederate States." This law specified that the five previously authorized brigadier general positions would be redesignated as the "full general" positions. Finally, these laws provided that promotion through the grade of colonel would be "according to seniority." General officers, however, were to be appointed "by selection from the Army."

When Rebel lawmakers specified that rank within each Confederate grade was to be based upon an officer's previous standing in the United States Army, they did not clearly and completely make provision for an important fact: United States Army regulations recognized three different types of grade. These were permanent (or line, or command of troops), brevet, and staff.

An officer's "permanent grade" was that which he held in the unit in which he was commissioned. (All officers below brigadier general were carried on the rolls of some unit in which they held their commissions. Promotion within the unit was by seniority.) "Brevet grades" were administrative devices that permitted an officer to be designated as holding a grade higher than his permanent grade. Many brevets were awarded for bravery performed at times when there was no permanent vacancy in the officer's unit into which he could be promoted. Others were bestowed upon officers for administrative reasons such as making it possible to assign an officer to some special duty calling for a higher grade than his permanent grade. "Staff grades" were grades held by virtue of assignment to a staff position for which a specific grade was required. In effect, both brevet and staff grades were devices for getting around legal limits on the number of officers who could hold a particular grade. When an officer was on duty with his unit, he functioned in his permanent grade. When away from the unit—on leave or detached for special duty—he went by his brevet or staff grade. Because of these different grades it was possible for a United States Army officer simultaneously to hold two or three grades, to outrank a fellow officer in one but not in another, and to be assigned to duty in any one of his grades under different circumstances. When a recently-resigned former United States officer joined the Secessionist army, should his standing in the Rebel military hierarchy be determined by his "old army" permanent grade, brevet grade, or staff grade? Confederate law was not crystal clear.

Since Joseph E. Johnston was a staff brigadier general by virtue of his 1860 appointment as Quartermaster General, he regarded himself as the highest-ranking officer who joined the Confederacy and reasoned, therefore, that he was the highest-ranking Rebel general.[18]

In early September 1861, Johnston's fragile ego received a severe jolt. Davis had finally gotten around to implementing the law of May 16, and Johnston found himself ranked fourth among Southern generals. The fact that Robert E. Lee was ranked third was, one suspects, even more galling to Johnston. On September 10, a furious Johnston sat down

---

[18]
    Johnston was clearly wrong on the point of who was the ranking former U.S. Army officer to take up arms for the Confederacy. That distinction belonged to David Emanual Twiggs of Georgia, who had been a brigadier general since June 1846, and a brevet major general since September of that year. Twiggs, however, was never a full general in the Rebel army—mostly because of his age (he was born in 1790), and his poor health. He did become a Confederate major general. Albert Sidney Johnston's appointment as a brevet brigadier general dated from November 1857.

at his desk to protest Davis' action. The general produced a bitter, 1,800-word, self-indulgent letter and then put it in his desk drawer where it smoldered for two days. On the twelfth, Johnston read over the document, dated and signed it, and sent it off to Richmond. Mailing that "ill-judged and foolish letter," observes biographer Symonds, "was the single worst decision of his professional career."

When Davis opened the envelope he found a long review of the relevant laws and Johnston's analysis of the rank of the five full generals. The document was obviously the product of a man who believed himself grievously wronged.

The president's decision as to his rank, wrote Johnston, had produced "surprise and mortification" in his mind. It was, he complained, "a violation of my rights as an officer, of the plighted faith of the Confederacy, and of the Constitution and laws of the land." He, therefore, entered an "earnest protest against the wrong which I conceive has been done me." Johnston pointed out that only his rank had been changed from what he regarded as the correct order. "It is plain then that this is a blow aimed at me only. . . .It seeks to tarnish my fair fame as a soldier and a man." It was "a studied indignity offered me."

Contrary to his usual practice, Davis—perhaps because he was ill at the time—did not offer a long legalistic rebuttal. On September 14, he sent Johnston a curt response of some three dozen words, branding the general's language "unusual," his argument "utterly one sided," and his "insinuations as unfounded as they are unbecoming."[19]

---

[19] Most of the writing about the controversy has involved labored and fruitless efforts to "prove" that one or the other of the principals was "right" in his interpretation of Johnston's status. As they often do, historians have taken a fairly simple matter and obfuscated it. The truth is that the question cannot be definitely answered in terms of whose interpretation of the law was correct because of Congress' failure to establish a clear policy regarding the different types of grade in the "Old Army." If one ranks officers only by their permanent grades, both Davis and Johnston were incorrect because Albert Sidney Johnston, whom Davis ranked second and Joseph E. Johnston placed third, would have been the ranking officer by virtue of his 1855 appointment as colonel. Samuel Cooper, whom Davis placed first and J. E. Johnston second, was a staff colonel as of July 1852. His permanent grade was captain. If one ranks by the highest grade held regardless of type, the order would have been A. S. Johnston, J. E. Johnston, Cooper, and Lee. Only Cooper and J. E. Johnston held staff grades. What Davis seems to have done was to rank Cooper by staff grade (he was a staff officer in both armies) and the others by their permanent grades (because they were troop commanders in the Rebel army). Davis once stated that he placed Lee over J. E. Johnston because Lee had ranked Johnston in the Virginia state army in which both served prior to becoming Confederate officers. See Varina Howell Davis, *Jefferson Davis: A Memoir by His Wife*, 2 vols. (New York, 1890), vol.

Neither Johnston nor Davis resurrected this disagreement during the war, but both men presented justifications in their post-1865 writings. The spat itself and the harsh tone of their 1861 correspondence combined with each man's hyperactive ego and fragile sense of self to undermine whatever possibility there might have been that the two would cooperate. Never, after mid-September 1861, would either man find it possible to trust or confide in the other.

Of Davis' reaction to his letter, Johnston later wrote, "It is said that it irritated him greatly, and that his irritation was freely expressed. The animosity against me that he is known to have entertained ever since was attributed by my acquaintances in public life, in Richmond at the time, to this letter."[20]

For the rest of the war Johnston would be constantly on guard lest Davis should discover some new way to humiliate, embarrass, and disgrace him—"to tarnish my fair fame as a soldier and a man." Within two years Johnston had come to feel at least borderline paranoia about his relations with the president. His wife and friends (and, almost certainly, he himself) had come to believe that Davis was scheming to disgrace him by bringing about his defeat on the battlefield.

2, pp. 138-158. For discussions of the issue, see *OR*, series IV, 1, pp. 605-608, 611; Symonds, *Johnston*, pp. 125-129; Govan and Livingood, *A Different Valor*, pp. 31-32, 66-71; William C. Davis, *Jefferson Davis: The Man and His Hour: A Biography* (New York, 1991), pp. 359-361; Davis, *Papers*, 7, pp. 336, 340. C. F. Eckhardt, "A Problem of Rank," *Civil War Times Illustrated*, 29, no. 6 (January-February, 1991), pp. 52-54, sheds some light on the confusing subject of brevets. Johnston's view is in his *Narrative*, pp. 70-73. The United States Army status of all these men can most conveniently be found in Francis B. Heitman, *Historical Register and Dictionary of the United States Army From Its Organization September 29, 1789, to March 2, 1903* (Gaithersburg, 1988). Newton, "Johnston and the Defense of Richmond," pp. 13-18, is the best discussion of the matter and points to a little-noticed section of the March 6, 1861, law which, Newton argues, fully justified Davis' decision. I am less sure than is Newton that this section settled the matter, but in either case, it is not clearly worded. The section, for example, permitted the use of brevets in determining rank in some situations but not in others. Johnston obviously believed that the section did not apply to his rank. Newton also presents in an appendix (p. 519) an even more seething paragraph that was omitted from the version of Johnston's letter that was sent to Davis.

20
    Johnston, *Narrative*, p. 73. See also the comments in Symonds, *Johnston*, p. 329. Newton, "Johnston and the Defense of Richmond," pp. 18-22 downplays the effect of this matter on the two men and attributes their growing antagonism to other factors—especially to the impact of Judah P. Benjamin on their relationship. Ibid., pp. 56-62. I believe that Newton underestimates the corrosive nature of the issue on the Davis-Johnston association.

For his part, Davis saw one example after another of Johnston's arrogance and incompetence. Over the following months the president would grow more and more disillusioned with Johnston. He was well aware that Johnston absolutely refused to keep the government informed about his plans and operations. By mid-1863 Davis seems to have convinced himself that the general was unable to command effectively and unwilling even to attempt to carry out government policy.

In his pain and bitterness Johnston did grow increasingly unwilling (perhaps unable) to cooperate with the government. He displayed a great deal of petty resentment at many of the orders, directives, suggestions, and inquiries that came from Richmond. Eventually, one senses, Johnston desired to sever the lines of communication between his headquarters and the capital. He adopted a cavalier attitude toward a number of matters that were of great concern to the president. It was almost as if he determined to detach himself from the Confederacy—to withdraw into what one scholar described as a "self-imposed isolation"—and to carry on the war in his own way with as little reference to the Richmond government as possible.

In late 1861, for example, Davis became enamored of a scheme to reorganize the army so that troops would be placed in brigades with other units from their state. Existing brigades had been thrown together on an ad hoc basis as the separate regiments arrived in Virginia. A brigade, therefore, might contain regiments from two or three states. Many soldiers were unhappy with such an arrangement, and Davis wrote that he received many a "disagreeable complaint" about the situation.

Creating state brigades, Davis thought, would stimulate the men's pride and improve morale. It would also—even though the president would never admit to embracing, or even being aware of, such a motive—have great political appeal. It would please the troops, their officers, the homefolk, and governors, congressmen, and other politicians from the state. It would mean that troops would almost always be commanded (at least through the brigade level) by officers from their own state. Davis was especially unhappy that regiments from his home state of Mississippi were scattered throughout the army.

Johnston, blind to Davis' political needs, saw no military reason for disturbing the existing organization of his army. He therefore was in no hurry to implement the president's wishes and—far worse—offered no real explanation for his delay. In May 1862, fourteen of the twenty-two brigades in his army still contained regiments from at least two states. "It [the delay] was foolish of him," admits biographer Symonds, "because it served mainly to diminish even further Davis' confidence in him."[21]

During the last eight months of Johnston's service in Virginia, many of the matters that arose between his headquarters, on the one hand, and the Confederate White House and War Department, on the other, were affected by the accelerating differences between the general and the president. In this atmosphere of mutual distrust normal differences of opinion became unbridged chasms across which there was no communication.

Johnston's political, military, and administrative mistakes—and he made many—that might have been chalked up to honest error, or simple inexperience with so large a command, or to inadequate support facilities were magnified by the lens of distrust. They were carefully cataloged as additional evidence of his incompetence or even of his disloyalty to the president. Messages from the government came increasingly to be resented by Johnston as unwarranted intrusions into matters best left to the army commander. Everything, it seemed, conspired to exacerbate the differences between Davis and Johnston.

Matters that aggravated the rift during the 1861-1862 period ranged from geo-political grand strategy to the mundane details of the daily administration of the army. The most serious and far reaching

---

21
Symonds, *Johnston*, pp. 133-135; Freeman, *Lee's Lieutenants*, 1, pp. 118-120, 207-208; Davis, *Davis*, p. 420; Jefferson Davis discussed the matter in *The Rise and Fall of the Confederate Government*, 2 vols. (New York, 1990), vol. 1, pp. 383-386. See Newton, "Johnston," p. 108, for comments on Davis' sensitivity to the need to balance general officer appointments among states. The 1861-1862 disputes between Davis and Johnston have been covered in many works. It would be pedantic to cite detailed specific sources for each of the examples discussed in the text. I have given sources for quotations in each section. For coverage of the winter quarrels, see Symonds, *Johnston*, pp. 125-159; Freeman, *Lee's Lieutenants*, 1, pp. 111-243; Lash, *Johnston and Confederate Rail Transport*, pp. 18-40; Davis, *Davis*, pp. 363-367, 410-416, 420-425; Govan and Livingood, *A Different Valor*, pp. 72-128, 138-144; and Newton, "Johnston and the Defense of Richmond," passim. The chapter titles in some of these works are as indicative of the deteriorating Davis-Johnston relationship as any details contained therein: "Johnston Passes a Dark Winter" and "Johnston Retreats Again," in Freeman, *Lee's Lieutenants*, 1, pp. 111-136, 148-155; and "Troubles With the War Office," in Govan and Livingood, *A Different Valor*, pp. 82-97.

disagreement was a fundamental difference about the basic strategy that the Rebels should follow. As an army commander, Johnston was concerned only with the area for which he was responsible. He believed that the Secessionists could not defend every mile of their border and that they should therefore concentrate their limited forces to fight major battles and protect important places. Johnston, wrote Douglas Southall Freeman, was "contemptuous of mere loss of ground" while he commanded in Virginia in the spring of 1862.

Johnston naturally thought that the most important part of the Confederacy was the area he had been assigned to defend. He therefore repeatedly urged Davis to strip troops from other commands and send them to reinforce the army in Virginia.[22]

Davis, on the other hand, was president of the entire country. As president he had to weigh other than military factors. Diplomatic, political, logistical, and psychological needs all seemed to dictate that the South hang on to as much of its territory as possible. Confederate state and local officials and the civilian population could hardly be expected to enthusiastically support a national government that abandoned them to the enemy. Members of Congress would be greatly displeased if the Confederacy made no effort to protect their constituents. Many troops would suffer demoralization and probably lose their ardor for the cause if the Rebel government evacuated their states and left their homes and families to the mercy of the Yankees.

In the winter of 1861-1862, for instance, Johnston urged Davis to bring Confederate troops from Georgia and the Carolinas to reinforce his army in Virginia. The president, however, was well aware of the fact that the Federals had already established footholds along the Confederacy's Atlantic coast from which they threatened to push west to cut the vital north-south railroad just a few miles inland.

---

[22] Lash, *Johnston and Confederate Rail Transport*, pp. 38-39; Govan and Livingood, *A Different Valor*, p. 89; Freeman, *Lee's Lieutenants*, 1, p. 192. In 1862 and 1863, when Johnston had gone to command in the Tennessee-Mississippi area, he urged that troops be taken from Virginia and sent to the West. The important point, it seems, was mobile. It followed Johnston as he moved about in the Confederacy. Johnston, in fact, was like almost every general. The vital point is the one he is charged with defending, and everything else should be subordinate to that purpose. As president, Davis had to worry about all the important points.

In April 1862, when Johnston and his army were transferred to the peninsula between the James and York rivers, he immediately inspected part of his new area of responsibility and rushed back to Richmond with the message that it could not long be held by the Southerners. He wanted to fall back and concentrate near the capital where he hoped to find an opportunity to fight. The government, on the other hand, wished to hold Norfolk and its great naval base for as long as it could—an impossibility if Johnston evacuated the lower peninsula. If the Rebels had to give up the peninsula, the government preferred to do so on a step-by-step basis, inflicting as many casualties as possible on the advancing Federals.

Meanwhile Lee, then acting as military adviser to Davis, argued for a strategy of using Confederate forces in the Shenandoah Valley to threaten the North and thereby induce the Yankees to siphon off troops from their army in Johnston's front. For political and military reasons, because he agreed with Lee's basic argument that it was to the Confederates' advantage to keep the enemy as far from Richmond as possible, and probably because he did not quite trust Johnston, Davis accepted Lee's recommendation. "Lee had Davis's ear and Johnston did not," notes Symonds. Lee also had a strategy far better attuned both to the realities of the situation facing the Confederacy and to Davis' own notions of how the Secessionists should conduct the war.[23]

For example, in the last weeks of Johnston's command and in the early summer when Lee had taken over, Davis did shift troops from the South Atlantic Coast area to Virginia. I have seen no direct evidence in

---

[23] Freeman, *Lee's Lieutenants*, 1, 148-154; Dowdey, *Lee*, pp. 188-191, 194-197; Symonds, *Johnston*, pp. 148-150, 152; and Davis, *Davis*, p. 414. Lee and Johnston aired their differences at an April 14 meeting at which Davis decided for the strategy advocated by Lee. See Newton, "Johnston and the Defense of Richmond," pp. 237-274. Newton also makes the point that Davis' original strategy had been that described in the text. After the early 1862 disasters in the West, however, Davis abandoned his original strategy in favor of a new scheme much closer to Johnston's views of how the war should be conducted. Once Lee arrived in Richmond, he took control of the war effort and implemented a strategy of opposing the Federals at as great a distance from Richmond as possible. Ibid., pp. 68-82. In chapters five and eight of his dissertation, Newton portrays Lee waging a skillful bureaucratic battle to dominate Davis' strategic thinking and to usurp control of the war in Virginia from Johnston. I believe that even if Lee did so, he was basically correct in his views. As the situation evolved in May 1862, Lee and Johnston both modified some of the aspects of what they advocated. As a result, their ideas became similar—at least as far as the local forces were concerned. Ibid., pp. 377-384.

the matter, but I suspect that this action was taken in part because of the widespread belief that the unhealthful summer climate of the Deep South would make it impossible for the Federals to conduct major operations there in June, July, and August. Confederate troops could therefore be moved from the area for use elsewhere without unduly exposing the region to the enemy. Transfer of Rebel troops to more healthful areas would also make it less likely that they would suffer so much from sickness.[24]

Johnston's handling of rail transport also served as an irritant in his 1861-1862 dealings with Davis. In June 1861, when he was still at Harpers Ferry, Johnston carried out a massive destruction of railroad property near Martinsburg, Virginia. Unfortunately for the Confederacy, the property belonged to the Baltimore & Ohio Railroad and that organization was not without friends in the Maryland Legislature. This egregious blunder by Johnston greatly strengthened the hand of Unionist politicians who were working assiduously to keep Maryland from joining the Confederacy.

In the early spring of 1862, when he hastily pulled his army back from its advanced positions in northern Virginia, Johnston failed to coordinate his movements with the railroads, and he neglected to see to it that his quartermaster and commissary officers worked in harmony. Johnston's inability to manage some of the elements of the withdrawal created "chaos on the railways of northern Virginia." As a result of what historian Jeffrey Lash calls "Johnston's. . .incompetence and negligence," the Secessionists had to destroy millions of dollars worth of food, clothing, ammunition, equipment, weapons, and railroad cars. Johnston, writes Lash, "adopted a defiant, noncooperative policy toward the Richmond authorities, and so almost willfully failed to use the Virginia railroads to save irreplaceable resources."

Prior to this withdrawal, Johnston was privately confident that he could remove most, if not all, of the army's vast accumulation of food,

---

[24]
    For general discussions of the influence of ideas about climate and health on the war, see Richard M. McMurry, "Marse Robert and the Fevers: A Note on the General as Strategist and on Medical Ideas as a Factor in Civil War Decision Making," *Civil War History*, Vol. 35 (1989), pp. 197-207; and Judith Lee Hallock, "'Lethal and Debilitating': The Southern Disease Environment as a Factor in Confederate Defeat," *Journal of Confederate History*, Vol. 7 (1991), pp. 51-61.

supplies, and equipment. At the same time in his official dealings with Richmond he maintained that the movement would necessitate the loss or destruction of great quantities of stores and equipment. He may have been practicing the old ploy of publicly proclaiming his assigned task to be impossible in order to escape blame if the effort failed or to claim undue credit if he succeeded.[25]

Sometimes third parties acted as catalysts on the accelerating Davis-Johnston feud. During the winter of 1861-1862 Judah P. Benjamin, who served as secretary of war from September 1861 to February 1862, was an especially irritating source of discontent. Benjamin, wrote Douglas Southall Freeman, was "a man with whom Johnston was doomed to clash ceaselessly." Symonds called Benjamin "an intolerable irritant to Johnston."

Judah Benjamin was a Louisiana politician who had had no military experience of any kind. He soon convinced himself, however, that he was competent to manage the Confederacy's military affairs. He was also exceedingly loyal to Davis (some would call him a sychophant), and he believed that no objection from an officer in the field should be allowed to offset a decision by the president. Benjamin was a skilled and in many ways arrogant lawyer. He dealt with Johnston as if he "were an adversary at the bar." Johnston was an awkward correspondent, and a self-confessed careless writer. "It was not difficult to get the better of the General," noted Freeman. "Johnston's irascibility and his lack of skill at dialectics made him appear, for some months, generally in the wrong." Benjamin's letters to Johnston were often condescending lectures on the general's conduct that "maddened and baffled" their recipient.

---

[25]
Lash, *Johnston and Confederate Rail Transport*, pp. 12-15, 27-34. Lash documents the fact that throughout the war Johnston displayed a "gross under-estimation" of how valuable railroad rolling stock was to the Confederacy. He also writes of Johnston's "one consistent approach to Southern railroads: he never hesitated to order the destruction of rolling stock or other railroad property." Ibid., pp. 14, 181, 182. Such promiscuous destruction of irreplaceable locomotives, cars, track, and other equipment exacerbated both Confederate transportation problems and Jefferson Davis' political difficulties. Railroad owners and state politicians (and sometimes they were the same individuals) were not pleased with the government when their property was wrecked with little or no attempt to save it. Newton, "Johnston and the Defense of Richmond," pp. 144-149, contends that the amount destroyed in the evacuation of Johnston's northern Virginia position has been greatly exaggerated.

The secretary dabbled in many military matters, often issuing orders directly to Johnston's subordinates and even granting furloughs to individual soldiers without consulting either Johnston or the unit commanders. When Johnston was consulted, his wishes were often ignored. On New Year's Day, 1862, a furious Johnston received an order from Benjamin to assign a particular enlisted man to a work detail. A decade after the war Johnston complained in his memoirs about "Mr. Benjamin's daily interference in its [the army's] administration and interior management." In a private letter written at the time, Johnston fumed about the "miserable little Jew" who seemed to be the source of so many of his troubles.

The best-known example of Benjamin's meddling in the army concerned Maj. Gen. Thomas J. "Stonewall" Jackson. That officer was Johnston's subordinate commanding Rebel forces in the lower Shenandoah Valley. During the winter he occupied Romney, Virginia (now in West Virginia), and stationed troops there to secure the area. When some of the men complained to Benjamin that their post at Romney subjected them to great discomfort, the secretary sent an order directly to Jackson to recall the troops. Jackson promptly wrote to Benjamin, through Johnston as required by army regulations, informing the secretary that he had received and obeyed the order and that if the secretary were going to try to manage his command from Richmond he wished to resign. Johnston and others joined the brouhaha, and in the end Jackson remained in the army and Benjamin did not bother him again. Had Johnston submitted his own resignation over this or some other incident, Davis would have had to do what he never liked to do—face up to and resolve the problem one way or the other. In this instance, as was the case in so many matters that vexed the Secessionists, Davis took no real action to deal with the underlying problem and the matter continued to fester.[26]

[26] The Benjamin-Jackson clash is covered in Freeman, *Lee's Lieutenants*, 1, pp. 122-130; Symonds, *Johnston*, p. 137; Govan and Livingood, *A Different Valor*, pp. 89-93; and Newton, "Johnston and the Defense of Richmond," pp. 22, 56-62. See also, Johnston, *Narrative*, pp. 87-94. Eli N. Evans, *Judah P. Benjamin: The Jewish Confederate* (New York, 1988), pp. 144-145, does not deal with the matter in any depth. Alfred M. Barbour, who became Johnston's chief quartermaster in December 1861, was another example of a third party who indirectly intensified the problems between Davis and Johnston. Barbour "proved incompetent, inefficient, and

One could go on compiling a long catalogue of the 1861-1862 Davis-Johnston incidents that seemed to erupt with every matter that arose between the two antagonists. The government reassigned general officers to and from the army without consultation with Johnston. The Furlough and Bounty Act of December 1861 occasioned some snide correspondence between Johnston and Benjamin over who had the responsibility for implementing it.

In February 1862 at a conference in Richmond, Johnston declared to Davis and his advisers that the position then held by his army was untenable. He also confessed such ignorance of the area to the army's rear that he was unable to specify to what point the army should retreat. The deliberations were held in strict secrecy. When Johnston returned to his hotel after the meeting, he found persons in the lobby discussing the deliberations that had taken place a short time earlier between himself and the government authorities. Neither the president nor the general could have gained much confidence in the other as a result of the day's events. Johnston had declared that he could not hold his position. It logically followed that he would have to fall back. Yet he had neglected the elementary step of studying the area in the rear of his army to locate a defensible line to which he could retreat. Davis' cabinet members had given ample proof that they could not be trusted with secret information.[27]

---

extravagantly wasteful of irreplaceable funds and resources." His appointment "represented one of the worst decisions that he [Johnston] made in the war." Barbour's general bungling of railroad matters in 1861-1862 embarrassed Johnston and led to intensified criticism of the government. The general, however, was not blameless. He and Barbour managed to create "what eventually became insuperable logistical problems" that turned Johnston's early 1862 withdrawal from advanced positions in northern Virginia into chaos. See Lash, *Johnston and Confederate Rail Transport*, pp. 22-28, 30. Louis T. Wigfall, at whose Richmond house Johnston lived while recovering from his Seven Pines wound, was a mortal enemy of President Davis and another person who acted as a catalyst to intensify the differences between the president and the general. See Symonds, *Johnston*, pp. 175-184, and *passim*.

[27] Symonds, *Johnston*, p. 145; Johnston, *Narrative*, p. 97; Newton, "Johnston and the Defense of Richmond," pp. 93-101, 132, 137-138. Newton doubts the truth of Davis' allegation (made in February 1865) that Johnston was ignorant of the area south of his army's position. It may have been that Johnston's experience of the previous day with politicians' inability to keep secrets led him to plead ignorance as a way of keeping details of his plans from becoming public. Ibid., pp.

At a dinner party one evening Johnston publicly and emphatically expressed the opinion that the Confederacy could not survive with Benjamin as secretary of war. Anti-Davis members of Congress were soon gleefully quoting the general in their incessant attacks on the administration. In March 1862 when he pulled his army back from Centreville, Virginia, Johnston did not inform Davis until after the event because he feared that the information would quickly become public. On May 31, 1862, the president went out to army headquarters to see Johnston. The general saw Davis arrive, pretended that he had not seen him, and rode off into the battle, where he was wounded.[28]

Although Davis sincerely regretted Johnston's Seven Pines wounds, the general's absence from the army in Virginia must have come as a relief to the harried chief executive. By the time Johnston fell, his differences with Davis had become so serious that it was unlikely that he and the president would ever have worked well together.

Robert E. Lee, in contrast to Johnston, proved to be a commander who understood the Confederacy's geo-political situation, his own role as an army commander, and—of greatest importance—his status relative to the president. He was also very skillful at working with others and within the system to get what he wanted. As historian William C. Davis has pointed out, Lee also had before him Johnston's example of how not to get along with Davis and he profited from his predecessor's experience. Lee labored to keep the chief executive informed of his

---

95-96, 185-189. In the spring of 1862, after Johnston was overruled in the matter of defending the lower peninsula, he held the fortified lines at Yorktown for several weeks—all the while convinced that he would soon have to abandon them. When he evacuated the position on May 3-4, 1862, he had made no provision to remove, destroy, or even disable the heavy guns at the site. Fifty-three such weapons were left to fall into Federal hands. Freeman, *Lee's Lieutenants*, 1, p. 155. In the period from late December 1863 to mid-May 1864, Johnston, then commanding the Army of Tennessee, was at Dalton, Georgia. Johnston believed that his position there could not be held, but he neglected to scout the area to the south. As a result, the Federals used an unguarded mountain gap (Snake Creek Gap) to flank him out of Dalton. A few days later Johnston retreated to Adairsville, where he believed the terrain would allow his army to hold its ground. Upon reaching the area, Johnston discovered that the ground did not offer the advantages he had anticipated, and he had to continue his retreat. Johnston, *Narrative*, pp. 277-278, 319-320. For more than four months Johnston had neglected to prepare for the situation that would inevitably arise if he were forced to abandon a position that he believed to be untenable.

28
Symonds, *Johnston*, pp. 138, 145-147, 170; Davis, *Davis*, pp. 411-412, 481; Newton, "Johnston and the Defense of Richmond," pp. 97-100.

situation and of what he was attempting to accomplish. He was careful to show proper deference to the president and to subordinate his military operations to the government's policies. Lee did not repeat Johnston's fatal mistake (after that general's May 1862 wound) of hobnobbing with anti-Davis politicians and newspapers and of allowing himself to be used by them in their attacks on the president and his government.

In the fall of 1862, for example, when Lee had the chance to institute a major reorganization of his army, he was careful to group regiments by states. A few weeks later he held his army in position at Fredericksburg rather than fall back to the North Anna River where, for purely military purposes, he preferred to make a stand. He did so because Davis did not want to abandon more territory.

When Davis found that he could trust Lee to follow the government's policies and to keep the authorities informed, he felt less need to watch over his general's shoulder and to intervene in the army's internal affairs. Davis also found that he could rely upon Lee for solid advice. The new commander had the moral courage to act without specific orders when the situation required him to do so. Like his Union counterpart, Abraham Lincoln, Davis at last found a general upon whom he could depend. The result was one of the most successful political-military teams in American history.[29]

While Davis and Lee were forging the powerful partnership that brought the Confederacy very close to independence, the president's relationship with Johnston continued to deteriorate. Johnston spent the summer of 1862 in Richmond recuperating from his Seven Pines wounds. During much of that time he and his wife lived in the house of Louis T. Wigfall, a former general in the Confederate army and then a

---

[29]
    Dowdey, *Lee* , pp. 326-327. In late 1862 and in the spring of 1863, for example, Johnston would not exercise his authority to order troops to move between Tennessee and Mississippi even though Davis had put him in command in the West to coordinate the defense of those two areas. In June 1864, Lee demonstrated his willingness to act on his own when there was not time to consult with Davis. Symonds, in *Johnston*, pp. 201-203, 213, defends Johnston's actions, but the point here is that Johnston would not use the authority that Davis gave him. See also, Dowdey, *Lee*, pp. 478-479.

senator from Texas. Wigfall was also emerging as a leader of the anti-Davis bloc in the Rebel Congress.

In November 1862 Johnston reported himself once again fit for duty. Davis assigned him to direct Confederate forces in a huge territorial command embracing Tennessee, Mississippi, and Alabama. The president envisioned Johnston's role as that of a coordinator who would move troops from one part of his command to another to meet crises as they arose.

Even before he left Richmond for the West, Johnston began to complain about the command arrangement to which he was assigned.[30] Once in the West, he again proved unwilling to assume responsibility and to exercise the authority Davis had given him. Concluding that he could not depend on Johnston, Davis once again began to give orders directly to some of Johnston's subordinates. By the summer of 1863, the misunderstanding between the two men was so great that in May, June, and early July, Johnston believed that his command had been reduced to the Rebel forces in Mississippi. Davis, on the other hand, thought that Johnston was also still in command of the forces in Tennessee.[31]

In Mississippi, in the spring and summer of 1863, Johnston once again was ignorant of or chose to ignore government railroad policy. Once again he was responsible for the loss of massive quantities of invaluable railroad equipment. Once again he and Davis were unable to reach agreement as to what policy the Rebels should pursue.[32]

Much the same thing happened in Georgia in 1864 when Johnston commanded the Confederate army defending the northern part of that state. He and Davis were never able to agree upon—or even to discuss seriously—a plan for the campaign or what the Confederate objective should be. Johnston once again proved oblivious to the president's

---

30
    Lash, *Johnston and Confederate Rail Transport*, pp. 44-45; Symonds, *Johnston*, p. 183.

31
    For examples, see Symonds, *Johnston*, pp. 208-209, 213-214, 221; Lash, *Johnston and Confederate Rail Transport*, p. 52.

32
    Lash writes that "The Grenada disaster, precipitated by Johnston's reckless unconcern for the safety of Mississippi rolling stock and his defiant disobedience of President Davis's orders to rescue that equipment. . .was devastating to the Confederate transportation system in the Southwest." Lash, *Johnston and Confederate Rail Transport*, pp. 73-103.

President Jefferson Davis
(National Archives)

political needs and to the geo-political importance of the area he was charged to defend. Davis again promoted and transferred some of Johnston's subordinates without consulting the general. Johnston again refused to keep the president informed of his plans and operations. Once again the result was a disaster for the Confederacy—the loss of northern Georgia, the important city of Atlanta, and whatever chance remained that the Confederacy could still gain its independence.[34]

The point to be understood is not that Davis was right about one disputed point and Johnston correct about another. Far too much time has been squandered on meaningless efforts to show that one or the other was right about some question that can never be answered. Nor is the point that Johnston, as the subordinate, had the responsibility to conform to the policy of his commander-in-chief or resign. The point is that almost from the beginning of the war, these two men were unable to communicate, to understand, and to trust one another. They were, therefore, unable to cooperate. Their personalities, their backgrounds, their antebellum experiences—*something*—made it impossible for them to do so under the stresses and strains of the war's first year.

All of the great disasters that came during Johnston's 1862-1864 command in the West were clearly adumbrated in the time that he directed operations in the Old Dominion. It could be said of Virginia in late 1861 and early 1862 that on those fields in those months were sown the seeds that in other months on other fields played a major role in the defeat and destruction of the Confederacy.

---

[34]
Lash comments, "Johnston [in 1864]...prepared to sacrifice the Deep South's most important railroad center after two months [May-June 1864] of offering feeble opposition to Sherman's advance." *Johnston and Confederate Rail Transport*, p. 152. For other comments on Johnston's conduct in the 1864 Georgia Campaign see Richard M. McMurry, "A Policy So Disastrous: Joseph E. Johnston's Atlanta Campaign," in Theodore P. Savas and David A. Woodbury, eds., *The Campaign For Atlanta & Sherman's March to the Sea*, 2 vols. (Campbell, 1994), vol. 2, pp. 223-248. For two other general essays treating Johnston and Davis and their roles in the war, see Richard M. McMurry, "'The Enemy at Richmond': Joseph E. Johnston and the Confederate Government," *Civil War History*, vol. 26 (1981), pp. 5-31; and Joseph T. Glatthaar, "'I Cannot Direct Both Parts of My Command at Once': Davis, Johnston and Confederate Failure in the West," in *Partners in Command: The Relationship Between Leaders in the Civil War* (New York, 1994), pp. 94-133.

Gen. Joseph E. Johnston
(*Generals in Gray*)

Edward Carr Franks

Ed Franks is an economist and a senior vice president at Trust Company of the West, a money management firm based in Los Angeles, California. He received his Ph.D. in 1980 from The RAND Graduate School for Public Policy Analysis, his M.S. from M.I.T. in 1976, and his B.A. from the University of California, San Diego, in 1974. This essay is dedicated to the memory of Tom Nolan, a founding member and guiding light of the Los Angeles Civil War Round Table. Tom's challenge in June of 1991 led to the research that resulted in this essay. He was a special man and is missed very much.

The Detachment of Longstreet Considered

Braxton Bragg, James Longstreet, and the Chattanooga Campaign

On November 4, 1863, during the partial investment of Chattanooga by the Army of Tennessee after the Battle of Chickamauga, Gen. Braxton Bragg—despite the intelligence that substantial Union reinforcements were approaching—detached Lt. Gen. James Longstreet's Corps to drive Maj. Gen. Ambrose Burnside's Federals out of East Tennessee. This decision has been consistently and vigorously condemned in the literature, both scholarly and popular. The overwhelming consensus is that the detachment of Longstreet was a terrible blunder and contributed directly and significantly to the humiliating defeat suffered by Bragg at Missionary Ridge three weeks later.

The purpose of this article is to consider the factors which may have motivated Bragg to make such a "blunder." The unfortunate outcome notwithstanding, the evidence points to three conclusions. First, the decision to clear East Tennessee was not only rational and reasonable, but possibly essential for the Confederates. Second, the force detached for the expedition under Longstreet was adequate for the task. And finally, President Jefferson Davis' intervention in this affair affected only the make-up of the detachment, not its existence, strength, or objective.

*   *   *

History has not been kind to Braxton Bragg. The general consensus on his handling of the Chattanooga Campaign was already well-established by the time his counterpart at Chattanooga, Maj. Gen. Ulysses S. Grant, argued in his 1885 memoirs that "Knoxville was of no use to the Confederates if the Federals held Chattanooga. . . .I have never been able to understand the wisdom of [the detachment of Longstreet]."[1] In his 1907 memoirs, Confederate Brig. Gen. Edward Porter Alexander, Longstreet's chief of artillery, went further in asserting that the detachment of Longstreet "cannot be excused or palliated. It was a monumental failure [of Bragg's] to appreciate the glaring weakness of his position."[2]

The banner of this negative refrain has been taken up and carried by professional historians since that time. Only Don C. Seitz, in his 1924 biography of Bragg, gave the general the benefit of the doubt by asserting that Bragg made the detachment against his better judgment and only after constant pressure from Longstreet. Seitz also argued that the move had some strategic merit to the extent that it prevented Burnside from joining Grant.[3] Robert Selph Henry, in his 1934 narrative

---

[1]
    Ulysses S. Grant, *Personal Memoirs of U. S. Grant,* 2 vols. (New York, 1885), vol. 2, pp. 96-97.

[2]
    Edward Porter Alexander, *Military Memoirs of a Confederate: A Critical Narrative* (New York, 1907), p. 480. In his unpublished notes, written a few years earlier but not published until 1989, Porter was more careful with his language: "To make [this detachment now], a second class move even if made forty days sooner & in ample force. . . .was as remarkable a piece of strategy as the war produced." Edward Porter Alexander, *Fighting for the Confederacy: The Personal Recollections of General Edward Porter Alexander,* edited by Gary W. Gallagher (Chapel Hill, 1989), p. 311.

[3]
    Don C. Seitz, *Braxton Bragg* (Columbia, 1924), pp. 390, 406.

on the Confederacy, observed in reference to Longstreet's detachment that "With all [Grant's] well directed activity going on below, Bragg began to scatter his forces." In 1941, Stanley Horn, in the first serious effort at a history of the Army of Tennessee, had no doubts—despite his admitted reliance on virtually no original manuscript material—that Bragg's move into East Tennessee was 'a wild goose chase. . .[a] foolhardy project. . . . Could a seasoned veteran like Bragg have failed to realize the folly of dividing his force in the presence of an ever stronger enemy?" Thirty years later, Thomas Lawrence Connelly, in a much more thoroughly researched (but perhaps overly interpreted) history of the Army of Tennessee, concluded that "the danger and the impractical nature of sending Longstreet had given way to personal motive. Bragg simply wanted to be rid of the man." Finally, James Lee McDonough, in his 1984 book on the siege of Chattanooga (which relied heavily on Connelly's work) concluded "It made no military sense, of course, unless one was blind, as Davis and Bragg apparently were, to the Union concentration at Chattanooga."[4]

Such a consistent assault over so many years by so many students of the conflict is striking. But has the detachment of Longstreet ever really been considered? Is it possible that a careful assessment of this detachment has been neglected because the subsequent defeats suffered by both Bragg and Longstreet made such an analysis seem redundant? In other words, have historians concluded that the detachment was a bad idea simply because of the bad results that followed? Or, conversely, is it possible that the detachment was a good idea despite the bad outcome?

Before proceeding with an analysis of James Longstreet's detachment from the Army of Tennessee, an appreciation of the general strategic situation as it existed in late October 1863 is necessary in order to provide a context within which to understand Bragg's decision to send Longstreet to Knoxville.

---

[4]
Robert Selph Henry, *Story of the Confederacy* (Indianapolis, 1934), p. 318; Stanley Horn, *The Army of Tennessee* (Indianapolis, 1941) p. 294; Thomas Lawrence Connelly, *Autumn of Glory* (Baton Rouge, 1971), p. 263; James Lee McDonough, *Chattanooga—A Death Grip on the Confederacy* (Knoxville, 1984), p. 98.

Major General George H. Thomas' Army of the Cumberland, which numbered approximately 53,000 men, was besieged within Chattanooga by Braxton Bragg's Army of Tennessee, whose 65,000 men occupied a 13-mile semi-circular line ranging from the northern tip of Missionary Ridge, northeast of town, to Lookout Mountain and beyond, southwest of town.[5]

Ambrose Burnside's 30,000 men of the Army of the Ohio occupied much of East Tennessee in detachments ranging from Loudon to Cumberland Gap to Bull's Gap, all within a 50-mile radius of Knoxville. Ten days earlier, Burnside's vanguard had stretched beyond Bristol, Tennessee, into southwestern Virginia, over 100 miles northeast of Knoxville, threatening Maj. Gen. Sam Jones and his 10,000 Confederates who were spread over the 100 miles from Abingdon to Dublin, Virginia. Burnside was attempting to rapidly concentrate his scattered forces on and around Knoxville in response to Bragg's extension of his right flank to the vicinity of Loudon, 30 miles southwest of Knoxville. This Confederate detachment consisted of a 16,000-man force under the command of Maj. Gen. Carter Littlepage Stevenson, a veteran of the Vicksburg Campaign. At the same time, Sam Jones' Rebels were advancing from Bristol in cooperation with Bragg's/Stevenson's move on Loudon, threatening both Cumberland Gap and Bull's Gap. Jones, in turn, was being threatened by Brig. Gen. William Averell's 10,000 Federals hovering on his right rear in the vicinity of Beverly and Charleston, in western Virginia. As bits and

---

[5]

In an effort to maximize comparability over time and between opponents, all estimates as to strength are "aggregate present of all arms, including artillery and cavalry," and all estimates are obtained from the U.S. War Department, *The War of the Rebellion: The Official Records of the Union and Confederate Armies,* 128 vols. (Washington, D.C., 1890-1901). All references are to Series I unless otherwise noted. Another common measure of strength is "effectives," which is the number of troops present for duty, equipped and available for deployment into line of battle. As a rough rule of thumb, this number is approximately 70% of the aggregate present of all arms for these armies during this period of the war. The relationship between aggregate present and effectives can be approximated as follows for both Northern and Southern armies: if aggregate present equals 100%, then present but sick equals 8%, present but under arrest equals 1%, present but detailed to extra-duty equals 8% (extra-duty includes foragers, pioneers, orderlies, staff, camp guards, provost marshals, teamsters, etc.), and present for duty but unequipped (without rifles, horses) equals 3%, thus yielding a figure of 80% present for duty, equipped. Total artillery equals approximately 5% to 6%, and total number of officers equals 5% to 7%, thus yielding anywhere from 67% to 70% for effectives, i.e., troops in line, both cavalry and infantry.

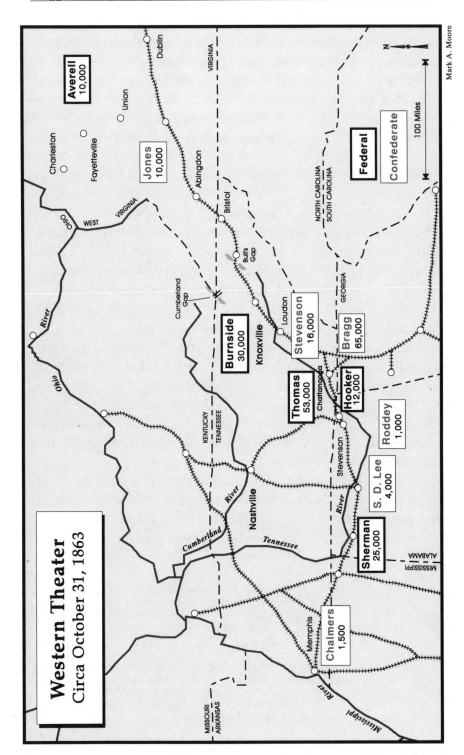

Mark A. Moore

Western Theater
Circa October 31, 1863

Averell
10,000

Jones
10,000

Burnside
30,000

Stevenson
16,000

Bragg
65,000

Thomas
53,000

Hooker
12,000

Roddey
1,000

S. D. Lee
4,000

Sherman
25,000

Chalmers
1,500

Federal

Confederate

100 Miles

N

pieces of the opposing forces maneuvered and threatened one another, substantial reinforcements for the beleaguered Union army in Chattanooga—25,000 men from Vicksburg and Corinth under Maj. Gen. William T. Sherman—were still south of the Tennessee River near the Mississippi line in the vicinity of Tuscumbia, Alabama. Sherman had recently been ordered by Grant to move to the rail junction at Stevenson, Alabama, in order to be in a position to intercept Bragg's right flank extension under Carter Stevenson, should this develop into a move on Nashville.[6]

Major General Joseph Hooker had just established his 12,000 Federals in Lookout Valley after Longstreet's failure to oust them at the battle of Wauhatchie in the pre-dawn of October 29, 1863. This development effectively raised the siege of Chattanooga by providing George Thomas with a more direct supply line to Bridgeport, which in turn made it possible for Thomas not only to maintain his own troops adequately, but also to receive and maintain additional troops.[7] With the raising of the siege, Bragg was forced to develop a new strategy, a key element of which was the evolution of the right flank demonstration (under Carter Stevenson) into a right flank offensive. In order to comply with the wishes of Jefferson Davis and Gen. Robert E. Lee, James Longstreet and his two divisions were assigned to this offensive, replacing Stevenson and his two divisions. In effect, Longstreet's men were swapped for Stevenson's.

Braxton Bragg was kept well informed of the location of the forces under Sherman and Hooker, and there seems to be little controversy on this point.[8] Most of Bragg's critics complain that he knew of the impending force disparity between his own army and the Federals in and

---

6
    U. S. Grant, "Chattanooga," in Robert U. Johnson and Clarence C. Buel, eds. *Battles and Leaders of the Civil War*, 4 vols. (New York, 1884-1889), vol. 3, pp. 691-694. Grant admitted that this move by Bragg in the direction of East Tennessee "alarmed the authorities at Washington" for the welfare of East Tennessee, and "caused [him] much uneasiness." Interestingly, Grant was quick to dismiss a similar move when it later involved Longstreet.

7
    For additional information on the fighting at Wauhatchie, see Douglas R. Cubbison, "Midnight Engagement: John Geary's White Star Division at Wauhatchie, Tennessee, October 28-29, 1863," *Civil War Regiments: A Journal of the American Civil War*, Vol. 4, No. 2, pp. 70-101.

8
    Horn, *Army of Tennessee*, p. 296, and Connelly, *Autumn of Glory*, pp. 232, 261.

around Chattanooga, and simply ignored it. The conventional wisdom is that Bragg detached Longstreet despite possessing knowledge of the imminent presence of 80,000 to 90,000 Federals at Chattanooga, as well as Burnside's 30,000 men in East Tennessee, which left him him with only about 36,000 effectives to combat this Federal concentration.[9] A careful examination of the written record, however, suggests otherwise.

On November 4, 1863, when Bragg shifted Longstreet's legions east, he knew, thanks to Gen. Joseph E. Johnston's Mississippi-based cavalry under Maj. Gen. Stephen D. Lee, that the vanguard of Sherman's 25,000 Federals had only just reached the Elk River, about 100 air miles from Chattanooga. Bragg also knew that most of Sherman's men were mired in mud for twenty miles back to Florence.[10] Bragg was also aware that Joe Hooker had about 12,000 men in Lookout Valley.[11]

With over seven weeks to observe Thomas in Chattanooga, it is reasonable to assume that Bragg formed an accurate estimate of his adversary's aggregate present, which was about 53,000 men.[12] Therefore, it is fair to assume that Bragg realized he was facing about 65,000 of all arms: George Thomas' 53,000 and Joe Hooker's 12,000, with W. T. Sherman's 20,000 or more soldiers en route to Chattanooga.

---

[9]
Horn, *Army of Tennessee*, p. 301; McDonough, *Chattanooga*, p. 100; Connelly, *Autumn of Glory*, pp. 262-263. The basis for this widely accepted conclusion may rest on a faulty presentation of the actual forces involved. For example, Connelly's estimate that Grant had 80,000 to 90,000 men appears to be based on Grant's aggregate present of all of his forces, whereas Connelly's estimate for Bragg of 36,000 men appears based on infantry effectives only.

[10]
Connelly, *Autumn of Glory*, p. 261, discusses Bragg's accurate assessment of the strength and location of Sherman and Hooker. As it turned out, Sherman's troops were not in position on the hills northeast of Chattanooga until eighteen days later, or November 23, despite the best efforts of Sherman and Grant to expedite their arrival. McDonough, *Chattanooga,* p. 118.

[11]
On October 3, 1863, Robert E. Lee estimated Hooker's strength at 12,000 troops in a note to President Davis, *OR* 34, pt. 2, p. 769, but his actual force was closer to 18,000 men before detachments to protect the railroad between Bridgeport and Nashville reduced it to about 12,000 aggregate by November 20. *OR* 31, pt 2, p. 12.

[12]
Ibid., p. 12. I was unable to find a definitive indication of Bragg's assessment of Thomas' strength during this entire period. Connelly *Autumn of Glory*, p. 232 cites *OR* 30, pt. 2, pp. 22-23; 30, pt. 4, pp. 696, 707, 711; 52, pt. 2, pp. 530-533; and ibid, pt. 2, pp. 752-754, 756-758, 766, 769-770, for Bragg's estimate immediately following the Battle of Chickamauga. None of these references reveal Bragg's assessment of General Rosecrans' force as of October 31, 1863.

Immediately prior to the detachment of Longstreet, Bragg's aggregate present as of October 31, 1863—exclusive of cavalry—was about 66,000 men.[13] His aggregate cavalry force probably numbered about 15,000.[14] Thus Bragg's army numbered an aggregate present of all arms of 81,000, or 56,000 after the detachment of Longstreet's combined force of infantry and cavalry, nine thousand fewer than Grant's 65,000 Federals.[15] Thus, immediately after the detachments, the force disparity between Bragg and Grant was insignificant.

Like Grant, Bragg's Army of Tennessee was also expecting rein-forcements. On October 27, President Davis ordered Lt. Gen. William J. Hardee and two infantry brigades transferred from Demopolis, Alabama, and two more brigades were promised by Gen. Joseph E. Johnston to Bragg on November 4. These brigades, totaling about 8,000 men aggregate present (or about 5,600 effectives), would soon augment Bragg's aggregate present of all arms to about 64,000, compared to Grant's 65,000.[16]

[13]
    OR 31, pt. 2, p. 656. This figure includes Carter Stevenson's 16,000 Rebels, which had been detached in stages toward Loudon, Tennessee, beginning on October 17. Most or all of these troops could rejoin Bragg within a couple of days or less if needed, and thus should be considered in setting the strength of his army.

[14]
    The figure of 15,000 was arrived at as follows: records indicate Bragg had 13,600 cavalry present for duty on October 7, 1863, ibid., 30, pt. 4, p. 733, and 11,753 present for duty on December 10, 1863. Ibid., pt. 2, p. 656. If we average these strengths for November 15, 1863, we arrive at 12,676. We would divide this sum by the same ratio of present for duty to aggregate present for duty observed in the December 10 return, or .84, which provides an aggregate total cavalry force of 15,090 men, allowing 1,000 men for Brig. Gen. Philip D. Roddey's detachment in northern Alabama.

[15]
    Coinciding with Longstreet's detachment of 16,200 men was the assignment to East Tennessee of five cavalry brigades, 9,400 men under Maj. Gen. Joseph Wheeler, who was ordered to cooperate with Longstreet. Ibid., 31, pt. 3, p. 656. This detachment left Bragg with about 5,600 aggregate cavalry in three brigades, or a total aggregate present of about 56,000, and Longstreet with some 25,000.

[16]
    The October 27 order involved the brigades of John C. Moore and John J. Pettus. Both were with the Army of Tennessee prior to the retreat to Dalton after the debacle on Missionary Ridge. Joseph E. Johnston, *Narrative of Military Operations During the Civil War* (New York, 1874), p. 261. On November 4, Johnston promised to send Bragg the brigades of William A. Quarles and William E. Baldwin from Maj. Gen. Dabney Maury's command at Mobile, Alabama. Ibid., p. 260. The effective strength of these units totaled about 2,700 men (Johnston, ibid, p. 569), thus yielding a likely aggregate present strength of about 1,900 men each (2,700 divided by .70% = 3,857, divided by 2 equals 1,928 in each brigade). Similar strengths are assumed for both Pettus and Moore, since no other reliable data regarding their strength has been located. President Davis, in his October 29

With the prospect of receiving additional infantry, Bragg's decision to detach Longstreet does not appear as reckless as historians have suggested—especially since Bragg did not intend to attack the Federals in their fortifications. "It would be murderous to assault the enemy's superior forces in his intrenchments," Bragg telegraphed Davis on October 1. "Our efforts will be devoted to drawing him out."[17] It was reasonable for Bragg to believe that his army was strong enough to hold the heights around Chattanooga at least until Sherman arrived to augment Grant. There was always the possibility, however, that Sherman would not reach Chattanooga. On October 27, for example, Grant was considering sending Sherman to Nashville. Three weeks later his destination was still open to speculation when on November 18, Longstreet argued that Sherman was heading for Knoxville.[18]

Even if Chattanooga was Sherman's objective, Bragg was still expecting the return of Longstreet, whose mission, at least according to Longstreet's memoirs, was to "crush Burnside and return before Sherman arrived."[19] The Army of Tennessee would only be outnumbered some 90,000 to 64,000 even if Sherman reinforced the Federals at Chattanooga before Longstreet returned to Bragg from Knoxville. Given Bragg's defensive strategy—and the odds regularly faced by Rebel armies throughout most of the war—these odds were not hopelessly long.[20]

---

letter to Bragg regarding the detachment of Longstreet, hinted that these reinforcements would be sent to him. Although ordered by Johnston on November 4 to join Bragg in response to that officer's telegram of the same day, only portions of these brigades had reached Chattanooga by the time the Army of Tennessee retreated into Georgia. Most of Baldwin's brigade of exchanged parolees from Vicksburg had arrived in time to take part in the fighting on Missionary Ridge, although it does not appear that any of these troops actually participated in the battle.

17
   OR 52, pt. 2, p. 534.

18
   Grant, "Chattanooga," pp. 691-693; *OR* 31, pt. 3, p. 733.

19
   Longstreet, *From Manassas to Appomattox* (Philadelphia, 1896), pp. 480-481.

20
   After leaving a strong detachment of soldiers at Athens to rebuild the railroad, Sherman arrived in Chattanooga with about 20,000 men. *OR* 31, pt. 2, p. 12.

Evidence that the disparity in numbers was not as great as often cited is supported by Longstreet himself, one of Bragg's most ardent critics. Anxious to retain Stevenson's Division for the campaign in East Tennessee, Longstreet asserted in a November 5 note to Bragg that, even if Bragg detached both Longstreet's Corps and Stevenson's Division, Grant's force would not exceed Bragg's. "I. . .cannot think [the enemy's force] exceeds your force without Stevenson's Division," speculated Longstreet.[21]

It is not clear whether Longstreet actually believed this to be the case, but it is certain that without Stevenson, Bragg would have been temporarily outnumbered by Grant 65,000 to 52,000 (Bragg was still awaiting the arrival of the four reinforcing infantry brigades). Even after the November 22 detachments of the divisions of Buckner and Patrick Cleburne (some 14,000 men) to reinforce Longstreet—which were made after the appearance of Sherman's 20,000 men—Bragg was still left with 50,000 soldiers to oppose Grant's 85,000 men. Given the long odds the Confederates faced throughout the war, Bragg had every reason to believe that his army was sufficient to resist a Federal assault, especially given Longstreet's anticipated return from Knoxville.[22]

Cleburne's Division, together with one of Buckner's brigades, about 9,000 men in all, were recalled to Chattanooga despite Longstreet's protest that Grant was simply launching a diversion to prevent Bragg from reinforcing him. As a result, Bragg was able to field approximately 59,000 men at Missionary Ridge on November 25 against Grant's 85,000. These figures should be contrasted with the gross disparity of forces suggested by Thomas Connelly, who postulated that Bragg had only 35,000 men to defend against 90,000 Federals. Therefore, a careful assessment of the opposing forces supports the contention that the

---

21
    Ibid., pt. 3, p. 633. Longstreet's note is especially interesting in light of his nearly simultaneous letter to Maj. Gen. Simon Bolivar Buckner, in which he complains that Bragg's current dispositions expose both Longstreet and Bragg to failure because of inadequate forces. Ibid., 52, pt. 2, pp. 559-560.

22
    The combined strength of 14,000 given for the divisions of Simon Buckner and Patrick Cleburne is from the return dated October 31, 1863. Ibid., 31, pt. 2, p. 656. This sum may have been smaller by November 22 because of the early November reorganization of the army conducted by Bragg.

disparity of force never reached unacceptable levels for Bragg's Army of Tennessee.[23]

* * *

As suggested above, the detachment of Longstreet's Corps for operations in East Tennessee was essentially an exchange of his corps for the troops operating under Carter Stevenson. Therefore the exchange merely maintained the status quo that already existed (i.e., Bragg's army was divided before the detachment and was still divided thereafter). Criticism of this exchange, if deserved, should focus on Bragg's original detachment on October 17, when he sent Stevenson and 16,150 men (two divisions of infantry and two brigades of cavalry) to extend his right flank as far as Loudon, within 30 miles of Knoxville and 70 miles from Chattanooga.[24]

Thus, Bragg's available force immediately *preceding* the detachment of Longstreet was 65,000, not 81,000. On November 4, when Bragg detached Longstreet's two divisions and three additional brigades of cavalry under Joseph Wheeler, he simultaneously recalled Stevenson's two divisions, but not the two cavalry brigades cooperating with Stevenson. Using the October 31 returns as a basis for calculation, the net effect of these transfers was simply to increase Bragg's extended right flank from 16,000 to 25,000, and to decrease Bragg's Chattanooga force from 65,000 to 56,000.

As previously established, Bragg was expecting reinforcements in the form of four infantry brigades: two of William J. Hardee from Demopolis, Alabama, and two more promised from Joe Johnston. The result of all this swapping, detaching, and transferring on Bragg's army around Chattanooga was the loss of three cavalry brigades and the

---

[23]
Ibid., pt. 3, p. 740; Connelly, *Autumn of Glory*, pp. 262, 267.

[24]
Carter Stevenson's strength is based upon the October 20, 1863, return showing 12,400 infantry and two cavalry brigades. *OR* 30, pt. 1, p. 765. Stevenson's position at Loudon is taken from his report of November 12, 1863. Ibid., 31, pt. 1, p. 8.

anticipated acquisition of four infantry brigades, a net loss of only about 1,000 troops.

Therefore, when Bragg sent Longstreet into East Tennessee, he had good reason to expect that this depletion would be temporary. When his reinforcements arrived from the Deep South, he would have 64,000 men, compared to his pre-detachment total of 65,000.

* * *

On September 23, 1863, after Bragg's victory at Chickamauga, Gen. Robert E. Lee suggested to Jefferson Davis that Longstreet be assigned to clear East Tennessee, reopen communications, and then return to Virginia.[25] After receiving Bragg's October 25 dispatch relating Stevenson's early success in East Tennessee, Davis expressed to Bragg four days later the hope that Stevenson's expedition might reopen communications with Virginia. Davis went on to suggest that if Bragg no longer considered the proposed—and thus far rain-delayed—left flank operations to be of "prime importance," he "might advantageously assign [Longstreet] to the task of expelling Burnside" from East Tennessee and thus "place him in position, according to circumstances, to hasten or delay [Longstreet's] return to. . .Lee."[26]

Many students of the war are unaware that Davis played a pivotal role in Bragg's decision to assign Longstreet to East Tennessee. Bragg discussed Davis' involvement in a post-war letter to E. T. Sykes, claiming that he had been planning an expedition to East Tennessee under Lt. Gen. John C. Breckinridge and only switched to Longstreet to comply with Davis' request. Bragg freely admitted, however, that he might not have "yielded [his] convictions to the President's policy" but for Longstreet's "disobedience of orders."[27] There seems to be general

25
   Armistead L. Long, *Memoirs of Robert E. Lee* (New York, 1886), p. 627.

26
   The mention of the proposed left flank operations corroborates Longstreet's recollection of the war council with Davis on October 11, 1863. Longstreet, *Manassas to Appomattox,* p. 468. See also Davis to Bragg, October 29, 1863, in Dunbar Rowland, *Jefferson Davis, Constitutionalist,* 10 vols. (Jackson, 1923), vol. 6, pp. 69-71.

27
   Bragg to E. T. Sykes, February 8. 1873, Polk Papers, University of the South, Sewanee,

agreement among historians that Bragg's displeasure with Longstreet was warranted. In her 1991 biography of Bragg, for example, historian Judith Hallock concludes that "Longstreet's intransigence, his incompetence, his subversive activities, and his refusal to serve Bragg as a trustworthy lieutenant boded ill [for Bragg]."[28]

Thus, despite Bragg's admitted and justified displeasure with Longstreet, he may not have sent him into East Tennessee without the intervention of Davis, who, in turn, might not have asked for Longstreet if Lee had not suggested it and if Carter Stevenson had not already enjoyed success in the eastern portion of the state.[29]

*   *   *

If Bragg's forces were already divided at the time of Longstreet's detachment, and if Longstreet's separation was essentially an exchange of forces that had little or no numerical impact on Bragg's army, then why has this exchange received so much criticism? Or conversely, if the detachment of Longstreet was such an obvious blunder, then why has there been so little criticism of the presumably equally odious detachment of Stevenson's divisions two weeks earlier? Was the

---

Tennessee. The "disobedience of orders" mentioned by Bragg refers to the events leading up to and including the fighting at Wauhatchie on the night of October 28-29, 1863. On October 25, Bragg ordered Longstreet to conduct a reconnaissance in the area, which Longstreet did not do. Two days later Bragg ordered Longstreet to dislodge the Federals at Brown's Ferry, and again Longstreet failed to act according to Bragg's wishes. On October 28, although Bragg ordered Longstreet to attack Joseph Hooker's Federals with four divisions, Longstreet assaulted with only one brigade. Bragg, in a letter to Davis, circa October 30, declared that Longstreet was disobedient, slow, and guilty of gross neglect. Even Edward P. Alexander, Longstreet's chief of artillery, declared his superior guilty of contributory negligence. Connelly, *Autumn of Glory*, pp. 255-261; E. P. Alexander, "Manuscript," vol. 41, Edward Porter Alexander Papers, Southern Historical Collection, University of North Carolina, Chapel Hill.

28
   Judith Lee Hallock, *Braxton Bragg and Confederate Defeat,* Volume II (Tuscaloosa, 1991), pp. 108, 122-124, 126.

29
   Bragg admitted to Davis that sending Longstreet would be a "great relief" to him. Seitz, *Braxton Bragg*, p. 392. One of Bragg's generals claims that Bragg told him he sent Longstreet into East Tennessee "to get rid of him." St. John R. Liddell's "Reminiscences," in Govan Papers, University of North Carolina, Chapel Hill.

operation under Stevenson a good idea and the Longstreet detachment a bad one? The Stevenson detachment was executed in response to a Union movement in East Tennessee and, judging by its immediate results, was successful. Stevenson's men were sent into the eastern portion of Tennessee to counter the thrust of a contingent of perhaps 18,000 men under Burnside that had pushed advance elements of Samuel Jones' Rebel force to within six miles of Abingdon, Virginia.[30]

By October 15, Jones' frantic messages to Richmond from Dublin, Virginia, 80 miles northeast of Abingdon, compelled Adjutant and Inspector General Samuel Cooper to forward Jones' pleas for assistance to Bragg. "BG Williams and his command reached Abingdon this morning," read one of Jones' dispatches. "The enemy are at Bristol and reported advancing. If you can send me any troops, I beg you to do it."[31]

Bragg responded to this threat on October 17 by ordering Stevenson's small division and two cavalry brigades "to press vigorously toward Knoxville, to press the enemy's rear and develop him, driving him back as far as their commands will allow." Bragg sent notice of this movement to Jones while at the same time notifying Cooper that he "[would] try to relieve General Jones by a move on the enemy's rear."[32] Five days later, on October 22, Bragg ordered Maj. Gen. Benjamin Cheatham's large infantry division, under the temporary command of

---

30
    On October 10, two divisions from Burnside's IX Corps, reinforced by Maj. Gen. Orlando B. Willcox's division and Brig. Gen. James M. Shackleford's cavalry, moved against a 1,500-man Confederate cavalry brigade under Brig. Gen. J. E. Williams near Blue Springs, about 60 miles northeast of Knoxville and ten miles southeast of Bull's Gap. Another brigade of Union cavalry was sent via Rogersville to intercept the enemy's retreat. Shackleford pursued the enemy beyond Bristol, supported by an infantry brigade under Col. William A. Hoskins at Jonesboro, 28 miles southwest of Bristol, with the rest of Willcox's division 22 miles below Hoskins' force at Greenville, yielding a total of perhaps 9,000 men within 50 miles of the Virginia border. In addition, 7,000 men from Brig. Gen. Robert B. Potter's IX Corps under Edward Ferraro and one or two additional cavalry brigades were just beyond Bull's Gap in the Morristown vicinity. These forces totaled about 18,000 men of all arms. OR 30, pt. 2, p. 547, 551-552. As of October 31, 1863, Sam Jones had less than 9,500 Rebels to cover the 175 miles of railroad stretching from Lynchburg to Bristol, and the 50 additional miles of track into East Tennessee as far as Bull's Gap. Ibid., 31, pt. 1, p. 613; 30, pt. 2, p. 639.

31
    Ibid., 30, pt. 4, p. 756. This note is referenced by Bragg in his orders to Stevenson on October 17, 1863.

32
    Ibid., 30, pt. 4, pp. 760, 761.

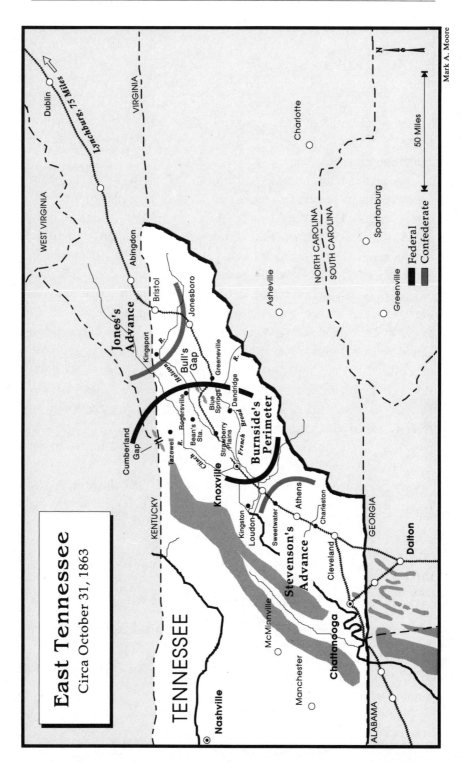

East Tennessee
Circa October 31, 1863

Mark A. Moore

Brig. Gen. John K. Jackson, to join Stevenson. By October 27, Bragg had over 16,000 men in two infantry divisions and two cavalry brigades between Athens and Loudon, a distance of 20 miles.[33] Two days later, Bragg reported to Davis—prematurely, as it turned out—that "Stevenson has driven Burnside back to Knoxville and is following." In actuality, Burnside retreated to Lenoir's Station, only six miles beyond the Tennessee River at Loudon.[34]

As planned, Stevenson's expedition caused Burnside to begin consolidating his forces. On October 29 Burnside relayed reports to both Gen. Henry W. Halleck and Grant that Bragg might be sending as many as 45,000 troops toward East Tennessee.[35] In response to these developments, Grant asked Halleck to order Maj. Gen. Benjamin F. Kelly to move out of West Virginia to threaten Jones' right flank, and ordered Sherman at Tuscumbia, Alabama, to hurry to the rail junction at Stevenson, Alabama, to be in position to beat Bragg (and/or Stevenson) to Nashville, should such a necessity arise.[36] By October 30, advance elements from Burnside's army had retreated 60 miles from Bristol back to Bull's Gap, ten miles beyond Blue Springs, from which point Burnside had launched his drive twenty days earlier. Sherman was hurrying to Stevenson, Alabama, to cover Nashville, Brig. Gen. William Averell was about to descend on Southwest Virginia, and Meade was preparing to push beyond the Rappahannock River and move against Lee and the Army of Northern Virginia.[37]

By November 10, after a sharp action at Rogersville with Jones' forces, Burnside fell back another 10 miles to Morristown, reducing his

[33]
     Ibid., 31, pt. 1, p. 8. Loudon is less than 30 miles from Knoxville and about 75 miles from Chattanooga.

[34]
     Ibid., 52, pt. 2, p. 555; ibid., 30, pt. 2, p. 574.

[35]
     Ibid., 31, pt. 1, p. 778. Two days earlier, Burnside had wired Grant that Lt. Gen. Richard S. Ewell was reported coming from Lee's army, although he was skeptical of the report. Ibid., p. 756.

[36]
     Ibid., 31, pt. 1, p. 770. In addition, Grant may have urged Halleck to encourage Meade to pressure Lee in order to counter any plans Lee might have for detaching forces to Jones in southwest Virginia.

[37]
     Ibid., 31, pt. 3, p. 607.

area of operations to about 30 miles on either side of Knoxville. At about the same time, Averell, with a force of 3,000 to 7,000 men, defeated Brig. Gen. John Echols' 1,400 men at Droop Mountain on November 6, 1863, but withdrew nonetheless, temporarily ending the threat to Jones' right flank.[38] With the possible exception of Meade's operations in Virginia, all of these events were the direct result of Bragg's decision to thrust Stevenson into East Tennessee. While the various side effects of the detachment may or may not have been desirable from Bragg's point of view, the primary objective, that of forcing Burnside's withdrawal from the area, was a signal success.

*   *   *

The exchange of Longstreet's men for Stevenson's divisions was not intended to create an independent command for Longstreet, and he did not believe he enjoyed such status until a week after his retreat toward southwestern Virginia, a full two weeks after Bragg's retreat from Missionary Ridge.[39] Bragg was certainly aware that the detachment might become permanent given the express desire of Davis "according to circumstances, [to] hasten or delay [Longstreet's] return to Lee."[40] The salient issue, however, is not whether Bragg or Davis intended to detach Longstreet permanently, but whether such a detachment created an independent command for Longstreet.

There are at least three reasons to believe that Bragg did not intend to create an independent command when he detached Longstreet. First,

38
  Ibid., 34, pt. 2, p. 862.

39
  Longstreet, *Manassas to Appomattox*, p. 512. On December 10, Longstreet received from Davis discretionary authority—at least to Longstreet's satisfaction—over the movement of all troops in the department of East Tennessee, thus allowing him to recall Brig. Gen. William T. Martin's cavalry division, which he had only the day before finally ordered back to Dalton in accordance with Bragg's November 26 order. *OR* 31, pt. 3, p. 760. The actual note from Davis to Longstreet, dated December 8, 1863 and printed in Rowland, *Jefferson Davis*, 6, p. 128, is not on its face quite so definitive.

40
  Ibid., pp. 69-71.

East Tennessee was clearly under Bragg's jurisdiction, as the recent controversy with Simon Buckner had established.[41] Second, no one suggested then or since that the earlier detachment of Carter Stevenson's 16,000 men altered the status of Bragg's authority over East Tennessee or Stevenson. Third, as his correspondence clearly indicates, Bragg considered Longstreet to be under his authority. For example, in his November 4 order sending Longstreet into East Tennessee, Bragg informed that officer that "your quick recall may be necessary."[42] In discussing the strategic ramifications and possibilities of the movement together with Stevenson's return to the Army of Tennessee, Bragg informed Longstreet on November 5 that "By means of the railroad I hope. . .to reinforce either point [Chattanooga or Knoxville] as necessary."[43] These are not the words of someone who had just yielded his authority to an officer of lesser rank. Davis harbored no doubts as to the relationship between Bragg and Longstreet. In a note to Bragg on November 20 in response to Longstreet's continued delays, the Confederate president wrote that, "The failure of Longstreet to keep you advised is unaccountable. You had better *order* him to report fully the events of each day [emphasis added]."[44]

Although some clues exist, Longstreet's perception of the detachment is more difficult to establish. According to Longstreet, on November 3, prior to his detachment, he met with Bragg and William J. Hardee to discuss strategy. He told these officers that his role would be to "crush Burnside and return [to Bragg]" before Sherman's arrival.[45] It

---

41
   Connelly, *Autumn of Glory*, p. 252; Rowland, *Jefferson Davis*, 6, p. 64. After Buckner and his division of infantry joined Bragg's army in October 1863, he lost both the command of his East Tennessee department, which was abolished, and his position as a corps commander.

42
   OR 31, pt 3, pp. 633.

43
   Ibid., p. 634.

44
   Ibid., 52, pt 2, p. 562.

45
   Longstreet, *Manassas to Appomattox,* pp. 480-481. Unfortunately, Hardee, who was present at this meeting, has no recollection of Longstreet proposing or agreeing to a return to Chattanooga after defeating Burnside. Hardee to Longstreet, April 8, 1864, in Hardee Papers, University of Alabama.

is difficult to determine how Longstreet could have concluded that he had an independent command given his stated objective. Even after Missionary Ridge, Longstreet's behavior suggests that he understood his continued responsibility to Bragg. On November 29, just after the failed assault on Fort Sanders at Knoxville, Longstreet received through Joe Wheeler an order from Bragg which was clearly discretionary: "General Bragg desires me to say he wishes you to fall back with your command upon Dalton if possible. If you find that impracticable [because of Sherman's line of march], he thinks you will have to fall back toward Virginia. In all events, he desires that you order all the cavalry to Dalton."[46]

The discretionary nature of these orders provided Longstreet with a unique opportunity to be rid of Bragg. According to E. P. Alexander, however, Longstreet spent the next few days holding councils "at which all possible routes [to Bragg] were minutely inquired into. . . .The unanimous conclusion was soon reached that it was extremely unwise to attempt to *obey* either the orders from Richmond or those from General Bragg, that we should seek to rejoin the army of the latter [emphasis added]. . .It was held to be the safest policy to keep up the siege of Knoxville" as long as possible and then retreat northeast only when Sherman was close at hand.[47] Such language suggests that Longstreet, as well as his lieutenants, accepted, if not embraced, Bragg's continued authority.

Contrary to Thomas Connelly's assertions, these observations support the contention that Longstreet—even after Missionary Ridge—had not seceded from Bragg's command, did not consider himself free from Bragg's authority, and had not, as Connelly wrote, "bowed out of the Chattanooga campaign."[48]

* * *

46
   OR 31, pt. 3, p. 760. This telegram, dated November 26, was delivered to Longstreet on November 29.

47
   Alexander, *Personal Recollections*, p. 329.

48
   Connelly, *Autumn of Glory*, pp. 265-267.

With the loss of Lookout Valley after the debacle at Wauhatchie on October 28-29, Bragg's only viable strategic option was to transform his right flank demonstration against Burnside into a right flank offensive against Grant at Chattanooga. The objective was no longer to "[drive Burnside] back as far as he will allow," but to "drive Burnside out of East Tennessee" in the hope that railroad communications with Virginia could be reestablished, thereby enabling a change of base by Bragg to Knoxville, if necessary, as a prelude to a turning movement against Grant's left rear.[49]

Bragg acknowledged early and often the appropriateness of an offensive flanking maneuver. On September 29 and twice on October 3, he promised the Confederate authorities in Richmond that he was readying his troops for a flanking move across the Tennessee River.[50] He also indicated to Davis on October 1 that a frontal attack would be "murderous" and that his efforts would be devoted to drawing the enemy out of their entrenchments.[51] Two weeks later, Bragg wrote to Gen. P. G. T. Beauregard that "your views [on an offensive move] are so in accordance with my own that a presentation of them. . .would be almost a renewal of my recommendations."[52] Bragg's enthusiasm for Beauregard's offensive proposal was confirmed by Armand Beauregard in his October 10 letter to his brother describing his recent meeting with Bragg.[53] The dilemma confronting Bragg was how best to draw out the enemy. To Bragg, this meant forcing the Federals either to attack him on the heights above Chattanooga, or to retreat out of that city. On October 11, a council of war that included President Davis apparently reached the consensus that Bragg should attempt to move by his left flank in the

[49]
See *OR* 30, pt. 4, p. 760-761 for Bragg's October 17 orders to Stevenson, and ibid., 31, pt. 3, pp. 633ff for Bragg's November 4 orders to Longstreet.

[50]
Bragg to Davis, September 29, 1863, and October 10, 1863, and Bragg to Cooper, October 3, 1863, in Bragg Papers, Western Reserve Collection.

[51]
OR 52, pt. 2, p. 534.

[52]
Ibid., 30, pt. 4, p. 745.

[53]
Ibid., 30, pt. 4, p. 733ff.

direction of Bridgeport. According to Longstreet, however, Bragg personally favored moving via his right, or upriver, to "cross the river and swing around toward the enemy's rear and force him out by that means."[54]

Bragg's apparent enthusiasm for a flanking maneuver was temporarily dampened by the time of his meeting with Davis on October 11. The recent deployment of Longstreet's troops into Lookout Valley, coupled with the limited success of Joe Wheeler's cavalry raid in the Sequatchie Valley, increased the prospects of an effective siege of Chattanooga.[55] According to Bragg, a flanking maneuver to sever the Federal line of supply through the mountains was unwarranted since it would uncover the Bridgeport supply route (the best line of supply for the Federals stationed in Chattanooga), which the Confederates controlled. With the loss of Lookout Valley and the consequent raising of the siege, however, this consideration was rendered moot.[56]

On October 31 Bragg met with Hardee, John C. Breckinridge, and Longstreet to discuss the feasibility of retaking Lookout Valley. All agreed that it would be impossible, thus conceding in effect that the siege was lifted.[57] Grant's force—which, with the arrival of Joe Hooker's men now slightly outnumbered Bragg—would soon receive substantial reinforcements from Sherman and/or Burnside. As a

---

54
Longstreet, *Manassas to Appomattox*, p 468. The consensus for the move around his left is corroborated in a message from Davis to Bragg dated October 29, 1863, in Rowland, *Jefferson Davis*, 6, pp. 69-71.

55
The effectiveness of the siege was implied by Grant in his memoirs when he noted Thomas' refusal to obey his order to attack on November 7, in part because of the condition of the horses. In other words, more than a week after the raising of the siege with the opening of the "Cracker Line," Federal horses were still too weak from chronic starvation to pull the guns. Grant, "Chattanooga," p. 694.

56
Seitz, *Bragg,* p. 376.

57
The necessity to detour 50 miles through Steven's Gap and Johnson's Crook made it difficult or impossible for the Confederates to recapture the valley. Micah Jenkins to Moxley Sorrel, October 31, 1863, in Micah Jenkins Papers, Perkins Library, Duke University. In a letter dated March 25, 1864, Longstreet agreed that Lookout Valley was irretrievably lost, but went on to say that it was "not essential. . .[because the enemy] supplied his army at that place some six weeks without it." *OR* 31, pt. 1, p. 218. This is a blatant example of obfuscation by Longstreet.

consequence, it would have been an exercise in futility for Bragg to concentrate his forces in the hopes of receiving a direct assault from Grant. Bragg understood that Grant, with river and railroad communications, could be reinforced to any extent necessary to offset any manpower augmentation that Bragg could reasonably support with his tenuous single rail line south to Atlanta. Furthermore, if Bragg did attempt a concentration, Grant could easily turn him with either Sherman or Burnside (or both) while holding him in place with Hooker and Thomas. Therefore, Bragg was compelled to either advance in some fashion or retreat, for sitting above Chattanooga was an invitation to Grant to seize the initiative. Given the current political situation in the Confederacy, Bragg had to advance. Voluntary retreat, or a "change of base" to the south, was not a viable option.

The issue, then, was whether to advance the Army of Tennessee by the left flank or by the right flank. Bragg's decision not to advance by the left flank, as contemplated since the October 11 war council with Davis, was probably due to a combination of sound reasons. With Hooker firmly entrenched in Lookout Valley and Sherman approaching from that direction, a move west did not appear feasible. In addition to these considerations, Union reinforcements from both the army and navy could be concentrated in the direction of the Stevenson-Bridgeport vicinity by both rail and river (the Tennessee River is broad and deep in most of Alabama). In other words, a move around the left would be tantamount to moving against and into Grant's strength. Southern logistical considerations were also a prime consideration for abandoning the move: Bragg would have neither rail nor river communications in that direction, the roads were little more than muddy mountain trails, and he would be extending and, at the same time, exposing, his own precarious logistical lifeline.

A move by his right flank, however, offered several advantages. First, Bragg would enjoy the use of the East Tennessee & Georgia Railroad (at least as far as Loudon), and as he extended his right flank, he would draw nearer to a second or alternative line of railroad communications from Virginia. Second, there were few Federals in East Tennessee of sufficient strength to vigorously oppose the movement, since Burnside and his forces were scattered across the eastern portion of

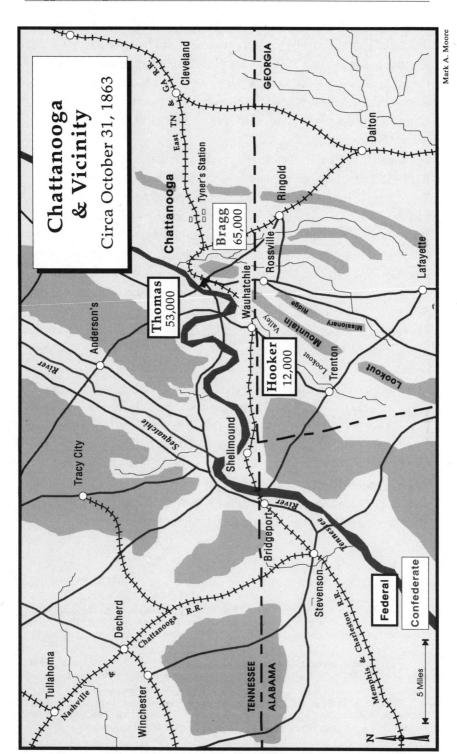

Chattanooga & Vicinity
Circa October 31, 1863

Mark A. Moore

Bragg 65,000
Thomas 53,000
Hooker 12,000

Cleveland
GEORGIA
Dalton
East TN & GA R.R.
Tyner's Station
Chattanooga
Ringold
Lafayette
Rossville
Wauhatchie
Missionary Ridge
Lookout Valley
Trenton
Lookout Mountain
Anderson's
River
Sequatchie
Shellmound
Tracy City
Bridgeport
Tennessee River
Stevenson
Memphis & Charleston R.R.
Decherd
Chattanooga R.R.
Tullahoma
Nashville &
Winchester
TENNESSEE
ALABAMA

Federal
Confederate

N
5 Miles

the state. Third, Burnside's supply problems and isolated location made
it unlikely that he could be significantly or quickly reinforced, even from
Grant. In addition, there was the very real prospect of cooperation from
Sam Jones in southwestern Virginia, who was receiving reinforcements
from Richmond and was advancing from Bristol as Burnside retreated
toward Knoxville.[58]

Thus Bragg's only viable offensive option was to advance by the
right flank, perhaps as a prelude to a general offensive into Middle
Tennessee.[59] Before he could attempt the movement, however, Bragg
had to extend his right flank [Longstreet] in order to join forces with
Sam Jones and clear Burnside from East Tennessee. Such an approach
offered two advantages over moving his entire army at one time. First,
an expedition into East Tennessee could open a second or alternative line
of communications with Virginia without unnecessarily exposing
Bragg's line of communications with Atlanta. Second, the elongation of
his right flank extension might induce Grant to attack Bragg on the
heights above Chattanooga, a position deemed "impregnable" by most
observers.[60]

If Burnside was cleared from East Tennessee, Bragg would have the
option of either recalling his divisions or changing his base of operations
to Knoxville. The latter would allow Bragg to march on Grant's left rear
or into Kentucky, as circumstances dictated. If such a move were
undertaken, thus uncovering Bragg's logistical line and the route to
Atlanta and the Deep South, it is doubtful Grant's 85,000-man army
would have advanced on Atlanta with Bragg's reunited and powerful
army of some 89,000 men hovering on his left rear.[61]

58
    Ibid., 34, pt. 2, p. 789.

59
    Alfred Guernsey agreed, writing in 1868 that "The only aggressive movement possible to him
was that which he now attempted against Burnside with Longstreet's column." Alfred H. Guernsey,
Harper's Pictorial History of the Great Rebellion, 2 vols. (New York, 1866), vol. 2, p. 557A.

60
    Grant did order George Thomas to attack Bragg's line to prevent him from strengthening his
right. Grant, "Chattanooga," p. 694. This issue is discussed in detail elsewhere in this essay.

61
    The Confederate figure of 89,000 is reached with the combination of Bragg's 64,000 men in
Chattanooga and Longstreet's 25,000 men from East Tennessee. The Federal estimate fuses George
Thomas' 53,000 men from the Army of the Cumberland with William T. Sherman's 20,000-man

The fact that Longstreet was assigned the task of extending Bragg's right flank appears to have been completely incidental to the evolution of Stevenson's right flank demonstration into a right flank offensive. Had President Davis not intervened, Bragg would have pursued the same strategy using Carter Stevenson—or as Bragg indicated after the war, John C. Breckinridge, Stevenson's corps commander.

Evidence that the movement's status had evolved from a simple demonstration into an offensive undertaking is provided in a November 5 message from Longstreet to Bragg in which Longstreet stated that if he was successful in clearing East Tennessee, then Bragg could either attack Chattanooga or move to join with Longstreet for an offensive.[62]

This language suggests that the possibility of a right flank offensive had at least been discussed. The key element to this plan, however, was the clearing of Burnside's Federals. Bragg hoped, and not unreasonably, that increasing his right flank detachment from 16,000 under Stevenson to 25,000 under Longstreet, coupled with the cooperation of Sam Jones, would bring about the speedy removal of Burnside from East Tennessee. Bragg's expectations are indicated in his November 5 note to Longstreet that "your [25,000 men]. . .will exceed considerably the highest estimate placed on the enemy."[63] The likelihood of Longstreet's receiving assistance from Jones was greatly enhanced by Jones' victory over Burnside at Rogersville on November 6, which pushed Burnside back

---

Army of the Tennessee and Joe Hooker's 12,000. All estimates are aggregate present; effectives can be approximated as 70% of aggregate numbers.

62

OR 31, pt. 2, p. 656; Bragg to E. T. Sykes, February 8, 1873, Polk Papers; *OR* 31, pt. 3, pp. 633ff.

63

Ibid., 31, pt. 3, p. 634. Longstreet claimed he would have "about fifteen thousand men, after deductions for camp guards and foraging parties." Longstreet, *Manassas to Appomattox*, p. 482. If we assume Longstreet meant effectives, then his 15,000-man estimate equates to an aggregate present of nearly 21,500, using the ratio of .70 for effectives to aggregate present. Bragg's expectation of cooperation from Sam Jones is partially acknowledged by Longstreet in his memoirs: "The remote contingent [Jones' men] that was to come from Southwest Virginia was an unknown quantity, not to be considered until it could report for service." Ibid.

beyond Bull's Gap. Jones' vanguard was now only 50 miles northeast of Knoxville.[64]

But did Longstreet outnumber Burnside? In a rather pessimistic letter dated November 11, Longstreet informed Bragg that "Information received yesterday confirms General Stevenson's report that the enemy's force about Knoxville is at least 23,000."[65] According to the November 30, 1863, returns for troops in East Tennessee, Burnside fielded 30,352 men "aggregate present" including 2,000 to 3,000 "home guards."[66] Of these, Burnside had sent Willcox's 6,000-man division, together with a brigade of 2,000 men from the XXIII Corps, to reinforce 2,500 Federals stationed at Cumberland Gap. This move was probably made in response to the recent debacle at Rogersville and the resulting concern for his line of communications. A large Federal force at Cumberland Gap would also threaten Sam Jones' right rear should he drive southwest towards Knoxville from Rogersville. With the transfer of Willcox and allowing for a small number of casualties from the fighting at Rogersville, Burnside was left with perhaps 19,000 men of all arms at Knoxville.[67] Bragg was obviously aware of the divided Federal situation in eastern Tennessee since he informed Longstreet in a November 11 message that Burnside had probably made substantial detachments from his base in Knoxville in response to Jones' activities.[68] The commander of the Army of Tennessee was correct in claiming that Longstreet's force

[64]
Bragg forwarded news of Jones' victory over Burnside to Longstreet in a message dated November 9. *OR* 31, pt. 3, p. 670.

[65]
Ibid., p. 681. Longstreet, *Manassas to Appomattox*, p. 482 refers to a letter from Burnside to Grant informing the latter that his force totaled about 22,300 men as of October 20. In neither case is it clear whether the figures represent aggregate, present for duty, or effectives.

[66]
OR 31, pt. 1, pp. 267, 680. See also, ibid., pt. 3, p. 292, which indicates that as of November 30, only eight of Burnside's infantry brigades were at Knoxville, with the remaining four presumably stationed in the vicinity of Cumberland Gap. Most of the Federal cavalry was probably at Knoxville, save perhaps one brigade stationed north of the city.

[67]
Burnside reported 12,000 "effectives," exclusive of new local recruits. This figure is comparable to my estimate of 19,000 "aggregate present" given the .67 to .70 ratio of effectives to aggregate. Brigadier General Richard C. Drum, "The Opposing Forces at Knoxville," in *Battles and Leaders*, 3, p. 752.

[68]
OR 31, pt. 3, p. 679.

exceeded Burnside's Knoxville garrison, and he was expecting 3,000 to 5,000 of Jones' men to join Longstreet, which would increase the odds in favor of the Confederates by an even wider margin. Bragg's expectation of expeditious success at Knoxville is substantiated by Longstreet himself in a curious letter to Simon Buckner dated November 5, 1863. In this letter, Longstreet stated that, "Twenty thousand men, well handled, could surely have captured Burnside and his forces."[69]

By the time of the failed assault on Knoxville's Fort Sanders on November 29, Longstreet had received from Sam Jones only two cavalry brigades under the command of Maj. Gen. Robert Ransom, about 3,500 troopers.[70] Additional reinforcements arrived on November 27 in the form of two of Simon Buckner's infantry brigades, 3,800 "aggregate present," under the command of Brig. Gen. Bushrod R. Johnson. Longstreet's potential assaulting column, which now numbered over 32,000 men, was opposed by Burnside's 19,000 Federals.[71]

A further indication of the adequacy of Longstreet's force for the task of reducing Knoxville and driving Burnside out of East Tennessee is provided by Edward Porter Alexander. Alexander's confidence in the success of the operation is revealed in his statement that, "It would have

69

Longstreet, *Manassas to Appomattox*, p. 484, and *OR* 52, pt. 2, p. 560. The letter's verb tense is curious since the note was purportedly written before Longstreet's attempt to seize or invest Knoxville. Even if Longstreet meant 20,000 effectives, his letter implies that with the 17,500 effectives he actually had, he should have been fairly confident of success, and that with the addition of Jones' troops, he should have been very confident of victory.

70

According to Longstreet, these reinforcements consisted of the brigades of Col. Henry L. Giltner and William E. Jones. Longstreet, *Manassas to Appomattox*, p. 502; *OR* 31, pt. 3, p. 613. The remaining troops from Ransom's Division were probably held back in the vicinity of Bean's Station to protect the Rebel right rear from the Federals at Cumberland Gap. Union reports to Burnside from Rogersville placed this force at 3,500 cavalry plus 3,500 infantry. *OR* 52, pt. 1, p. 492. This is consistent with the size of Ransom's Division. Sam Jones was not able to send all the troops in his department (about 11,000) because Averell was hovering on his right rear. Despite Lee's assurances to the contrary, Averell conducted a raid between November 6-13 with about 7,000 men and nearly reached Union, West Virginia, 30 miles from the railroad at Dublin's Station (Jones' headquarters). He was stalled in the fighting at Droop Mountain on November 6. Averell managed to break the railroad at Salem (Roanoke) in December, demonstrating the real threat Jones faced. *Civil War Times Illus*, March 1989; *OR* 34, pt. 2, p. 812.

71

The "effective" strength of Buckner's [Johnson's] two brigades was 2,625. *OR* 31, pt. 1, p. 532; Longstreet, *Manassas to Appomattox*, p. 503.

been impossible, I think, to find on the continent another earthwork [Fort Sanders] so advantageously situated for attack. No military engineer could ask for an easier task." Even as late as December 2, several days after the botched assault, his confidence remained undiminished as he "urged a renewal of the attack upon Ft. Sanders. [Longstreet] readily agreed and I started to organize it in such a way that it could not fail."[72]

Given the strength of Longstreet's command and the dispersed nature of Burnside's forces, Bragg appears to have had good reason to expect that East Tennessee would quickly be cleared of Burnside's Federals. After Burnside was eliminated or driven out of the region, Bragg would then be in a position, if warranted, to carry out a change of base to Knoxville in order to turn Grant out of Chattanooga. If for some reason Longstreet was delayed, Bragg's Army of Tennessee—which was expecting reinforcements from the Deep South—occupied a good defensive position and adequate force to hold it even without Longstreet. It was not unreasonable for Bragg to conclude that he could hold off Grant—with or without Sherman—until Longstreet succeeded or if necessary, until he could recall Longstreet.

* * *

Another aspect of the Chattanooga Campaign that is uniformly overlooked regards the necessity of reopening railroad communications with Virginia, which may have been logistically imperative for Bragg. Commissary General Lucius B. Northrop made it clear to Gen. Samuel Cooper on October 7 that "the recovery of East Tennessee [which would necessarily result in the reopening of the East Tennessee & Georgia Railroad] is absolutely necessary to the subsistence of Bragg's Army."[73] Up until that time, it apparently had not been seriously contemplated that the Army of Tennessee would have to be supplied from the eastern seaboard states. The retreat from Middle Tennessee forced Bragg into northern Georgia, an area incapable of offering much in the way of local

[72]
   Alexander, *Personal Recollections*, pp. 322-329.

[73]
    OR 30, pt. 4, p. 714.

subsistence. This new base of operations forced the Confederacy's Western army to depend on a single congested railroad line to Atlanta that was not adequate to maintain the army or provide for significant reinforcements. Northrop's concerns were validated by the inadequacy of the railroad between Tyner's Station and Loudon, and by Bragg's complaints to Richmond of the slowness with which troops were being forwarded from Atlanta (it took three weeks to forward two battalions).[74]

These circumstances suggest that Bragg was under considerable logistical pressure—independent of any other strategic considerations—to reestablish communications with Virginia in order to satisfy his current and future logistical requirements.

*   *   *

Given all of these factors, what went wrong with Braxton Bragg's plan? As in all campaigns in every war, the enemy had something to do with it. Ulysses Grant ordered George Thomas to launch a full-scale assault on Bragg on November 7 in order to draw Longstreet back to Chattanooga. By that date, Sherman's 20,000 men were still two weeks away from reaching Grant, Bragg still possessed Buckner's men (Bushrod Johnson's Division), Longstreet's 25,000 were only just underway for East Tennessee, and Joe Hooker's 12,000 Federals were still separated from Grant by Lookout Mountain. Given these factors, Thomas' 53,000 men would have been pitted against Bragg's 56,000, with Longstreet's divisions available to Bragg on short notice.[75] Furthermore, the attack was to have been against that portion of

---

74
   Ibid., 31, pt. 3, pp. 633ff; ibid., pt. 3, p. 699.

75
   The figure of 56,000 for Bragg's army assumes that the brigades of John C. Moore, John J. Pettus, William A. Quarles, and William E. Baldwin, which were still en route to join the Army of Tennessee, had not yet joined Bragg. In fact, Quarles and Baldwin did not entrain for Atlanta until November 21 & 22, respectively. *OR* 31, pt. 3, p. 740. This delay was by design, since Joseph Johnston was only willing to send these brigades, and Bragg probably only willing to feed them, if a battle was imminent. Ibid., pt. 3, p. 643.

Missionary Ridge held by Maj. Gen. Patrick Ronayne Cleburne, where Sherman's division later assaulted and was so roughly handled two weeks later. Unfortunately for Bragg and the Confederacy, Thomas refused to obey the order to attack, asserting that it was impossible to comply with the order because of the worn condition of the artillery horses. Under the circumstances, it seems likely that such an attack would have resulted in a damaging setback for Grant.[76]

A time-honored military truism is that subordinates do not always follow timetables, schedules, or their commander's wishes. If Longstreet had taken Knoxville quickly—as Bragg had reason to expect—the commander of the Army of Tennessee would have had two viable options. First, he could have recalled Longstreet to Chattanooga, which would have virtually equalized (numerically) the opposing forces. Second, he could have moved to join Longstreet at Knoxville, posing a serious threat to Grant's left-rear. When Bragg was finally routed off the heights of Missionary Ridge and driven back into northern Georgia, Longstreet was still four days away from delivering his assault against Fort Sanders—despite having been in front of Knoxville for one week and away from Bragg for three weeks. Longstreet did not act as quickly as the circumstances dictated.

There is much evidence that Longstreet could have moved more quickly to carry out his task. He took two weeks to get to Knoxville from Chattanooga, while Buckner's reinforcing division made the trip in five days. Similarly, Longstreet's entire force took eight days to traverse the distance from Tyner's Station to Sweetwater, arriving at the latter destination on November 12. In contrast to this slothful exhibition, Stevenson had made the same trip in mid-October against enemy opposition in just five days, and on November 10, he made the return trip in less than one day.[77] Longstreet's constant complaints from Sweetwater about a lack of transportation mystified Bragg. On November 12, apparently intending to ensure that the record would suggest that Longstreet was to blame for any delays, Bragg telegraphed:

[76]
   Grant, "Chattanooga," p. 694.

[77]
   See Stevenson's report, *OR* 31, pt. 1, p. 8.

"Your several dispatches of to-day astonish me. . .transportation in abundance was on the road and subject to your orders. I regret that it has not been energetically used. The means being furnished, you were expected to handle your own troops, and I cannot understand your constant applications for me to furnish them."[78] Longstreet moved out the next day.

Other evidence exists that suggests that Longstreet could have turned in a better performance. In early 1864, Maj. Gen. Lafayette McLaws, a division commander in Longstreet's Corps, accused his superior of intentionally delaying his move on Knoxville so he would not have to return to Chattanooga.[79] Even Longstreet admitted that the delays "he [was] suffering" gave him time to seek reinforcements.[80] These delays, coupled with a negative attitude about the move on Knoxville—Longstreet's November 5 letter to Buckner predicts failure for both Bragg and Longstreet—ultimately spelled doom for Bragg's design to oust Burnside and thereafter turn on Grant.[81] While he may not have been responsible for some of the delays, he was perhaps not working as hard as he might have to overcome them. Worse, some of his actions may have been designed to ensure the accuracy of his prediction to Buckner. A greater tragedy than Longstreet's slowness was his failure to seize the success that was within his grasp before Knoxville. His protests to the contrary notwithstanding, the force under his command was more than adequate for the task at hand long before the November 29 assault on Fort Sanders. Consequently, if Longstreet delayed for

---

78
Ibid., 31, pt. 3, p. 686.

79
McLaws to Bragg, February 25, 1864, in Bragg Papers, Western Reserve. This letter is also additional evidence that Longstreet's return to Bragg had been part of the original plan.

80
See Seitz, *Bragg*, p. 393, for a letter dated November 11, 1863, from Longstreet to unidentified correspondent.

81
Longstreet, *Manassas to Appomattox*, p. 484. This letter is also found in *OR* 52, pt. 2, pp. 559-560. The tone of this letter to Buckner suggests that it may have been written after the fact to pad the record.

reinforcements, his delay was not only fatal to Bragg's plans, but likely unnecessary.[82]

Despite the detachment of Longstreet, Bragg should have been able to maintain his position on Missionary Ridge—even after the arrival of William T. Sherman's reinforcements. The Federals did not enjoy an overwhelming preponderance in numbers even after Sherman joined Grant. By November 23, rather than being outnumbered nearly three to one, as suggested by a coterie of historians including Stanley Horn, Thomas Connelly, and James Lee McDonough, Bragg's 56,000 Confederates confronted about 85,000 opponents under Grant, odds of roughly 2 to 3.[83]

Bragg's apparent complacency under the circumstances is thus easier to understand. It must also be remembered that on the evening of November 24, after Federals under Joe Hooker captured Lookout Mountain, both John C. Breckinridge and William J. Hardee, two competent and well-respected military men, expressed complete confidence in the strength of the Confederate position on Missionary Ridge.[84]

Even Grant believed that Bragg should have been able to hold his position on Missionary Ridge. The Union commander wrote in his memoirs that "the victory at Chattanooga was won against great odds, considering the advantage the enemy had of position," and was due, in

[82]
    It is, however, to Longstreet's credit that he was able to maintain this force in East Tennessee, reopen the railroad to Virginia as far as Morristown, within 40 miles of Knoxville, by mid-January, and remain within 20 to 60 miles of Knoxville, constantly threatening Burnside, until he was recalled to Virginia by Lee on April 7, 1864. The engagement at Bean's Station, circa December 15, 1863, allowed Longstreet to remain in the Knoxville vicinity for the rest of the winter, where his presence was such a constant source of alarm that Grant was compelled to visit Knoxville personally at the end of December. Only at the end of January did Grant give up on the notion of expelling Longstreet. Longstreet, *Manassas to Appomattox,* pp. 507-547.

[83]
    See earlier discussion on Union strength. Bragg's army numbered 56,000 men after Longstreet's detachment and the subsequent transfer of 4,000 men from Simon Buckner's command to Longstreet in East Tennessee. Bragg also received some 4,000 reinforcements in the form of two of the four brigades he had been expecting for some time (the brigades of Baldwin and Quarles, about 4,000 men, did not arrive in time to participate in the Missionary Ridge engagement).

[84]
    Captain Irving A. Buck, in "Cleburne and His Division at Missionary Ridge," *Southern Historical Society Papers,* 52 vols. (1880), vol. 8, p. 466.

part, to Bragg's "grave [mistake]. . .in placing so much of his force on the plain in front of his *impregnable position* [emphasis added]."[85]

Despite his tactical deployment blunders, Bragg might still have prevailed on November 25 had Grant's revised battle plan not gone awry. Grant intended the assault by George Thomas on Missionary Ridge (Bragg's center) to be only a demonstration to prevent Bragg from sending additional reinforcements from his center to his right flank at Tunnel Hill. There, Sherman's attacking divisions—Grant's main thrust to dislodge Bragg's army—were stalled by Patrick Cleburne's Confederates. If Grant's battle plan had been adhered to, the Federals might never have discovered Bragg's faulty deployment of troops in his center. Grant's good fortune on November 25 is best summed up by Union Maj. Gen. William F. Smith, who observed some years later that "the assault on the center before either flank was turned was never seriously contemplated, and was made without plan [and] without orders. . . ."[86]

Conclusion

The critical event in understanding Braxton Bragg's decision to clear East Tennessee is the acceptance by Bragg and his generals of the lifting of the siege of Chattanooga brought about by the loss of Lookout Valley at the end of October. Up to that time Bragg had hoped, with good reason, to force William Rosecrans—who had not yet been replaced by George Thomas as the commander of the Army of the Cumberland—either to attack his strong positions around the city or

---

[85] Grant, "Chattanooga," p. 709; See John Hoffman, *The Confederate Collapse at the Battle of Missionary Ridge* (Dayton, 1985), for the best discussion of Bragg's faulty deployment of troops on November 25, 1864.

[86] Cleburne's reinforcements were actually coming from Bragg's left flank, not his center. Thus, not only was Grant's battle plan not followed, but it was based on faulty intelligence. See McDonough, *Chattanooga*, pp. 161-165, for a detailed discussion of these events; William F. Smith, "Comments on General Grant's Chattanooga," *Battles and Leaders*, 3, p. 717.

retreat out of Chattanooga. A Union attack almost certainly would have failed, and a retreat to a new and more secure base would have handed Bragg and the Confederacy much of Middle Tennessee. But the defeat at Wauhatchie on October 28-29 upset this Confederate balance of power. The loss of Lookout Valley meant that Grant's force—which with the addition of Joe Hooker's divisions now slightly outnumbered Bragg's army—would also receive substantial reinforcements from at least Sherman and possibly Burnside as well. It would have been foolhardy for Bragg, in the hope of receiving a direct assault from Grant, to have concentrated his forces in response to this development. He realized that the re-establishment of Union river and railroad communications would allow Grant to reinforce his army to the extent necessary to offset any force that Bragg could likely support with his tenuous single rail line. Furthermore, if Bragg did completely concentrate his forces, Grant could easily turn his position with either Sherman, Burnside, or both, while holding him in place with the troops of Hooker and Thomas.

Therefore, the loss of Lookout Valley significantly altered the strategic situation around Chattanooga, forcing Bragg to either advance against the Federals, either directly or indirectly, or to retreat. Since retreat was not a viable option, the question became one of whether to advance by the left flank or the right.

Bragg's decision not to advance by the left flank, as had been contemplated since the October 11 meeting with Davis, was probably due to a combination of reasons. First, Hooker was entrenched in Lookout Valley, and Sherman's men were approaching from beyond Bragg's left flank. Additional Union reinforcements could be concentrated, via rail and water, relatively easily in the vicinity of Stevenson and Bridgeport. Thus a move in that direction would have shifted Bragg's men into Union strength. Another consideration was that Bragg did not enjoy either rail or river communications in that direction, and the roads on his left consisted of little more than muddy mountain byways. Finally, extending his army to the left exposed his precarious logistical line with Atlanta. A move to the right, however, offered several advantages. Bragg would have had the use of the East Tennessee and Georgia Railroad, at least as far as Loudon. As he further extended his right flank, he would draw nearer to a second or alternative line of railroad and wagon communications from Virginia. Only Burnside was there to oppose him, and his forces were scattered all over East Tennessee. Also, Burnside's supply problems and remoteness from reinforcements made it unlikely that he could be significantly reinforced, even from Grant. In addition, there was the very real prospect of cooperation from Sam Jones' Rebels in southwestern Virginia, who were advancing from Bristol into Burnside's enclave. Rather than shift east the Army of Tennessee in its entirety, Bragg decided to extend his right flank to clear East Tennessee quickly with the cooperation of Sam Jones. A movement of his entire army would have unnecessarily exposed his line of communications with Atlanta prior to the establishment of an alternative line of communications with Virginia. In addition, the elongation of Bragg's right flank might induce Grant to rashly attack Bragg's weakened line before Sherman's arrival.

If successful in clearing East Tennessee, Bragg would have been in a position to move his whole force northeast toward Knoxville, uncover his Atlanta line, and threaten, perhaps indefinitely, Grant's communications with Nashville and points north. Such a threat, exclusive of other significant political concerns, would have probably caused Grant to hesitate advancing on Atlanta. If Sherman and other Union reinforcements arrived before Burnside was dealt with in East Tennessee, Bragg, given his strong position and adequate force, felt he could hold off Grant until Burnside was cleared from around Knoxville or, if necessary, recall Longstreet's men.

Finally, Longstreet's assignment to this extension of the right flank was completely incidental to the development of Bragg's decision to move by the right. The siege of Chattanooga had just been raised by the loss of Lookout Valley, and Bragg's only viable remaining strategic option was to advance by the right flank. By this time, Bragg had already made a substantial right flank detachment under Carter Stevenson, and it was President Davis' request to Bragg that resulted in Longstreet being assigned to the task already underway with Stevenson. Bragg indicated in a letter sent after the war that he intended to send John C. Breckinridge (as a replacement for Stevenson) against Knoxville instead of Longstreet.

Lt. Gen. James Longstreet
(*Generals in Gray*)

Gen. Braxton Bragg
(*Generals in Gray*)

The purpose of this article is to present a rational scenario that explains how Bragg could embark on such a seemingly irrational policy that came to be so universally condemned. The evidence presented herein suggests—the unfavorable outcome for the Confederates notwithstanding—that Bragg's decision to clear East Tennessee was not only rational and reasonable, but possibly essential; that the force detached for this expedition was more than adequate; and that President Davis' intervention affected only the membership of the detachment, not its existence, strength, or objective. Bragg's decision to attempt to clear East Tennessee was militarily sound.

Marion V. Armstrong

Vince Armstrong, a native of Maryland with a life-long interest in military history, holds advanced degrees from the University of Southern California and Old Dominion University. He has served since 1969 in the United States Army as an officer and civilian employee in Vietnam, Korea, Germany, and various posts throughout the U.S. He regularly lectures on military topics and frequently conducts battlefield tours. Mr. Armstrong is currently beginning a second career as an historian in Nashville, Tennessee, where he is preparing a series of book-length studies reassessing the actions of the various Federal corps at Antietam for Savas Woodbury Publishers.

A Failure of Command?

A Reassessment of the Generalship of Edwin V. Sumner and the Federal II Corps at the Battle of Antietam

Historians have almost uniformly maligned the performance of Maj. Gen. Edwin V. Sumner at the September 17, 1862 Battle of Antietam. Sumner, who commanded the II Corps of the Army of the Potomac at Antietam, has been ill-treated in the history books on four different counts. First, for immediately sending Maj. Gen. John Sedgwick's Second Division into action in the West Woods as it arrived upon the battlefield between 8:40 and 9:00 a.m.; second, for forming that division for the attack in three brigade lines of battle in tandem; third, for failing to exercise effective control over his remaining two divisions; and lastly, for failing to resume offensive operations with the combined forces on the right of the Federal line after Sedgwick's repulse from the West Woods. A careful review of the situation as it existed on the battlefield during those hours, however, coupled with an appreciation of what

Maj. Gen. Edwin V. Sumner
(Library of Congress)

Sumner knew of it, suggests that in these actions his generalship was not as culpable as many believe.

At the time of the Battle of Antietam, Major General Sumner was at the acme of a Regular Army career that spanned forty-two years of continuous active service. At sixty-five he was the oldest general officer in the Army of the Potomac. Directly commissioned in the 2nd Infantry in 1819, he was made a captain of dragoons in 1833 and thereafter served almost continuously on the frontier. His record as a cavalry commander under Winfield Scott during the war with Mexico was one of distinction, earning him Scott's respect and brevet promotions to lieutenant colonel and colonel. Advancement in the Regular Army continued after the war, when he was made colonel of the 1st Cavalry in 1855, and commander of Fort Leavenworth from 1855 to 1857, a position that placed him in the maelstrom of "bleeding Kansas." He moved to St. Louis in 1858, where he assumed command of the Department of the West. In 1861 he was selected by General-in-Chief Scott as the senior officer to escort President-elect Abraham Lincoln from Springfield, Illinois to Washington, D.C. Edwin Sumner was made a brigadier general in the Regular Army on March 16, 1861, and sent to San Francisco to replace Southerner Albert Sidney Johnston in command of The Department of the Pacific. He was recalled to Washington late in the year, appointed to command a division in the Army of the Potomac, and subsequently, the II Corps of that army when Lincoln directed the organization of corps in his General War Order Number 2 on March 8, 1862.[1]

Sumner's reputation in the Old Army was that of a soldier who could be relied upon to carry out orders regardless of the obstacles, although that reputation did not necessarily extend to include imagination or inventiveness in carrying them out. Whatever his shortcomings, however, Edwin V. Sumner did not lack in courage. At

---

[1] U.S. War Department, *War of the Rebellion: The Official Records of the Union and Confederate Armies*, 128 vols. (Washington, D.C., 1890-1901), series I, vol. 51, Pt. 1, p. 507. Hereinafter cited as *OR*. All references are to series I unless otherwise noted.

the Mexican War Battle of Cerro Gordo, when a company of overly enthusiastic infantry charged under the guns of the main Mexican defensive position and was pinned down, Sumner immediately led his mounted riflemen in a second charge to extract them. The tactic resulted less in the rescue of the infantrymen than in placing the mounted riflemen in the same jeopardy, but both units managed to hold their forward position with small loss until an opportunity to withdraw presented itself. In Scott's ill-advised attack on Molino Del Rey, Sumner, with 270 cavalrymen, was given the mission of protecting the left flank of the American advance from 4,000 Mexican horsemen. When half of this greatly superior force moved threateningly forward, Sumner unhesitatingly lead his small command in a charge across a ravine against the oncoming Mexicans. Faced with this onslaught and under fire from American artillery, the Mexicans withdrew without actually crossing sabres with Sumner's dragoons. The only drawback to this exceptional demonstration of determination and courage was that in executing the charge Sumner lead his troopers within short range of the Mexican infantry line and lost some 44 men and 104 horses.[2]

Back on the frontier Sumner showed himself to be a more than competent officer and leader, capable of independently conducting campaigns against large bands of marauding Indians over extensive territory with infantry, cavalry, and artillery combined in multiple columns. Of just such a campaign conducted by Sumner against the Cheyenne in 1857, Percival Green Lowe, one of Sumner's soldiers, wrote, "he did the best that an earnest preserving commander could do and I think that the general verdict of his command was that he did well, and that is the highest court by which a man can be tried."[3] As Lowe indicates, Sumner was carefully observed by the soldiers under him. Their nickname for him was "Bull," an appellation derived from his

---

[2]
Justin H. Smith, *The War With Mexico*, 2 vols. (Gloucester, 1919), vol. 2, pp. 52, 144-146: John S. D. Eisenhower, *So Far From God: The U.S. War With Mexico, 1846-1848* (New York, 1989), pp. 278-279, 334, 336.

[3]
Percival Green Lowe, *Five Years a Dragoon and Other Adventures on the Great Plains* (Kansas City, 1906), p. 297.

great booming voice which, it was said, could be heard clearly from one end of a regiment to the other, even in the din of combat. Another story, though, had it that the sobriquet was in actuality "Bull-Head," a less flattering nickname arising out of a rumor that a musket ball had been seen to bounce off of his head without doing noticeable damage.[4]

As a corps commander in the Army of the Potomac, Sumner was something of an anomaly. The II Corps would become one of the best trained, best lead, and most reliable in the army. Sumner was its first commander and as such his direction of the nascent corps was of great and lasting influence. Francis A. Walker, one of the corps' staff officers and later its historian, ascribes to Sumner's soldierly qualities a full measure of credit for making the corps everything it would become. Walker wrote, "The history of the Second Corps cannot be written without full and explicit recognition of the influence which its first commander exerted, especially upon the younger officers and soldiers of the corps, in that highly plastic state of mind which belonged to the early months of the war."[5]

George B. McClellan, the commander of the Army of the Potomac and Sumner's immediate superior, recognized the value of Sumner's soldierly qualities. He was not happy, however, to have Sumner as his senior corps commander, the officer who would assume immediate command of the army should some calamity befall McClellan. After the rear guard action before Williamsburg on May 5, 1862—which, due to the army commander's reproachable absence, was directed by Sumner—McClellan wrote his wife, "Sumner had proved that he was even a greater fool than I had supposed & had come within an ace of having us defeated."[6] McClellan went on to take full credit for saving

---

4
    Stephen W. Sears, *Landscape Turned Red, The Battle of Antietam* (New York, 1983), p. 216; David Lavender, *Bent's Fort* (New York, 1954), pp. 319-320.

5
    Francis A. Walker, *History of the Second Army Corps in the Army of the Potomac* (New York, 1887), p. 11.

6
    Stephen W. Sears, *The Civil War Papers of George B. McClellan, Selected Correspondence, 1860-1865* (New York, 1989), p. 257.

the day and the army. While Sumner's direction of the Williamsburg fight left him open to constructive criticism, there were extenuating circumstances involved and the day did not go nearly as badly for the Unionists as McClellan indicated.

McClellan's tune changed, if only briefly, after the May 31, 1862 Battle of Fair Oaks, where Sumner pulled the Young Napoleon's fat from the fire. Arriving before Richmond, McClellan carelessly advanced the III and IV corps across the Chickahominy River, where they were attacked in force and in serious danger of being destroyed by Joseph E. Johnston's Confederate army. To the advantage of the Confederates, a tremendous storm the night prior to the battle had raised such a flood in the river that the isolated units were all but effectively cut off from support. Hearing the sound of battle, Sumner called his corps to arms and moved them to the flooded river crossings. It was not long before McClellan sent orders for Sumner to go to the aid of the endangered force, if possible, but the bridges that he needed to cross the Chickahominy were severely damaged by the flood and the engineer officers present told him that a crossing was impossible. "Impossible!" Sumner roared. "I tell you I can cross. I am ordered."[7] With that he pushed across his two divisions and continued his march to Fair Oaks, arriving on the right flank of the IV Corps just in time to keep it from being overwhelmed. In dispatches to the Secretary of War, McClellan complimented Sumner by saying that, "He displayed the utmost energy in bringing his troops into action, & handled them with the utmost courage in action. He repulsed every attack of the enemy, & drove him wherever he could get at him."[8]

At Savage's Station on June 29, Sumner again demonstrated his qualities as a fighting general by successfully conducting a rear guard action as McClellan withdrew the rest of the army toward the James River. But Sumner believed that the Army of the Potomac could and

[7]
  Richard Elliott Winslow, *General John Sedgwick, The Story of a Union Corps Commander* (Presidio, 1982), p. 16.

[8]
  Sears, *McClellan Papers*, p. 286.

should stand and fight, and moved away from Savage Station that night only after being ordered to do so directly by McClellan. Throughout the remainder of the Peninsula Campaign, Sumner continued to be seriously disappointed with McClellan's lack of initiative and aggressiveness. Uncharacteristic of the apolitical professional soldier that he was, Sumner went so far as to express his concern to a politically influential friend in Washington asking him to "represent this in the right quarter."[9]

Whatever misgivings McClellan had concerning Sumner's abilities as a corps commander, they were not aired officially. McClellan made no disparaging remarks in his official reports concerning Sumner's performance and did not attempt to have Sumner removed or reassigned away from the Army of the Potomac. During both the Peninsula and Maryland campaigns, McClellan paid due regard to Sumner as his senior corps commander. Whenever two or more of the corps were operating beyond his direct control, McClellan habitually appointed Sumner as the overall commander. When Secretary of War Edwin Stanton nominated Sumner and McClellan's other corps commanders for promotion to major general on July 5, 1862, McClellan made no objection.[10]

In the eyes of his soldiers, most of whom were volunteers and knew nothing of military ways, Sumner was a wonder. He was a man steeped in military policy, process, and practice and he conducted the affairs of the II Corps and its soldiers accordingly. An officer of the Irish Brigade remembered Sumner as an "accomplished soldier of more than forty years' experience: cool, thoroughly trained, and competent for all the emergencies of war."[11] Sumner understood soldiers and their needs, and saw to it that they were met. But what the soldiers would remember most about Edwin V. Sumner was that he was a fighter who would not hesitate to commit himself and his command to battle when he believed

---

9
    OR 11, pt. 3, p. 356.

10
    Ibid., 51, pt. 1, p. 716.

11
    David P. Conyngham, *The Irish Brigade and Its Campaigns: With Some Account of the Corcoran Legion, and Sketches of the Principal Officers* (Boston, 1869), p. 105.

it was necessary. Among them it was said that if McClellan went to the front there would be no battle that day, but if "Old Man Sumner goes to the front, look out for a fight."[12]

The Battle of Antietam, September 17, 1862

Sumner's fighting blood was up on the morning of September 17, 1862. Better than his commander, he understood that the rebellion was not going to be brought to an end without a terrible and decisive victory on the battlefield, and on that morning the opportunity seemed at hand. General Robert E. Lee and his Army of Northern Virginia, forced on September 14 from the passes creasing the summit of South Mountain, had taken up a defensive position west of Antietam Creek on the high ground between that stream and the Potomac River only a mile farther to the west. Despite being well outnumbered, Lee remained in position throughout September 15 and 16 as McClellan slowly assembled the Army of the Potomac on the east bank of Antietam Creek. As the hours passed and the Army of Northern Virginia stood its ground, it became clear to most observers that Lee was going to make a stand against McClellan with his back against the Potomac River.

McClellan finally determined on September 16 that he must attack Lee. Late in the afternoon he sent the I Corps under "Fighting" Maj. Gen. Joe Hooker across Antietam Creek, supposedly to gain the left flank of the Rebel position and to prepare the way for an attack on the morning of the 17th. The extent and the objective of that attack were unclear to McClellan's corps commanders then, and remain unclear today. In a confusing and rambling statement written in his initial report on October 15, 1862, McClellan recalled his plan of battle by saying, "The design was to make the main attack upon the enemy's left—at least to create a diversion in favor of the main attack, with the hope of something more by assailing the enemy's right—and, as soon as one or

---

12
  Frederick L. Hitchcock, *War from the Inside: The Story of the 132nd Regiment Pennsylvania Volunteer Infantry in the War for the Suppression of the Rebellion, 1862-1863* (Philadelphia, 1904), p. 40.

both of the flank movements were fully successful, to attack their center with any reserve I might then have on hand."[13]

McClellan did not consult with or confide many of the details of his plan of battle to his II Corps commander. Sumner knew only that Hooker had crossed Antietam Creek in the late afternoon and would move against the enemy left flank, and that if this attack were successful, it would set the stage for an advance by the V and IX Corps. By special order published on September 14, Sumner had taken command of his own and Maj. Gen. Joseph K. F. Mansfield's XII Corps, both of which were bivouacked for the night of the 16th in the vicinity of Keédysville, only a mile from where Hooker crossed the Antietam. The three divisions of Sumner's corps were commanded by Maj. Gen. John Sedgwick, Brig. Gen. William H. French, and Brig. Gen. Israel B. Richardson. Late in the evening, Sumner received orders from army headquarters to send Mansfield's corps forward immediately to support Hooker's and to have the II Corps ready to march at an hour before daylight. In obedience to those orders, Mansfield's corps marched at 11:30 p.m., while Sumner allowed his own men to sleep until 2:00 a.m. before they were ordered up to make breakfast and to prepare to move.[14]

Although Sumner had the three divisions of his own II Corps ready to march to the front at first light as McClellan had directed, no orders were forthcoming. From the direction of the Rebel left flank came the unmistakable sounds of a bitterly-fought contest, indicating that the I and perhaps the XII Corps were pressing their attacks alone. Anxious minutes passed but still no orders to move to the front were received. Sumner grew increasingly impatient knowing that those two corps acting alone could not hope to be successful attacking the whole of Lee's army. McClellan might be letting an opportunity for decisive victory slip

---

13
   OR 19, pt. 1, p. 30.

14
   Ibid., p. 275, pt. 2, p. 290; U.S. Senate, *Report of the Joint Committee on the Conduct of the War,* 3 vols. (Washington, D.C., 1863), vol. 1, p. 368; Charles D. Page, *History of the Fourteenth Regiment, Connecticut Vol. Infantry* (Meriden, 1906), p. 34.

away in the piecemeal commitment to battle of the Army of the Potomac.[15]

By 6:00 a.m. Sumner could stand the wait no longer. Together with his son Samuel, a captain serving as his aide-de-camp, he mounted and rode to army headquarters at the nearby Pry Farm to see McClellan and to get the orders he needed to move the II Corps to the scene of action. McClellan's staff, however, kept Sumner from seeing the army commander, an affront that probably rankled the old soldier. The word was that all was going well, Hooker was driving them, and the action was only that of a rear guard. McClellan, they said, had been up most of the night attending to the details of his plan of battle and was resting and could not be disturbed. Sumner chaffed at the continuing delay.[16]

After waiting for well over an hour, Sumner was finally given orders at 7:20 a.m. to move to the front and support the combined assaults of Hooker and Mansfield—but he was to take just two of his three divisions. Major General Richardson's brigades were to remain in position as a tactical reserve until Brig. Gen. George W. Morell's division of Maj. Gen. Fitz John Porter's V Corps could be brought forward to replace it. Withholding an entire division made little sense to Sumner, since Morell's division was only a mile away and could be brought forward in a matter of minutes. He did not stop to protest the order, however; Richardson would be following soon enough.[17]

With two miles to march before reaching the battle front, Sedgwick's division was already formed on the Boonsboro-Shepherdstown Pike, with French's brigades directly behind it. A few shouted words of command and the regiments were up and moving. No time was to be lost finding and following country lanes. The men marched due west, cross-country, through fields and wood lots, breaking fences as they

15
    Samuel S. Sumner, "The Antietam Campaign," in *Papers of the Military Historical Society of Massachusetts*, 15 vols. (Boston, 1895-1918), vol. 14, p. 10.

16
    Ibid.; *OR* 19, pt. 1, p. 275; Stephen W. Sears, *George B. McClellan, The Young Napoleon* (New York, 1988), p. 305.

17
    Sumner, "Antietam Campaign," p. 10; *OR* 19, pt. 1, p. 275.

were reached. The infantrymen crossed Antietam Creek at a ford prepared by the army's engineers exactly one mile below the Upper Bridge, taking it in their stride without changing formation.[18]

The formation in both divisions was the same: three brigades moving parallel to each other, each brigade in a column of regiments, the regiments marching by the right flank. Sumner chose this formation to facilitate getting into the attack formation that he expected to use once he reached the front. As he understood it, Hooker and Mansfield had begun their assault at about 6:00 a.m. and were successfully attacking south along the Hagerstown Pike toward the village of Sharpsburg. If that were true, Sumner's II Corps (less Richardson's division) would arrive at the front either on the left flank or in the rear of the I and XII Corps. In either case, one simple command, "front!," would put each division in three tandem lines of battle, one brigade in each line. Sedgwick's division would be on the right, French's on the left. From that point the II Corps could take over the assault either by attacking on the left of the I and XII Corps or by passing through them from the rear.[19]

As the II Corps ascended the undulating slope west of Antietam Creek toward the spine of high ground between that stream and the Potomac River, Sumner began to suspect that all might not be going as well as he had been lead to believe. Rather than rolling off to the south and southwest, the battle seemed to be directly ahead of his advance (west), concentrated in and beyond a fairly large body of woods (the East Woods). From what he could tell at this distance, the fighting might even be shifting to the north. As a precaution, Sumner directed Sedgwick to deploy his division into assault formation. The brigade columns of regiments were brought around to the right, marching north

---

18
   Ibid., 19, pp. 172-173. Sedgwick's Second Division was composed of the brigades of Brig. Gens. Willis A. Gorman, Oliver O. Howard, and Napoleon J. T. Dana. French's Third Division was composed of the brigades of Brig. Gens. Nathan Kimball and Max Weber, and Col. Dwight Morris; Sumner, "Antietam Campaign," p. 10; *OR* 19, pt. 1, pp. 275, 313.

19
   Max Weber to Antietam Battlefield Board, December 10, 1892, Ezra Carman Papers, copy at Antietam National Battlefield; Sumner, "Antietam Campaign," p. 10; *Committee on the Conduct of the War*, 1, p. 368; *OR* 19, Pt. 1, p. 305.

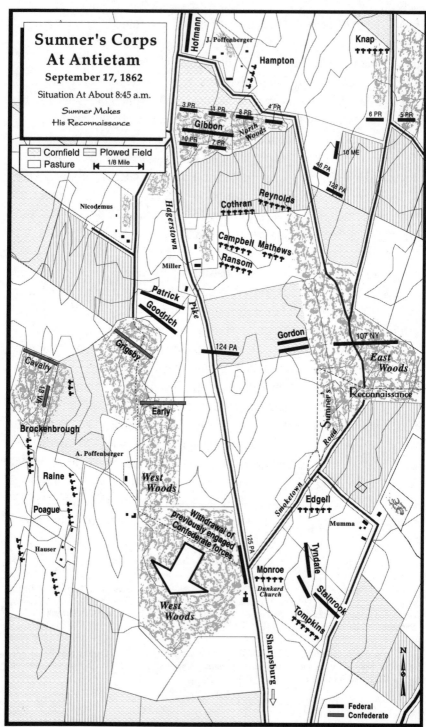

**Sumner's Corps
At Antietam**

September 17, 1862

Situation At About 8:45 a.m.

*Sumner Makes
His Reconnaissance*

- Cornfield
- Pasture
- Plowed Field
- 1/8 Mile

Federal
Confederate

Mark A. Moore

until every file turned the corner. The command "front!" was given, the lines were dressed to the right, and the division continued its march to battle in a column of brigades, each brigade in one line of battle with 50 to 70 yards between them. As Sedgwick's division approached within a few hundred yards of the large body of woods, artillery shells began to fall in its ranks. The fire was long range and not very harmful, most of it coming from some distant point beyond the woods.[20]

As the advance of Sedgwick's division continued toward the woods, Sumner encountered a group of soldiers carrying the wounded I Corps Commander, Joseph Hooker, to the rear. By this time Hooker had lost a great deal of blood and may have only been half conscious. No one made a record of the dialogue that passed between the two men, but if Sumner did not talk directly with the wounded officer, it is reasonable to assume he received a synopsis of the situation from one of the staff officers accompanying Hooker. Hooker later testified before Congress that at his meeting with Sumner, he was upbeat concerning the progress that his corps had made and the potential for driving "the Rebel army into the Potomac, or to destroy it."[21]

Hooker had launched his I Corps assault south along the Hagerstown Turnpike toward the high ground above Sharpsburg at about 6:00 a.m. Despite heavy resistance, his corps managed to advance about one mile, driving the Confederates back to near a small white church that represented the objective of the assault. Powerful Southern counterattacks, however, staggered the I Corps driving it back to its starting point. Hooker then sent an urgent call to the XII Corps for assistance. Together with Brig. Gen. Alpheus Williams, who had

---

[20] *OR* 19, pt. 1, pp. 305, 310-311, 319-320. The reports of all three of Sedgwick's brigade commanders agree that the division was deployed into line of battle and came under artillery fire prior to reaching the East Woods. Oliver O. Howard, however, is mistaken when he says that the division faced to the south. The fighting in the woodlot ahead, though, had largely subsided and the officers could see what appeared to be formations of Federal infantrymen leaving its southern end, preceded by less organized knots of enemy infantry. At this point Sumner was riding well in advance of Sedgwick's division in an attempt to understand the unfolding action and determine how best to employ his 15,200 infantrymen against an as yet largely unseen enemy.

[21] *Committee on the Conduct of the War*, 1, p. 582.

succeeded the mortally wounded Mansfield in command of the XII Corps, he worked out a plan of support and a design for the renewal of the assault. Hooker later testified that as he was carried from the field (he was wounded soon after talking to Williams), he believed that a continuation of the XII Corps assault southward toward Sharpsburg would receive support from the V and IX Corps, which he assumed would be driving on Sharpsburg from the east and southeast. It is therefore reasonable to postulate that Sumner may have come away from his meeting with Hooker with the understanding that the I Corps was pretty well used up, and the XII Corps was deployed and continuing the attack on the right in accordance with McClellan's battle plan.[22]

After his meeting with Hooker, Sumner turned and spurred his horse in an attempt to catch up with the leading brigade of Sedgwick's division, which was approaching the woods. As he rode up he could see that the woodlot was completely clear of Rebels, making an assault through the timber unnecessary. Sumner entered the woods ahead of the division, conducting his own reconnaissance. At the same time, he sent staff officers to gather information concerning the fluid situation in his front and to find whatever general officers were now in command of the I and XII Corps. As he rode west through the woods, he came upon the dead, dying, and wounded soldiers from both sides. In some places, it was possible to discern where the lines of battle had been by the ranks of dead and wounded men who fell where they had stood. There were also hundreds of unwounded Federal soldiers milling about. Many were helping wounded comrades to the rear, while others had simply lost their units or themselves in the shock of combat. On the western side of the woods, small groups of soldiers collected behind trees and fired their weapons to the west and southwest. These torn squads of soldiers were all that remained of regiments that only an hour earlier had moved forward in strong lines of battle. These clumps of Federals now formed an expedient albeit disjoined line of battle. One Federal regiment, still

22
    Ibid., pp. 368-369, 581-582; *OR* 19, pt. 1, pp. 219, 275, 475; George W. Smalley, "Antietam," *New York Tribune*, September 19, 1862; reprinted, *New York Times*, September 20, 1862, p. 2.

intact and nearly unbloodied, was passing rapidly through the woods to the south in battle formation.[23]

The scene that greeted Sumner as he approached the west side of the woods was just as confused. Beyond the woodlot was a large open area of pasture and corn covered with the dead and wounded. Hundreds more wounded and lost soldiers were making their way slowly to the rear across this terrain. To the west and southwest he could see a collection of disorganized Rebels retiring over a ridge toward a half-hidden woodlot that looked to be about 800 yards distant.

Standing directly in front of him at the southeast corner of a large cornfield was a brigade of Federal infantry that apparently had been engaged in driving a Rebel force from the open area. The brigade was formed in two lines of battle with two regiments in each line. While the regiments in front appeared comparatively fresh, the two rear regiments were obviously bloodied, indicating that the brigade had just been reformed.[24]

The line of the reformed brigade was extended to the west and northwest by a very large regiment, whose line vanished over a ridge of high ground that ran northeast to southwest through the center of the open area.[25] Although the terrain obscured his view of the regiment's right flank, Sumner could tell that it was still actively engaged with the enemy, who were apparently disputing its advance toward the western woods. From the sound and smoke of the small arms fire, Sumner concluded that the regiment was supported on its right by additional Federal troops who were attacking toward the north end of the distant

---

[23]
    Smalley, "Antietam," p. 2; *Committee on the Conduct of the War*, 1, p. 368; Oliver Otis Howard, *Autobiography of Oliver Otis Howard, Major General United States Army*, 2 vols. (New York, 1908), vol. 1, p. 295; *OR* 19, pt. 1, p. 502. The regiment Sumner saw passing through the woods was the 107th New York, Brig. Gen. George H. Gordon's brigade, Alpheus Williams' division, XII Corps.

[24]
    OR 19, pt. 1, p. 495; John Gibbon, *Personal Recollections of the Civil War* (New York, 1928), p. 87. The brigade in the edge of the cornfield was Gordon's, minus the 107th New York.

[25]
    OR 19, pt. 1, p. 491; Ezra A. Carman, "History of the Antietam Campaign," Microfilm, Antietam National Battlefield, chp. 17, p. 26. The regiment extending Gordon's right flank was the 124th Pennsylvania, Brig. Gen. Samuel W. Crawford's brigade, Williams' division, XII Corps.

western woods.[26] In addition to these troops, five hundred yards to his right front were several Federal batteries on the ridge at the center of the open area. At least one of these batteries and an additional section of two guns were firing toward the western woods in support of the attacking infantry, while the others were in the process of limbering up and moving to the rear.[27]

Looking back to the south, Sumner found his view blocked by a second ridge running to the southwest, parallel to the one in the center of the open area. Down the swale created by these two ridges, however, he could see all the way to the western woodlot. Just in front of the woods was a road running off to the south in the direction of Sharpsburg, disappearing from view behind the southernmost ridge. From what Sumner knew of this area, this major thoroughfare could only be the Hagerstown Pike. A country road, bordered on the north by a zig-zag rail fence and on the south by a heavier post and rail fence, joined the Hagerstown Pike at the end of the swale. This road extended from the southern point of the eastern woods southwest across the open area along the crest and slope of the southern ridge.[28] Sumner had crossed this road only minutes before while passing through the eastern woods. Directly beyond the junction of the two roads, set back a few yards into the western woods, was a small white building that looked to be either a

---

26
   Marsena Rudolph Patrick, *Inside Lincoln's Army: The Diary of Marsena Rudolph Patrick, Provost Marshal General, Army of the Potomac*, edited by David S. Sparks (New York, 1964), p. 149. The Federals extending the flank of the 124th Pennsylvania were from Col. William B. Goodrich's brigade, Brig. Gen. George S. Greene's division, XII Corps and Brig. Gen. Marsena R. Patrick's brigade, Brig. Gen. Abner Doubleday's division, I Corps.

27
   OR 19, pt. 1, pp. 227, 269-270. The guns firing from this position were from Capt. John A. Reynolds' 1st New York Light, Battery L, and a section from Capt. Joseph B. Campbell's 4th United States, Battery B, under the command of Lt. James Stewart, both of Doubleday's division, I Corps. The remaining artillery, Capt. Dunbar R. Ransom's 5th United States, Battery C (Brig. Gen. George G. Meade's division), and Capt. Ezra Matthews' 1st Pennsylvania Light Artillery, Battery F (Brig. Gen. James B. Ricketts' division), both I Corps units, had been in this position for some time and were just withdrawing. Captain George W. Cothran's Battery M, 1st New York Light Artillery (Greene's division, XII Corps) had also been in this position, but by this time was moving toward the East Woods.

28
   This was the Smoketown Road.

church or a school house.[29] A large body of Federal infantry, perhaps a small brigade, was just entering the woods in the vicinity of this building. It did not appear to Sumner that these men were meeting with any significant Confederate opposition.[30] A number of Rebel prisoners were being marched to the rear along the country road that intersected the Hagerstown Pike.[31]

In order to get a better view of what was transpiring to the south, Sumner cantered along the tree line until he reached the southern end of the eastern woods and the crest of the ridge that was blocking his view in that direction. From this point he could see well to the south, all the way to the village of Sharpsburg, although a few hundred yards farther to the southwest the ridge turned directly south ending in a knoll that blocked his view in that direction. In the distance, Confederate infantry could be seen withdrawing in some disorder.

His new vantage point revealed other valuable information. Only a few yards in front appeared to be an entire division of Federal infantry lying down in battle formation. The orientation of their lines was in a quarter-circle, with their left flank facing to the south, their center to the southwest, and their right to the west. Situated below the ridge and its terminating knoll, these prone men were protected from Confederate artillery fire being directed at the open area from somewhere beyond the western woods and from the southwest. Ahead of these troops were two batteries of artillery. The first, a battery of six guns, was located in front of the left flank of the infantry. It was engaging a Confederate battery located just 300 yards farther to the south. The second unit, also a battery of six guns, was positioned on the opposite side of the ridge in front of the division's right flank, just east of the Hagerstown Pike

---

29
    This was the Dunker (Dunkard) Church, the earlier focal point of Hooker's I Corps assault.

30
    This body of troops was the 125th Pennsylvania (Crawford's brigade, Williams' division, XII Corps), a new nine-month regiment enlisted just weeks before. It was much larger than the average regiment on the field at Sharpsburg since it had not yet been depleted by sickness or hard campaigning.

31
    OR 19, pt. 1, pp. 506, 508, 509. Many of the regimental reports of Greene's division, XII Corps, mention capturing a large number of prisoners at this point.

opposite the white building. This battery was firing to the southwest across the turnpike at a target blocked from Sunmer's view by the intervening knoll. Almost directly in front of Sumner beyond the country road and about 200 yards to the rear of the battery near the white building was yet a third Federal six-gun battery. This battery was firing in the same direction and apparently at the same target as the battery in front of the white building.[32]

At about this time Sumner's staff officers began to return. One brought word that the only general officer of the I Corps who could be located was Brig. Gen. James B. Ricketts, commanding the Second Division. Ricketts sent discouraging information about the condition of the battered I Corps, telling Sumner's staffers that he could not raise more than 300 men from its ranks. Another staff officer brought confirmation that Major General Mansfield was seriously wounded and had been taken from the field. Staff officers from the XII Corps also arrived and appealed to Sumner for assistance in holding the positions that they had gained.[33]

Sumner's observations, coupled with this information, led him to conclude that the I Corps had been entirely used up, and that the troops which he could see in the open area between the eastern and western woodlots and below the ridge to the south were those of the XII Corps, which had been brought up to continue the assault that the I Corps had begun early in the morning. He also concluded that the assault of the XII Corps had reached its climax. The troops in the open area were no

---

[32]
   Committee on the Conduct of the War, 1, p. 368; *OR* 19, pt. 1, pp. 227-228, 308, 505, 509; Carman, "History of the Antietam Campaign," pp. 7-8. The troops lying down behind the ridge were Lt. Col. Hector Tyndale's and Col. Henry J. Stainrook's brigades (Greene's division, XII Corps). The battery on their left front was one of Sumner's own, Battery A, 1st Rhode Island Light Artillery, under the command of Capt John A. Tompkins. This battery had been sent forward during the night of September 16 prior to the arrival of the II Corps, and had been under the direction of Joe Hooker. We do not know whether Sumner knew this unit was a II Corps battery. The other two batteries were, respectively, Capt. J. Albert Monroe's 1st Rhode Island Light, Battery D, and Lt. Frederick M. Edgell's New Hampshire Light, First Battery, both of the I Corps. Monroe's was firing from across the Hagerstown Pike in front of the Dunker Church, and Edgell's was unlimbered to its left rear.

[33]
   Committee on the Conduct of the War, 1, p. 368; Samuel S. Sumner to George B. Davis, April 4, 1897, John C. Ropes Research Files, Military Historical Society Collection, Boston University.

longer moving forward and appeared as if they were about to withdraw into the woods. Those to the south of the open area were holding their position and obviously attempting to reorganize. Furthermore, the firing at the northern end of the western woodlot was beginning to die away, which could mean either the Federal troops had driven the Rebels out of the woods, or that they were simply discontinuing their assault. At the same time, there appeared to be no fighting in the vicinity of the white building, where only moments before he had watched as a body of Federal infantry entered the woods around the structure. Still, the battery across the turnpike from the white building, together with the guns behind it, were continuing to fire to the southwest over the Hagerstown Pike.

If Sumner felt any dilemma concerning the situation he quickly resolved it. It was clear that McClellan's plan for driving the Rebel left flank south against the advance of the V and IX Corps had been partially successful. The II Corps was sent over Antietam Creek specifically to support and continue that assault, and it had arrived at the right moment and at the right place. The key to winning the battle on this flank appeared to be the capture of the western woodlot into which the Rebels had been driven. If the timber was allowed to remain in Confederate hands, it would act as a redoubt, blocking further Federal advances. If the woodlot was taken and held by the Federals, however, its capture would deny the Rebels a formidable, cohesive defensive line north of Sharpsburg and force them to fall back toward the Potomac River, where they would be boxed in by Fitz John Porter's V Corps and Ambrose Burnside's IX Corps, both of which Sumner assumed would be advancing against the enemy from the east.

Furthermore, the woods were practically in Federal hands. The southern end was occupied by Federal troops and the fighting had died down at the northern end of the timber. Between these two forces there was no evidence, as far as Sumner could see, of any Rebel activity or any Federal force. If Sedgwick's division was committed into that gap, it would go into the woods on the right flank of the troops at the white building and on the left flank of the troops assaulting into the northern end of the woods. Moreover, it would enter the woods on the flank and rear of any Rebel force that might still be opposing the Federals at the northern end of the woods. Sedgwick's flanks, in turn, would be protected by the Federal troops at either end of the woods.

Not a moment was to be lost. Sumner galloped back into the eastern woodlot, found Sedgwick, and gave him the necessary orders for the advance. Sedgwick, in the meantime, had drawn up his division in the woods. With a few brief orders shouted to the brigadiers, he redressed the lines for a continuation of the advance across the open fields to the west. The division, still in three long lines of battle, began moving toward its objective point at the double-quick.[34]

Sumner spurred his horse forward to follow closely behind Brig. Gen. Willis A. Gorman's brigade, which was leading Sedgwick's advance toward the western woods. As they started out across the open area, passing in front of the brigade of troops at the edge of the cornfield, Sumner looked back expecting to see the second of Sedgwick's brigades, Brig. Gen. Napoleon J. T. Dana's, emerging from the woods. Dana's and Sedgwick's last brigade, under Brig. Gen. Oliver O. Howard, were supposed to follow Gorman at intervals of only 50 to 60 yards. But to Sumner's astonishment Dana's brigade was nowhere to be seen. In a loud and excited voice he exclaimed, "Where is my second line?" Brigadier General John B. Gibbon, a brigade commander of the I Corps who overheard Sumner's exclamation, rode up and offered his services as a messenger. Instead of asking Gibbon to go in search of the missing brigade—a staff officer had already galloped off on that errand—Sumner asked him to assist Maj. F. N. Clarke, the II Corps chief of artillery, in the placement of the corps' batteries. Sumner indicated that Major Clarke would be with the batteries in the vicinity of the woods that they had just passed through, and Gibbon turned and rode off in that direction.[35]

After dispatching Gibbon, Sumner turned and spurred his horse to catch up with Gorman's advancing regiments. He rode in the direction of

---

[34]
    George B. Davis, "The Antietam Campaign," in *Papers of the Military Historical Society of Massachusetts*, vol. 3, pp. 61-62.

[35]
    Gibbon, *Personal Recollections*, pp. 87-88.

the right flank of the brigade line so that when it crossed the ridge, he would be able to observe the terrain and learn what was transpiring in the vicinity of the northern end of the western woods. As he caught up with the infantrymen, Sumner noticed that the 1st Minnesota marching on the right of the brigade line, was advancing with its colors furled and cased. To Sumner, advancing against the enemy without the flags unfurled was unthinkable. Men going into battle were to be inspired by those standards, which represented the honor and esprit of the regiment. "In God's name, what are you fighting for?" he roared in a voice that could be heard by the entire regiment. "Unfurl those colors," he yelled, prompting the color bearers to uncase and display the pride of their regiment.[36]

As Gorman's line of battle continued its advance, it crossed the crest of the ridge and the Hagerstown Turnpike just beyond. Ahead of his right flank regiments, several pasture fields interposed a space of 300 yards between the road and the treeline. This open area allowed Sumner to see that west of the ridge the ground fell away rapidly into a deep and wide ravine. In front of Gorman's center, though, the pasture was just 200 yards wide bringing the woodline nearly to the crest of the ridge. This pasture continued south for 400 yards at which point the woods extended all the way out to the turnpike. It was in this area that Gorman's left flank regiments were crossing the road and preparing to enter the tree line. South of that point, the woods bordered the turnpike all the way to the white building.

Sumner was no doubt pleased to see that Federal troops did indeed occupy the area on Gorman's right between the crest of the ridge and the western expanse of woods. As it crossed the turnpike, the right flank of Gorman's brigade passed over several companies of a Pennsylvania regiment, and in continuing across the pasture and down into the ravine passed diagonally in front of two other Federal brigades. These brigades, which had been fighting in tandem in a southwesterly direction across the pasture toward the northern end of the woods, had already pushed

[36]
    Carman, "History of the Antietam Campaign," p. 26.

their skirmishers into the timber. As Sumner expected, enemy resistance to Gorman's advance was virtually nonexistent, and the brigade swept on to the west and disappeared into the trees.[37]

Although the remaining two brigades of Sedgwick's division were to have followed Gorman at intervals of no more than 50 or 60 yards, a series of events conspired to cause a delay in their advance. As Napoloen Dana's brigade—the second line of Sedgwick's three-line advance—moved from the eastern woods, it came up against the rear of the brigade (George H. Gordon's) that Sumner had seen reforming its ranks in the cornfield some minutes earlier. This brigade was no longer standing in line, however, but was instead lying on the ground. Dana, believing that it was Gorman's brigade, ordered his regiments to lie down behind it, a move that halted the advance of Howard's brigade as well. No sooner was this done than one of Sumner's or Sedgwick's staff officers, or perhaps Sedgwick himself, noticed what Dana was about and ordered him to get his brigade up and moving again in the direction of the western woodlot.[38]

Matters were even more confused in Howard's ranks. As the one-armed general was ordering his brigade up to move across the open area behind Dana, one of Sumner's staff officers galloped up and ordered him to send a regiment to support the brigades that Sumner had seen in the vicinity of the northern end of the western woods. Howard stopped his brigade and ordered away the 71st Pennsylvania, which had been anchoring the right side of the brigade's line of battle. No sooner had the Pennsylvanians started off, however, than heavy small arms fire was heard from deep in the western woods, indicating that Gorman's brigade had finally made contact with the enemy. At this moment, Sedgwick appeared and ordered Howard to close up with his whole brigade in support of the other brigades of the division. Howard delayed his ad-

[37] *OR* 19, pt. 1, pp. 244, 314, 317, 514, 515; Patrick, *Inside Lincoln's Army*, p. 149; Carman, "History of the Antietam Campaign," pp. 26, 51. The troops near the turnpike belonged to the 124th Pennsylvania. The brigades in the vicinity of the northern end of the woodlot were William Goodrich's and Marsena Patrick's brigades.

[38] *OR* 19, pt. 1, p. 320. Dana ordered his men to lay down behind Gordon's brigade.

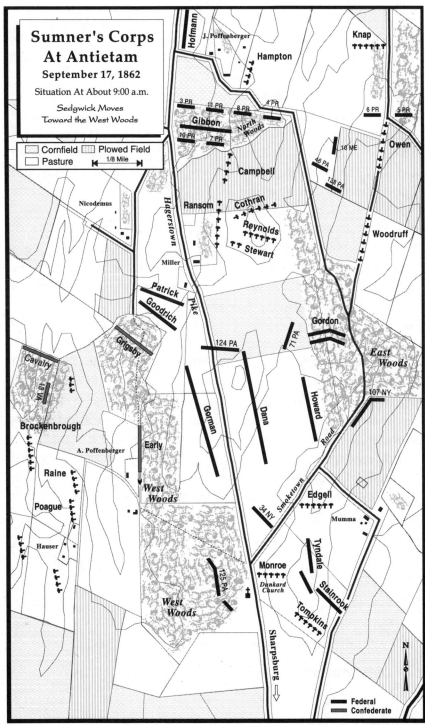

Sumner's Corps
At Antietam
September 17, 1862

Situation At About 9:00 a.m.

Sedgwick Moves
Toward the West Woods

Cornfield · Plowed Field
Pasture · 1/8 Mile

Mark A. Moore

vance just long enough for the 71st Pennsylvania to return to its position in line before he moved his brigade over the crest of the ridge, across the Hagerstown Turnpike, and on toward the western woods which Gorman and Dana had already entered.[39]

While Sedgwick was sorting out the confusion that had stopped two of his three brigades, Gorman continued his drive into and through the western woods. He was still confronted with little resistance, even though he could see Confederate infantry retiring ahead of him in some disorder. These retreating Rebels were apparently the troops who had been contesting the advance of the Federal infantry attacking toward the northern extension of the western woodlot. As Sumner had expected, Gorman's advance had swept in on the Confederate right flank and rear, forcing the Southerners to withdraw hurriedly to the west. Gorman pressed his brigade forward through the woods and deeper into the ravine. As it approached the western edge of the woods, Gorman's brigade came under fire from a line of Confederate infantry deployed amongst the buildings, haystacks, hedgerows, fences, and orchard trees of a small farm situated on the edge of the woods and at the deepest part of the ravine.[40] The Confederate infantry was supported by several batteries and some additional infantry positioned in a cornfield which covered the slope and high ground on the western side of the ravine that overlooked the farm and the woods. Gorman continued to push his regiments forward until they were all on the edge of the woods. Here they opened a heavy musketry fire on the well-covered Confederate line. The contest was fought at close range—as close as fifteen yards in some places. Although Gorman did not later recollect the firing as "rapid," it was very deadly.[41]

[39]
  Ibid., p. 305.

[40]
  This is the Alfred Poffenberger Farm. The Confederate troops were a remnant of J. R. Jones' Division, less than 300 strong, who had been rallied by Col. Andrew J. Grigsby.

[41]
  Ibid., pp. 311, 313; Carman, "History of the Antietam Campaign," pp. 27, 54.

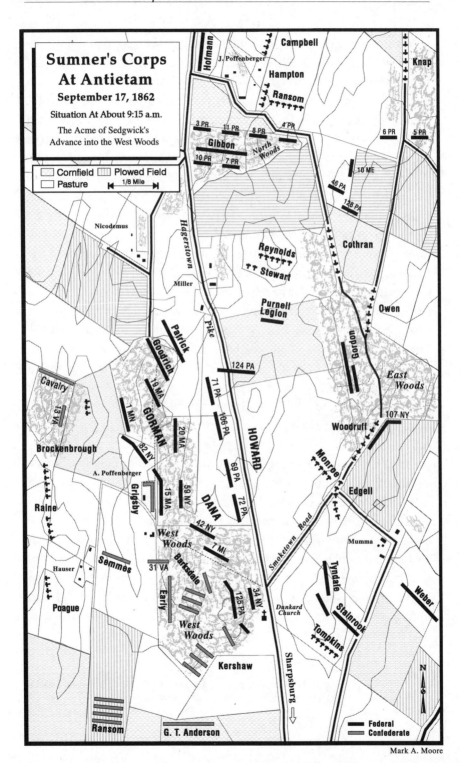

**Sumner's Corps
At Antietam**
September 17, 1862

Situation At About 9:15 a.m.

The Acme of Sedgwick's
Advance into the West Woods

Cornfield | Plowed Field
Pasture | 1/8 Mile

Campbell

Knap

Hofmann

J. Poffenberger

Hampton

Ransom

3 PR | 11 PR | 8 PR | 4 PR
Gibbon | North Woods
10 PR | 7 PR

6 PR | 5 PR

10 ME

46 PA

138 PA

Nicodemus

Reynolds

Stewart

Cothran

Hagerstown

Miller

Purnell Legion

Owen

Patrick

Goodrich

Pike

124 PA

East Woods

Cavalry

19 MA

71 PA

Gordon

13 VA

1 MN

GORMAN

106 PA

HOWARD

107 NY

Woodruff

Brockenbrough

20 MA

82 NY

69 PA

Monroe

A. Poffenberger

Grigsby

15 MA

59 NY

72 PA

DANA

Edgell

Raine

42 NY

West Woods

7 MI

Mumma

Semmes

31 VA

Barksdale

Tyndale

Hauser

Early

34 NY

Weber

Stainrook

Poague

125 PA

Dunkard Church

West Woods

Tompkins

Kershaw

Smoketown Road

Sharpsburg

N

Ransom

G. T. Anderson

Federal
Confederate

Mark A. Moore

From Sumner's point of view, things were moving forward nicely. Gorman's brigade had cleared the western woodlot of what little Confederate resistance remained, filled the gap between the Federal units in the northern and southern ends of the woods, and had set the stage for continuing the assault south toward Sharpsburg in accordance with McClellan's plan of battle. The problem now was to marshal the forces necessary for that advance. Riding behind Gorman's line of battle, Sumner picked his way south and east through the open woods until he returned to the crest of the ridge, where he observed Dana's brigade crossing the Hagerstown Pike and the pasture beyond before entering the woodlot to close up behind Gorman. As Dana's men entered the smoky timber, Sumner crossed the lower pasture to the east and reached the turnpike, where he turned his horse's head south and rode toward the small white building. As he approached the building, he noted that the Federal battery which had been in position across the turnpike from it was gone as well as the battery that had been in position to its rear.[42] The Federal infantry he had seen lying down in battle formation on the eastern slope of the ridge at the southern end of the open area was still in position and did not appear to be preparing to renew the assault any time soon. From what he could tell, Sumner could also tell that the battery firing from the left-front of the prone infantry was still in position and actively engaged.

In a short time Sumner reached the small white building, which stood near the southern edge of the western woods in which Gorman was currently engaged. From this vantage point he could see down the Hagerstown Pike nearly to the village of Sharpsburg. His view of the terrain west of the road, however, was restricted by the woods, which continued south a short distance beyond the church and only very gradually pulled away from the road. Five hundred yards in the direction of Sharpsburg Sumner could see Confederate guns being withdrawn from a position they had occupied just west of the pike. Immediately

---

[42]
OR 19, pt 1, p. 228. Captain Monroe's report indicates that his and Lieutenant Edgell's batteries remained in position near the Dunker Church only a short time.

across the road from where the guns were withdrawing, Confederate infantry was being hastily formed into a line of battle along a farm lane that intersected the Hagerstown Pike from the east. This line of battle, however, was thin and without support so far as Sumner could see.[43]

Of more significance to Sumner, however, was the fact that no other large bodies of troops from either the I or XII Corps were immediately available to renew the assault south toward Sharpsburg. His own Third Division, under William H. French, had been following behind Sedgwick, and it was reasonable for Sumner to assume that French was probably near the eastern woodlot by now. Accordingly, he decided to order French's division across the open area to close up on Sedgwick's left flank in the vicinity of the church. From that point, both divisions, side by side, would continue the attack south toward Sharpsburg, where they would link up with the V and IX Corps coming into the town from the east and southeast. Support for the two divisions of the II Corps could be found in the troops lying down on the eastern slope of the ridge, the Federals Sumner had seen enter the woods in the vicinity of the white building, and those that Gorman had passed as he entered the western woodlot. From where Sumner was sitting he could see no Confederate force capable of stopping such a powerful thrust. Accordingly, he sent his son and several other aides to find French and communicate his plan of attack. Aides were also sent to locate and order the commander of the troops across from the church to get his men ready to move.[44]

43
  OR 19, pt. 1, pp. 845, 1022-1023, 1036-1037. The guns were those of Col. Stephen D. Lee's artillery battalion. They had been forced from their original position east of the Dunker Church by the advance of Greene's division, the infantry that Sumner had observed lying down. The Confederate infantry he could see being formed into line of battle were from Col. Alfred H. Colquitt's Brigade of D. H. Hill's Division. After fighting the advance of the I and XII Corps, what was left of Colquitt's Brigade was falling back and being rallied in the west end of the farm lane that would afterwards be known as the Sunken Road or Bloody Lane.

44
  Ibid., pp. 510, 512; Sumner letter, April 4, 1897. Captain Sumner's letter places Edwin Sumner in front of the Dunker Church at the time that he called for French's division to go into action on the left of Sedgwick. The reports of Col. James C. Lane, commander of the 102nd New York Infantry (Col. Henry J. Stainrook's brigade, Greene's division, XII Corps) in the *OR*, establish that Sumner attempted to elicit support from elements of George Greene's division at this time.

After deciding upon a strategy of attack for Sedgwick's and French's divisions, Sumner set off to find Sedgwick to discuss his plan for pushing the assault southward. Sumner also wanted to see for himself how the situation was developing in front of Gorman's brigade. The firing on the west side of the woodlot was still heavy and continuous, indicating that Gorman probably had not been able to move forward beyond the ravine. Sumner rode north up the turnpike about 300 yards, where he found Howard's brigade crossing the road and preparing to move across a pasture into the woods to catch up with Gorman and Dana.[45]

Moving ahead of Howard's regiments, Sumner crossed the southern end of the pasture and entered the western woodlot at the point where the firing indicated the fighting was heaviest. He was confronted almost immediately by an excited Lt. Col. John W. Kimball, commander of the 15th Massachusetts of Gorman's brigade. Kimball reported to Sumner that the 59th New York of Dana's brigade, which had been in position 30 or 40 yards behind the 15th Massachusetts, had moved forward and was firing into the rear of the Bay Staters, killing and wounding many of them. Kimball had been unable to get the New Yorkers to either advance to the front or stop shooting into the rear of his regiment and he pleaded with Sumner to do something about it. The II Corps commander sought out the right flank of the 59th New York and bellowed an order for its commander to cease firing and to move his regiment back to its former position well to the rear of the 15th Massachusetts. Although Sumner's orders were eventually executed, the command resulted in a great deal of confusion in the ranks of the 59th New York.[46]

45
    OR 19, pt. 1, p. 305. Howard's delay in following Dana's brigade has already been discussed.
46
    OR 19, pt. 1, p. 313; Carman, "History of the Antietam Campaign," pp. 44-45. According to Carman, this incident occurred after the discovery of the Confederate attack on Sedgwick's left. Colonel Kimball's report, however, states otherwise. The forward movement of the 59th New York was probably in response to the fire delivered by the Confederate infantry engaged with Gorman's brigade. Once the New Yorkers were attacked by the Confederates assaulting Sedgwick's left, they fell back to the right and rear.

As the New Yorkers began moving to the rear, Gorman found Sumner and pointed out to him that the left flank regiments of the two rear brigades—the 7th Michigan of Dana's brigade and the 72nd Pennsylvania of Howard's—had been broken by an enemy force coming up through the woods on the left of the division. The shattered regiments were streaming to the rear nearly in a panic. Gorman also told Sumner that his brigade could not hold its position unless support of its left and rear was reestablished. The situation had indeed suddenly changed for the worse. Looking back toward the road, Sumner could see the pasture he had crossed only minutes before was now filled with hundreds of disorganized II Corps soldiers fleeing for the rear.[47]

It did not take long to realize that an enemy force of unknown strength had moved into the southern end of the woods and was now driving north into the left flank and rear of Sedgwick's division. Perhaps the Confederates had broken the line from the front or they may have maneuvered between Sedgwick's regiments and the Federal troops that had preceded him into the woods near the white building. There was no time for speculation on the cause of the looming disaster; he had to act quickly to stem the growing rout. He turned and rode toward Howard's brigade, most of which was lying down just a few yards north of where he was. As he rode behind these regiments, he tried to get them up and moving through shouted orders and gestures. "Back boys," he kept calling to them, "for God's sake move back; you are in a bad fix."[48]

Sumner found Howard behind the right portion of his brigade line. Although he shouted to him that he must immediately take up a new position, changing the front of his brigade to the left, the noise of the approaching fight was so loud that even "Bull" Sumner could not make himself heard above the din. Howard eventually understood what his corps commander wanted of him and the position that he was to take up only by the gestures that Sumner was making. By the time Sumner communicated the advancing danger of the Confederate assault to

[47] *OR* 19, pt. 1, p. 311.

[48] Carman, "History of the Antietam Campaign," p. 42; Sears, *Landscape Turned Red*, p. 226.

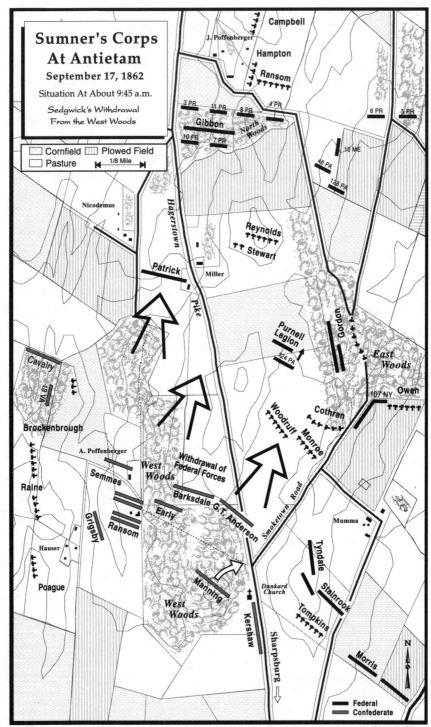

**Sumner's Corps
At Antietam**
September 17, 1862

Situation At About 9:45 a.m.

*Sedgwick's Withdrawal
From the West Woods*

Cornfield ▦ Plowed Field
Pasture ▯ ⟼ 1/8 Mile

Mark A. Moore

Howard, additional left flank regiments from both the second and third brigade lines had collapsed and were streaming through the lower pasture, over the Hagerstown Pike, and across the open area to the north and east. Although Howard realized at the time that his task of stopping the Confederate onslaught would be nearly impossible, he set himself to his work. He later noted that he could not help thinking at the time that if he had his old brigade, or that if he had had more time to drill his current regiments, he could fulfill Sumner's orders.[49]

After delivering his orders, Sumner turned away from Howard and rode back toward the vortex of the crisis to see what he could do to rally the broken regiments and get them and the others out of harm's way. He rode quickly and calmly among the retreating soldiers, exhorting them to make their stand while assisting officers in getting their commands formed and moving to the rear in an orderly fashion. One soldier in the ranks of the 59th New York remembered that his regiment was completely flanked on the left and rear when Sumner personally rode in through a terrific fire and brought them out. The commander of the 69th Pennsylvania of Gorman's brigade, Col. Joshua T. Owen, also recorded Sumner's brave act: "General Sumner appeared in person in the midst of a most deadly shower of shot and shell, and an order was received to fall back."[50]

Regiments and pieces of regiments made valiant efforts at reforming and making a stand as the Rebel attack gained momentum. Howard managed for several minutes to get the 106th Pennsylvania to hold a position behind a rail fence that ran across the northern end of the lower pasture from the woods to the pike, the same position that Sumner had ordered Howard to attempt to hold. From there the 106th checked, if

---

[49] *OR* 19, pt. I, p. 306; Carman, "History of the Antietam Campaign," p. 42; Howard, *Autobiography*, 1, pp. 296-297; Oliver O. Howard, "Personal Reminiscences of the War of the Rebellion," *National Tribune*, April 3, 1884, p. 1. Howard lost an arm commanding a brigade in Israel Richardson's division at the Battle of Seven Pines on May 31, 1862. He had returned to active service and was placed at the head of a brigade in Sedgwick's division only a few weeks before the Battle of Antietam.

[50] James Peacock, as quoted by Jonathan Peacock to Erastus Peacock, October 27, 1862, photocopy of letter at Antietam National Battlefield; *OR* 19, pt. 1, p. 318.

only for a moment, the onrush of Confederates in their front, firing volleys at them as they left the woods and started across the pasture. The regiments on the right of the original division formation were fortunate in that they had additional time to change their position before the danger reached them. Colonel Alfred Sully of the 1st Minnesota, Gorman's brigade, managed to move his regiment in good order to a position just outside and north of the woods, where he was joined by the 82nd New York, also of Gorman's brigade, and the 19th Massachusetts of Dana's brigade. Together these three regiments withdrew slowly to the north, fighting the Confederates every step of the way.[51]

Howard would later recall that "Sumner and every officer of nerve made extraordinary efforts to rally the men and make head[way] against the advancing enemy, but that was impossible till we had traversed the open space for now we had the enemy's artillery and infantry both pursuing and flanking our broken brigades by rapid and deadly volleys."[52] In withdrawing across the open area, those regiments that had been in the immediate vicinity of the small church retired northeast in the direction of the eastern woodlot, where Sedgwick had originally formed his division for its advance. The path of their retreat was dictated primarily by the direction of the Confederate assault, which fell more directly across their front than on their flank. The balance of the division's regiments, however, attacked more heavily on their left flanks, retired generally to the north along the Hagerstown Pike toward another woodlot which stretched across the northern end of the open area about one half of a mile above the western woods.

As the withdrawing regiments continued their retreat, Sumner dispatched staff officers to locate units to assist in stopping the pursuing Confederates. Several staff members managed to find and alert commanders in the I and XII Corps of the sweeping Rebel attack that threatened to unravel the morning's achievements. One of the most

---

51
    OR 19, pt. 1, pp. 307, 314, 317, 323; Carman, "History of the Antietam Campaign," pp. 43, 48.

52
    Howard, "Reminiscences," p. 1.

active and effective of these officers was Maj. F. N. Clarke, Sumner's II Corps chief of artillery. Even as Sedgwick's division was making its assault toward and into the western woods, Clarke had been busy positioning batteries to support the attack. With Sedgwick's thrust in a shambles and his men streaming in retreat across the fields, Clarke attempted to position every gun he could find to make the crossing of the open area as difficult as possible for the Confederates. Brigadier General Gibbon of Hooker's I Corps, who had personally observed the beginning of the withdrawal, responded by forming his brigade in the northern woodlot and refusing to allow any of Sedgwick's men to pass to the rear. Another I Corps officer, division commander Maj. Gen. Abner Doubleday, sent Lt. Col. John William Hofmann with his brigade and a section of artillery into position to the west of the northern woods and the Hagerstown Pike, where they provided support for Colonel Sully and his ad hoc command as they continued their fighting withdrawal northward.[53]

As men of the I and II Corps joined together to stem the tide of defeat, Brig. Gen. George S. Greene pushed his XII Corps division of two brigades forward into the fray. His men entered the western woods in the vicinity of the white church, driving back the Confederates who had attacked and driven out the Federal troops in that area. It was Greene's division Sumner had seen lying down in the open area below the ridge across the turnpike from the church. Greene's attack into the western woodlot, however, seems to have been more a spontaneous response to the Confederate rush into the open area in front of his division than it was to any request for assistance from Sumner. Earlier in the day, before the arrival of Sedgwick, Greene had attacked south through the eastern woods, driving the occupying Confederates south and west. He had continued his attack south, halting in the open area below the eastern woodlot to reorganize his regiments and bring up more ammunition. It was at this point and in this position that Sumner had first observed Greene's prone brigades. With replenished cartridge

---

[53]
 OR 19, pt. 1, pp. 236, 476-477; Carman, "History of the Antietam Campaign," pp. 1-2.

boxes, Greene pushed back the advancing Rebels and entered the woods (probably without realizing that Sedgwick's division had already been driven out of the timber). With Sumner in the vicinity of the northern woodlot a mile to the north of the church, it is reasonably certain that the II Corps leader was unaware of Greene's advance into the western woods.[54]

One XII Corps unit that responded to Sumner's call for assistance in stemming the Confederate onslaught was Brig. Gen. George H. Gordon's brigade. Gordon's men, ordered forward from their position in the eastern woodlot by Brigadier General Williams, were the soldiers Sumner had seen standing in the cornfield at the edge of the eastern woodlot just before Sedgwick's advance. After Sedgwick passed by on his way to the western woods, Gordon, under orders from Williams, withdrew his brigade into the woodlot and reformed it facing to the west. It now moved out of these woods and started across the open area, threatening the right and rear of the Confederate units pursuing Sedgwick beyond the Hagerstown Pike. Two of Gordon's five regiments managed to advance to the turnpike, where, as they attempted to cross the road's bordering fences, they received a heavy fire from the western woods that forced them to fall back on the remaining regiments of the brigade and seek shelter on the eastern slope of the ridge dividing the open area. After holding that position for no more than a few minutes, Gordon ordered the entire brigade back to the eastern woods, where it remained in support of the batteries being assembled there by Major Clarke and other officers.[55]

The Confederate pursuit of Sedgwick's division continued north of the western woods for a few hundred yards before Federal resistance and a loss of momentum halted the counterattack. The Southerners fell back across the fields, taking up a position in the western woods. The general fighting that had engulfed this portion of the field since dawn ended for a few minutes as both sides sought to consolidate their positions and

---

54
  OR 19, pt. 1, p. 505.

55
  Ibid., pp. 477, 495-496.

reform their broken and exhausted regiments in preparation for a continuation of the battle. It was probably at this time that Sumner began to realize the full extent of the disaster that had befallen Sedgwick's division within the western woods. Not only were the regiments of the division scattered over a mile of terrain from the southern tip of the eastern woods to the northern edge of the northern woods, but both Sedgwick and Dana were wounded and out of action, as were three of the division's thirteen regimental commanders. The real catastrophe, however, was the tremendous number of casualties the division had suffered. Even in regiments that were under control and reforming, less than half the number of men who a few hours before crossed Antietam Creek appeared to be present in the ranks.[56]

As the senior officer present, Sumner now assumed command of all Federal units on the northern portion of the battlefield. After locating a signal station in the vicinity of the Northern woods and sending an urgent message to army headquarters seeking reinforcements, Sumner began establishing a hasty defensive line to resist any further attacks. Available to him for this purpose were the broken remnants of the I and XII Corps, together with the remains of Sedgwick's division from his own corps. With the help of his staff and other general officers, he went about the field collecting whatever units he could find, ordering their commanders to get their men up and into position.[57]

The resultant hastily-formed line of battle was positioned as a consequence of the fighting up to this point in the battle. It ran from the southern and western edge of the eastern woods north to the southern and western edge of the northern woodlot, then north along the Hagerstown Pike. This makeshift line was crowded with artillery, especially in front of the eastern woods and along the turnpike north of the northern woodlot. The northern extension of the line along the

---

56
OR 19, pt. 1, pp. 192-193, 276, 308; Dwight E. Stinson, Jr., "Operations of Sedgwick's Division in the West Woods," Antietam National Battlefield, 1962, pp. 38-40. Stinson figures the final percentage of casualties in Sedgwick's division at 42 percent.

57
Ibid., pp. 134, 226, 312, 321; Patrick, *Inside Lincoln's Army*, p. 150.

turnpike reflected Sumner's growing concern for the extreme right flank of the Federal position. The Confederate force that pursued Sedgwick beyond the western woods had appeared most threatening on the right. Hofmann's brigade, which had been put into position on the extreme right during Sedgwick's withdrawal, was able to remain there only about thirty minutes before enemy infantry and cavalry threatened his flank.[58]

The Confederates opposite Sumner's right flank were establishing two batteries on a prominent ridge directly west of the northern woods. Morever, Sumner was probably aware of the speculation at army headquarters that Lee had concealed his main strength in the ravines and woodlots west of the crown of land between Antietam Creek and the Potomac. If so, this force would surely launch an attack if an opportunity presented itself.[59] As Sumner went about overseeing the organization of his defensive line, he observed the battered condition of the I and XII Corps units and learned some of the details of other fighting that had taken place while he was in the western woods with Sedgwick's division. French, whose division Sumner had ordered to follow to the front and form on the left of Sedgwick, had instead shifted his line of advance far to the left, or south, after reaching the eastern woods. After marching for some distance, French became engaged with a Confederate line of battle posted in a sunken farm lane at about the same time that Sedgwick was being attacked on his left flank in the western woods. The last division of the II Corps under Israel Richardson, which had been held back by McClellan while Sumner's other two divisions marched to the front, had come up and taken over the fight for the sunken road after French's division was repulsed in a series of assaults against that position. After throwing in and using up two of his own brigades, Richardson was positioning his third brigade on the flank of the sunken road to drive off the last of the thin line of Confederates still holding it.[60]

58
  OR 19, pt. 1, p. 236.

59
  Smalley, "Antietam," p. 1; Sears, *Landscape Turned Red*, pp. 173, 270.

60
  OR 19, pt. 1, pp. 277, 323. Although French believed that he had gone into action on the left

Having initiated the establishment of a defensive line, Sumner set up his headquarters in a field near the northern woods. Almost immediately a request for reinforcements came in from the XII Corps. Greene, from his advanced position in the western woods—he did not yet realize just how advanced he was—appealed to Williams for more men and guns. Williams sent two regiments and a battery, all that he felt he could spare, before asking Sumner for additional troops. Sumner, more concerned with reestablishing control over the exhausted Federals on the field and setting up a strong defensive line on the right, had none to send. There were indications, however, that substantial reinforcements were on the way. Major General William B. Franklin, commander of the VI Corps, had reached the battlefield at about mid-morning. Soon thereafter, he had two divisions in position west of Antietam Creek behind the Federal right and was in the process of crossing his third. Sumner sent immediately to have these troops brought up to the front.[61]

The first VI Corps unit to arrive at the front was the division of Maj. Gen. William F. "Baldy" Smith, which had marched up from the Antietam along a route that was a little north of the one followed earlier by Sumner and Sedgwick. In the front of Smith's division was Brig. Gen. Winfield S. Hancock's brigade, followed by the brigades of Col. William H. Irwin and Brig. Gen. William T. H. Brooks. As the division approached the eastern woods, Sumner and members of his staff were on hand to direct it into position. Hancock's regiments were quickly sent through the woods to the open area to support three of the batteries placed in that vicinity by Major Clarke. Irwin's brigade was sent through the woods to take position on Hancock's left in support of batteries in the open area near the southern end of the eastern woodlot, while Brooks' brigade was held in reserve east of the woods.

---

of Sedgwick's division, he was really on the left of Greene's division.

[61] *OR* 19, pt. 1, pp. 376, 402, 505; Carman, "History of the Antietam Campaign," p. 2.

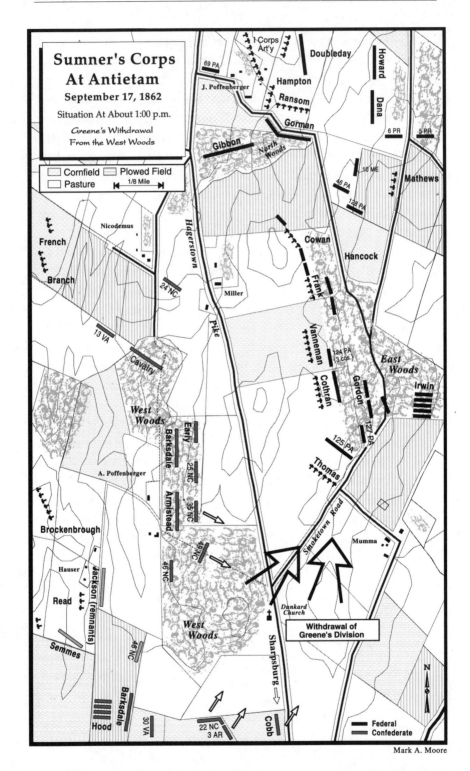

Sumner's Corps
At Antietam
September 17, 1862
Situation At About 1:00 p.m.

*Greene's Withdrawal
From the West Woods*

Cornfield   Plowed Field
Pasture   1/8 Mile

Withdrawal of
Greene's Division

Federal
Confederate

Mark A. Moore

As Hancock moved from the woods into the open area he found that his infantrymen had to drive off Rebel skirmishers who were working their way through a large cornfield. Concerned over a body of infantry and two artillery batteries across the open area in the fringes of the western woods, Hancock asked Sumner for one more regiment. Sumner granted this request, probably because it fit his plan for the defensive line. The regiment sent to Hancock was the 20th Massachusetts of Dana's brigade.[62] As Irwin's brigade was moving off to its assigned position on Hancock's left, the battle in the western woods and across the southern end of the open area erupted again. As the fighting increased in intensity, Greene's division streamed out of the western woods in the vicinity of the white building in considerable confusion, crossing the open fields toward the eastern woods. Confederate infantry in two separate columns followed on the heels of Greene's retreating men, one from the woods north of the church and the other—the larger of the two attacking Rebel forces—attacking east across the southern end of the open fields from a position south of the western woods.

Initially it appeared as if this new Southern assault would be successful in further disrupting and pushing back the Federal right, for in addition to Greene's routed division, several regiments and a Federal battery in the path of the Confederates were driven off the field. The Federal response, however, was quick and effective. From the area of the sunken farm lane, cleared of the enemy only a few minutes before, several regiments from Richardson's division were sent to blunt the Confederate assault. Irwin's brigade, which was just reaching its position near the southern end of the eastern woodlot, was ideally situated for a counterattack on the left flank of the northernmost Confederate column. This combined pressure broke the Rebel assault, forcing the Southerners back to the west of the turnpike, to the south of the western woods. Irwin's brigade pursued them until it was opposite the white building,

OR 19, pt. 1, pp. 376-377, 402, 406-407; Ibid., pp. 406-407; *Committee on the Conduct of the War*, 1, p. 626.

where the brigade received such heavy fire from the woods that it was forced to fall back to the shelter of the ridge in the open area.[63]

This demonstration of Confederate strength and resolve, although it had little consequence other than clearing the western woods of Greene's troops, served to revive Sumner's concern for the Federal right flank. He was now convinced that the Confederates had the capability of launching a successful attack against the Federal right. The first order of business had to be ensuring that any such attack could be defeated. Accordingly he continued his efforts at strengthening the defensive line on the right. But Sumner had not as yet entirely given up hope of mustering sufficient strength to renew the assault against the Confederate left and driving them toward the Potomac. If the corps of Fitz John Porter and Ambrose Burnside proved to be successful in their drive toward Sharpsburg, their advance would make the Confederate position north of the town (opposite Sumner's corps) untenable. If Porter and Burnside were successful in their dual thrusts, Sumner's troops on the northern portion of the field must be prepared to advance.

As Sumner considered the disposition of his troops, Franklin rode up and the two generals discussed the situation as they understood it. Franklin later reported that at this conference Sumner seemed much depressed as he explained the condition of the I and XII Corps and how Sedgwick's fine division had been routed and driven from the western woodlot with great loss. Sumner told Franklin that the I, II, and XII Corps were entirely used up and nothing more could be expected of them that day. At this point, the second of Franklin's divisions under Maj. Gen. Henry W. Slocum began to arrive at the front, and Franklin broke off the conference with Sumner to see to its placement. Sumner attended to a few more of the details of strengthening the defensive line

---

[63]
  OR 19, pt. 1, pp. 278, 290, 402, 408, 409; *Committee on the Conduct of the War*, 1, p. 626; Hitchcock, *War From the Inside*, p. 64; David Hunter Strother, *A Virginia Yankee in the Civil War: The Diaries of David Hunter Strother*, edited by Cecil D. Eby, Jr. (Chapel Hill, 1961), pp. 110-111. The northern Confederate column was the 49th North Carolina of Walker's Division. The southern column consisted of Col. Thomas R.R. Cobb's Brigade of McLaws' Division, and the 3rd Arkansas and 27th North Carolina, two regiments of Walker's Division, all under the command of Col. John R. Cooke.

and then mounted and rode off to ensure the proper placement of Slocum's division. The first unit of that division he came across was Col.
Joseph J. Bartlett's brigade. Bartlett had not received orders concerning
the placement of his brigade. Since Brooks' brigade of Smith's
division—which Sumner had previously designated as a reserve—had
been sent off to support French during the crisis of the recent
Confederate advance, Sumner directed Bartlett to go to the right in place
of Brooks.[64]

Sumner then learned, possibly from Bartlett, that Franklin had the
other two brigades of Slocum's division in hand and was forming them
for an immediate attack across the open area with the objective of
retaking the woods in the vicinity of the white building. Bartlett's
brigade was slated to participate in this attack as a reserve. Realizing the
utter recklessness of such a venture, Sumner rode off to find Franklin.
When he did he ordered the VI Corps commander not to make the
attack.

Franklin was unhappy with this interference and the two corps
commanders debated the issue for some minutes, the discussion at times
becoming heated. Franklin insisted that the attack would be successful,
but Sumner maintained that Franklin had the only fresh body of troops
on that part of the field, and that if they were beaten back, as those
before had been, the right of the Federal line could not be held. As the
senior officer present Sumner assumed full responsibility for the
decision and would not allow Franklin to take his brigades forward.
Franklin, still convinced that the assault should be made, asked Maj.
Herbert von Hammerstein, a member of McClellan's staff present at the
time, to explain the situation to McClellan and get his decision.
Hammerstein agreed to carry the message and rode off toward army
headquarters.[65]

64
   OR 19, pt. I, p. 377; William B. Franklin, "Notes on Crampton's Gap and Antietam," *Battles and Leaders of the Civil War*, 2, p. 597.

65
   OR 19, pt. 1, p. 377; Franklin, "Notes," p. 597; *Committee on the Conduct of the War*, I, p. 626.

After his encounter with Franklin, Sumner went back to his own headquarters to confer with his staff and the commanders from the I, II, and XII Corps and to review and reconsider his situation. The question of whether to resume the offensive on the right with all of the troops available, as opposed to another piecemeal assault as Franklin was proposing, very much troubled him. McClellan's plan of battle—and Sumner's orders from McClellan, which he could not ignore—called for delivering the army's main attack from the right. The condition of the units and troops on that portion of the field, however, convinced Sumner that there was little possibility of success in resuming the offensive, and every possibility of disaster.

As Sumner was deep in these somber thoughts he was approached by Lt. James H. Wilson, another of McClellan's staff officers. Wilson had just come from army headquarters carrying new information and orders. He told Sumner that his orders were "to get his men up and hold his position at all hazards" as Burnside had forced his way across Antietam Creek south of Sharpsburg and was advancing west. Sumner realized that Burnside's success could set up a situation which would call for an offensive on the Federal right to support him and/or to exploit his success. But the orders that Lieutenant Wilson delivered did not address retaking the offensive, nor did they indicate that McClellan understood the critical condition of the units on the right of the line. Sumner sent Wilson back to McClellan with the whole perplexing question. He told Wilson, "Go back, young man, and ask General McClellan if I shall make a simultaneous advance with my whole line at the risk of not being able to rally a man on this side of the creek if I am driven back." Wilson, who did not understand all that was comprehended in the question, tried to point out to Sumner that his orders did not mention an advance. But Sumner, who was in no mood to debate the situation with a boy of a lieutenant, cut him off and repeated the question Wilson was to address to McClellan before sending him on his way.[66]

---

[66]
James Harrison Wilson, *Under the Old Flag: Recollections of Military Operations in the War for the Union*, 2 vols. (New York, 1912), vol. 1, pp. 112-113. Wilson, who would later serve in the

By this time it was nearly 1:30 in the afternoon. Almost five hours had slipped past since Sumner had ordered Sedgwick's division to make its assault toward the western woodlot. Although the field of battle was still relatively quiet following the last attack from the western woods by the enemy, the Confederates continued to show signs that they might renew the battle with a general offensive against the Federal right. The western woods contained undisclosed numbers of Confederate infantry, and their cavalry was active west of the Federal right flank. Additionally, they seemed to be attempting to reposition their artillery so as to be able to support a new attack. Guns were appearing in front of the woods and several batteries had only recently been driven from a high hill to the west, a position which the Confederates had been using to advantage all day. The Confederate guns were driven off by the massed Federal batteries located just east of the Hagerstown Pike and a little north of the northern woodlot. Sumner had assembled over forty guns in this sector, a giant battery set up nearly hub to hub on which he pinned his hopes of crushing any Confederate advance against the extreme Federal right flank.[67]

Lieutenant Wilson, who had ridden to army headquarters and had delivered Sumner's message to McClellan, returned after an absence of only about one-half hour. McClellan sent Wilson back to Sumner with orders to risk nothing, but to hold his present position at all hazards. Sumner may have felt some initial relief at knowing that the commander understood the situation and did not expect him to continue the offensive. But then Wilson continued, repeating verbatim the rest of

---

Western Theater with Ulysses S. Grant, was promoted to brigader general in 1863. He moved east with Grant in 1864 and led a division of cavalry in Virginia before returning west, where he gained prominence by defeating Lt. Gen. Nathan Bedford Forrest at Selma, Alabama, during the war's final days.

67
OR 19, Pt. 1, p. 377; Franklin, "Notes," p. 597. After Greene's division was driven out, the Confederates occupied the West Woods with what was left of Hood's and McLaws' divisions and Brig. Gen. Lewis A. Armistead's Brigade of Maj. Gen. Richard H. Anderson's Division. To the northwest of the woods the cavalry brigades of Brig. Gen. Wade Hampton and Brig. Gen. Fitzhugh Lee, supported by Capt. John Pelham's three batteries of horse artillery, were very active.

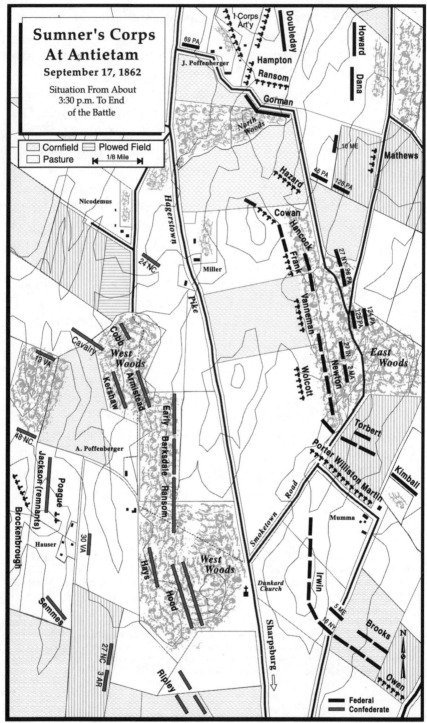

Sumner's Corps At Antietam
September 17, 1862
Situation From About
3:30 p.m. To End
of the Battle

Cornfield Plowed Field
Pasture 1/8 Mile

Mark A. Moore

McClellan's directive: "Tell the general to crowd every man and gun into ranks, and, if he thinks it practicable, he may advance Franklin to carry the woods in front, holding the rest of the line with his own command, assisted by those of Banks and Hooker." The ambiguousness of the final portion of McClellan's message revealed that McClellan did not understand the true situation on the right flank of the Union army. The verbal dispatch angered Sumner, especially since it was repeated in front of Franklin and the other generals who were assembled at his headquarters. "Go back, young man," snapped Sumner, "and tell General McClellan I have no command. Tell him my command, Banks' command and Hooker's command are all cut up and demoralized. Tell him General Franklin has the only organized command on this part of the field!" This time Wilson did not attempt to talk back to the exasperated II Corps leader. The staffer mounted his horse and started for army headquarters with Sumner's message.[68]

Sumner returned to conferring with the other generals, listening to their reports on the conditions of their commands and considering what he should do. A sudden flurry of activity in the form of "Little Mac" himself interrupted this conference. Major Hammerstein had found McClellan at his headquarters at the Pry house, where he told him of Franklin's plan for renewing the offensive on the right and Sumner's veto of the assault.

McClellan, energized by the idea of a renewed attack after hearing so many reports of a repulse on the right, decided to go to the front to see for himself what could be done. McClellan met with both Sumner and Franklin together, with both generals making a case for their respective positions. Having now seen for himself the battered condition of the four Federal corps on the army's right flank, McClellan accepted Sumner's argument for remaining on the defensive. Things had gone so well on other parts of the field, reasoned the army commander, that he did not care to risk making an attack on the right at this time. McClellan stated, however, that he intended to renew the battle in the morning. Neither

68
    Wilson, *Under the Old Flag*, 1, pp. 113-114.

Sumner nor Franklin objected. Having made his decision McClellan remounted and rode back to his headquarters.[69]

With McClellan's departure the Battle of Antietam essentially came to an end for Sumner. Fighting on the left of the Federal line involving Burnside's IX Corps continued until late afternoon. Just as Lieutenant Wilson had reported, Burnside made significant progress in his drive west, with some of his regiments actually reaching the high ground south of Sharpsburg. He was close to cutting the Confederate army off from its single ford across the Potomac River when a last-minute Confederate counterattack by the troops of A. P. Hill's Division, which arrived on the field after an arduous forced march from Harpers Ferry, ended the Federal thrust toward Sharpsburg.

The remainder of the afternoon on the right was quiet, with only a few minor flare-ups of action. Franklin saw McClellan once again late in the day and urged him to consider making the initial effort on the following morning against the ridge to the west of the Federal right flank, which the Confederates had used to great advantage as an artillery position. He pointed out that from that high ground Federal artillery could command the western woods and the entire Confederate left would be turned. McClellan agreed and told Franklin to make the attack. But even before troops could be moved into position the order was countermanded by McClellan.[70]

During the night of September 17-18, Sumner and the other officers of the I, II, and XII Corps continued to organize what soldiers and units they could find. As the morning of the 18th arrived, no orders for renewing the battle were issued. That morning McClellan again came to the front and met with Sumner and Franklin. Sumner, based on his assessment of the Federal forces at hand, continued to urge McClellan to remain on the defensive while Franklin counseled attack. McClellan told the two generals he was expecting reinforcements, which would ensure the success of a new offensive. The reinforcements arrived but

---

[69]
 Committee on the Conduct of the War, 1, pp. 626-627; Franklin, "Notes," p. 597.

[70]
 Committee on the Conduct of the War, 1, pp. 626-627; Franklin, "Notes," p. 597.

McClellan postponed the attack to the following day. While thousands of fresh Union troops sat idle, a truce for picking up the wounded was arranged, a task that occupied the remainder of September 18. During the night of September 18, Lee quietly withdrew his army across the Potomac River over Boteler's Ford to the relative safety of northern Virginia. McClellan made only a halfhearted attempt to follow his enemy, and the Maryland Campaign came to an end.[71]

* * *

Recriminations

The first charge leveled against Sumner for his generalship at Antietam was that he recklessly committed Sedgwick's division to an assault on the West Woods without a full appreciation of the situation in his front or the attendant risks of such an attack. He made this attack, so state his detractors, against the sound advice of general officers who had witnessed and/or participated in the fighting on that portion of the field. The implication of this indictment is that Sumner was headstrong in ignoring the advice of other generals and impetuous in ordering Sedgwick forward. The first person to make this charge was probably Brig. Gen. Alpheus Williams in letters to his daughters and a brother-in-law only a few days after the battle. Williams was upset that the XII Corps, and its general officers in particular, was not receiving its fair share of the praise for its role in the battle. He complained that "Generals are amazingly puffed who are not ten minutes on the field. Corps are praised for services done by others." His reference is to Edwin Sumner and the II Corps. Williams went on to criticize Sumner, stating, "Hundreds of lives were foolishly sacrificed by generals I see most praised, generals who would come up with their commands and pitch in at the first point

71
Franklin, "Notes," p. 597.

without consultation with those who knew the ground or without reconnoitering or looking for the effective points of attack."[72]

In 1882, Francis W. Palfrey, who was severely wounded and captured at the Battle of Antietam while serving as lieutenant colonel of the 20th Massachusetts of Dana's brigade, published *The Antietam and Fredericksburg* as part of Scribner's Campaigns of the Civil War Series. In this work, Palfrey accused Sumner of marching Sedgwick's division into an ambush. Palfrey says of the movement, "What General Sumner may have expected or even hoped to accomplish by his rash advance, it is difficult to conjecture. It is impossible that he can have been ignorant that French had not come up upon his [Sedgwick's] left." Palfrey speculates that the reason for the movement may have resulted from Sumner's long experience as a cavalryman on the frontier: "His old cavalry training may possibly have planted in his mind some notions as to charging and cutting one's way out."[73] Palfrey delivered a paper before the Military Historical Society of Massachusetts in 1885 with the intent of strengthening and revising his published account of the battle, but he had not changed his mind concerning Sumner and had nothing new to add or correct concerning Sumner's decision to advance Sedgwick's division into the West Woods.[74]

Francis A. Walker, the historian of the II Corps and also a veteran of the battle, agreed with Palfrey's assessment of Sumner's generalship at Antietam. In his 1887 *History of the Second Army Corps in the Army of the Potomac*, Walker merely echoed Palfrey by writing that Sumner's experience on the frontier had much to do with his impetuous decision to commit Sedgwick's division. "All his life in the cavalry, he has the instincts of a cavalry commander. What shall stay him?" Walker was particularly critical of Sumner for making the charge with Sedgwick's

---

72
    Alpheus S. Williams, *From the Cannon's Mouth: The Civil War Letters of General Alpheus S. Williams*, edited by Milo M. Quaife (Detroit, 1959), pp. 133, 135.

73
    Francis Winthrop Palfrey, *The Antietam and Fredericksburg* (New York, 1882), p. 88.

74
    Francis Winthrop Palfrey, "The Battle of Antietam," in *Papers of the Miltary Historical Society of Massachusetts*, 15 vols. (Boston, 1895-1918), vol. 3, p. 1.

division without waiting for the divisions of French or Richardson to come up. "Richardson, indeed," Walker stated, "could be up in forty minutes; and half that time would serve to draw French in toward Sedgwick's left. But Sumner does not wait."[75]

Modern historians have based their assessments of Sumner's decision largely on the accounts written by Williams, Palfrey, and Walker. James V. Murfin, in *The Gleam of Bayonets: The Battle of Antietam and the Maryland Campaign of 1862*, quoted heavily from Palfrey. Murfin concluded that Sumner was ignorant of the situation—especially of the position of I and XII Corps troops when he committed Sedgwick to battle—and that if he had taken more time for reconnaissance the decision to commit Sedgwick might have been executed differently. According to Murfin, "As it was, he did not see them and so forged ahead on his own."[76]

Stephen W. Sears, in his well-received *Landscape Turned Red: The Battle of Antietam*, considered Williams' statement about generals "who would come up with their commands and pitch in at the first point without consultation with those who knew the ground or without reconnoitering or looking for the effective points of attack" an "apt summary of Sumner's actions." Based on Williams' account, Sears surmises that Sumner refused to listen to the officers already on the field (especially Williams) and that he "devised a plan of action based almost entirely on misapprehension."[77]

As we have seen, however, Sumner's decision to order Sedgwick's division into the West Woods was the right decision made at the right time. Moreover, it was made after his own reconnaissance, which gave him sufficient knowledge of the field (the terrain and the troops) to make such a decision. Sumner must be judged not by the ultimate disaster

75
   Walker, *Second Army Corps*, p. 102.

76
   James V. Murfin, *The Gleam of Bayonets: The Battle of Antietam and the Maryland Campaign of 1862* (New York, 1965), pp. 233-235.

77
   Sears, *Landscape Turned Red*, p. 222.

that befell Sedgwick's division in the West Woods, but rather on his understanding of McClellan's plan of battle and by what he knew of the situation at the time he ordered Sedgwick forward into the timber.

When Sumner ordered Sedgwick to begin his assault across the open fields, the West Woods was the key terrain feature on that portion of the battlefield. This body of woods was on the western edge of the crown of land between Antietam Creek and the Potomac River, situated at least in part on some of the highest terrain in the area. Only one ridge intervened west and southwest of the woods before the land began to drop off into the basin of the Potomac River less than 3000 yards away at its nearest point.[78]

Because of an eastward bend in the river directly behind the battlefield, there was only a 2000 yard gap between the west end of the village of Sharpsburg and the Potomac River. Moreover, there was little or no possibility of crossing the Potomac north of Sharpsburg. The only exit from the battlefield for the Confederates was Boteler's Ford, two miles southwest of the town. The West Woods, therefore, had to be held if the Confederates expected to maintain a defensive line north of Sharpsburg. The loss of the woods would have effectively cut the Confederate army in two and would have forced the Confederates into a disasterous withdrawal across the lone Potomac ford.[79]

Confederate forces available in the vicinity of the West Woods at the time of Sedgwick's assault were woefully inadequate to defend against an attack by a full Federal division the size of Sedgwick's. As Sumner crossed Antietam Creek with Sedgwick's division and climbed the slopes toward the battlefield, Maj. Gen. Thomas J. "Stonewall"

[78]
     This ridge is often referred to as "Hauser's Ridge," named after a farm located just west of the West Woods. It formed the western side of the ravine in the West Woods and was the high ground that Gorman's brigade was facing as it reached the acme of its advance in that body of timber.

[79]
     OR 19, pt. 1, p. 970; John G. Walker, "Sharpsburg," Battles and Leaders, 2, pp. 677-678. Brig. Gen. Jubal Early, a Rebel brigade commander who fought in the West Woods, believed that the loss of those woods would have been followed by a decisive Confederate defeat and the "probable destruction of our army." Jubal A. Early, War Memoirs: Autobiographical Sketch and Narrative of the War Between the States (Bloomington, 1960), p. 149.

Jackson, commanding the Confederate left, was busy searching for troops to defend the critical West Woods. Three divisions and three brigades of a fourth had already been used up defending the West Woods and the adjacent fields to the east and northeast.[80]

The only troops which Jackson could find to continue the defense of the West Woods were a remnant of John R. Jones' Division, about 200 to 300 men rallied under the command of Col. Andrew Grigsby, and a brigade of less than 1,200 men under Brig. Gen. Jubal A. Early. While Sumner was on the edge of the East Woods surveying the field and trying to decide what he should do, this small Confederate force was in the northern end of the West Woods defending against an encroachment by Goodrich's and Patrick's I Corps brigades (this was the fighting that Sumner could detect beyond the ridge in the center of the open area but could not directly observe). The remainder of the West Woods south of Grigsby and Early did not contain any substantial body of organized Confederate troops, a circumstance correctly surmised by Sumner.[81]

Sumner, of course, could not have known all of the details of the terrain and of the Confederate situation at the time that he made his decision to commit Sedgwick's division to an assault into the West Woods. For that matter, neither could any other Federal general officer on the field. What Sumner did know was that he had been sent with his corps to support and continue the attack against the Confederate left flank as an integral part of McClellan's overall plan. He believed as well that that plan included an attack on the Confederate center and right flank by Fitz John Porter's V Corps and Ambrose Burnside's IX Corps, respectively. Sumner also knew from area maps and his own eyes that he had reached the highest ground between Antietam Creek and the

80
    OR 19, pt 1, p. 956. These were the divisions of Alexander Lawton, John R. Jones, and John Bell Hood. The brigades were Roswell Ripley's, Alfred Colquitt's, and Samuel Garland's, the latter under the command of Col. Duncan K. McRae. All three brigades were part of Daniel H. Hill's Division.

81
    OR 19, pt. 1, pp. 956, 970.

Potomac River, and that the latter was considerably less than a mile in the Confederate rear.[82]

What impressed Sumner most, however, and what would become the basis of his decision regarding Sedgwick, was the Federal situation on the right flank of the army. He could see and later learned that Hooker's I Corps was used up and effectively out of the fight, and that the XII Corps had reached, at least for the time being, the acme of its advance. But that advance represented a significant Federal tactical advantage, for it advanced the Federal right wing to within a mile of Sharpsburg and gave the Federals possession of the high plateau north of the town which could be used as a platform for a continuation of the attack. He could not abandon this accomplishment any more than he could abandon the army commander's plan of battle. The one flaw in the tactical situation that Sumner could discern was the gap in the Federal line between the Federal troops around the Dunker Church and those in the vicinity of the northern end of the West Woods. This interval, which essentially encompassed the West Woods, was extremely dangerous since it gave the Confederates a concealed avenue of approach into the Federal rear. The gap had to be plugged with troops, and it had to be plugged immediately. Sumner utilized Sedgwick's division, the only available body of troops capable of accomplishing the task.

Sumner was severely criticized by some early students of the battle for committing Sedgwick's division into the West Woods, but he was not without his defenders. George B. Davis, a Civil War veteran (though not of Antietam) and post-war career army officer who rose to be the army's Judge-Advocate General, believed that Sumner made the right decision. Davis was an authority on the fighting at Antietam and eventually became the president of the Antietam Battlefield Board, during which one of his duties was laying out and marking the battlefield as a national monument. In 1897 he appeared before the Military Historical Society of Massachusetts to read a paper on the Antietam Campaign. In that paper, Davis reiterated the XII Corps' need for support and the desperate

---

[82] *Committee on the Conduct of the War*, 1, p. 368-369.

situation of the Confederates at the time that Sumner made his decision to commit Sedgwick. Davis concluded:

> As the only success which had attended the Union arms on that part of the field had been that just gained by the XII Corps, it was obvious that that success should be followed up before the enemy could recover from its effects and resume the offensive. His resolution had to be taken, and was taken, on the instant. He formed Sedgwick's splendid division in column of assault, three brigades deep, and launched it against the shaken Confederate left.[83]

The second criticism directed at Sumner for his performance at Antietam centers on the formation of Sedgwick's division during its assault into the West Woods. This formation placed each brigade, with its regiments side by side in a single line of battle, one behind the other with only 50 to 70 yards between them. There is little doubt that Sumner, as corps commander (and not Sedgwick) was the source of this formation because both Sedgwick's and French's divisions approached the battlefield prepared to form in this manner as soon as they made contact with the enemy. Moreover, Richardson's division, which followed its II Corps companions once released by McClellan, also marched and formed in similar manner before entering combat.[84]

The most outspoken critic of Sumner's choice of formations was Francis Palfrey. He believed that more than any other factor, this deployment accounted for the disaster that befell Sedgwick's division in the West Woods. He noted that this formation left the flanks of the division exposed and vulnerable to attack, and that with the brigade lines advancing so close together, fire directed at the leading brigade would also have an effect on the two trailing brigades. Palfrey concluded "There is nothing more helpless than a column of long lines with short intervals between them, if they have anything to do other than to press straight forward with no thought of anything but the enemy before them.

---

[83]
    Davis, "The Antietam Campaign," pp. 61-62.

[84]
    OR 19, pt. 1, pp. 277, 285, 305, 311, 319, 323; Weber to Antietam Battlefield Board, December 10, 1892.

They cannot take care of their own flanks, and if they are attacked there, disaster is certain."[85]

In his history of the II Corps, Francis Walker criticized Sumner's choice of formation for the same reasons as Palfrey. Walker pointed out that once contact was made with the enemy, "all three lines will be almost equally under fire at once, and their losses must be enormously increased." But the primary reason for Sedgwick's discomfiture in the West Woods, he believed, was due to the lack of protection that the formation afforded to Sedgwick's flanks. Walker wrote, "A line of battle struck that way is the weakest thing in the world. Each of Sedgwick's brigades was comprised of fifteen hundred men, but at its extreme left flank each had the strength of two men."[86]

Unlike their criticism of Sumner for his decision to commit Sedgwick's division to the West Woods, the points that Palfrey and Walker raised concerning his choice of formation were valid. The formation had many characteristics which made it a poor choice for almost any tactical situation. First, it limited the division's fighting potential—its firepower and shock action—to only one direction (the front). Even then, only one brigade, just one-third of the division, would be in a position to engage the enemy in that direction. The other two brigades could only stand and wait their turn. As both Palfrey and Walker correctly pointed out, if the rear two brigades were closed up on the forward brigade, both would certainly suffer the effects of fire directed at the leading brigade without being able to fire back at the enemy.[87] Second, the flanks of the formation were completely vulnerable to attack. In this formation, virtually none of the division's firepower could be directed toward its flanks without turning the flank regiments to face in the desired direction. In the tactical terminology of the day, this maneuver was called "changing front." The tactical manuals had several procedures for

[85]
Palfrey, *The Antietam and Fredericksburg*, pp. 83-84, 89.

[86]
Walker, *Second Army Corps*, pp. 102-106.

[87]
Palfrey, *The Antietam and Fredericksburg*, pp. 83-84; Walker, *Second Army Corps*, p. 102.

allowing a regiment in line of battle, as Sedgwick's regiments were, to change front to the right or left. But these procedures required time and were difficult to perform even under the best of drill field conditions, let alone under fire. A regiment changing front also required a great deal of space perpendicular to its original line of battle, something Sedgwick's regiments did not have because of the close proximity of the brigades to each other once they reached the West Woods. To overcome this problem, Sumner could have had the regiments of the two trailing brigades formed in column. There were a number of appropriate column formations, and deploying a regiment from a column to a line of battle in almost any direction was an easier matter than changing front in line of battle. If the regiments of the two rear brigades had been in a column of almost any kind, their maneuverability would have been greatly enhanced. As it was, the division could do only one thing well, and that was to move to the front.

Lastly, the formation of Sedgwick's division created problems of control which detracted greatly from its ability to fight. Each brigade was in a single line of battle that covered a front of almost 800 yards. Each of these single lengthy lines was under the command of one individual (the brigade commander) who in order to control his brigade had to be able to see his regiments and communicate with his regimental commanders either by voice or by sending a mounted staff officer. Given the distance over which each brigade was stretched, this was a nearly impossible task. In the reality of this situation, the brigade commanders could effectively control only a segment of their brigades at a time, which meant that the division system of command and control was also seriously diminished by this arrangement.[88]

In defense of Sumner and the formation that he selected, it should be noted that the Civil War, particularly during the war's early years, was fought in an era of tactical transition. Because of the introduction of rifled firearms to the infantry, the tactics of shock action were yielding to the tactics of firepower. Tactics that had been successfully utilized

---

[88] Stinson, "Operations of Sedgwick's Division in the West Woods," p. 34.

during previous wars were no longer feasible on battlefields dominated by longer range and more accurate rifle fire. Commanders often experimented in battle with different combinations of formations. Sumner's deployment of Sedgwick's division allowed for the delivery of a full brigade of firepower in front of the division while presenting the appearence of far-reaching strength, a not inconsequential combination at a time when display could still be counted as an element of combat power. Brigadier General Gibbon of the I Corps, who would prove himself a competent commander and tactician on many later battlefields, wrote, "When I saw Sedgwick's division going into action in such splendid style I felt that it was destined to carry everything before it."[89]

To what degree, then, did Sedgwick's formation contribute to his defeat within the West Woods? Consideration of this question necessarily requires a review of what happened to Sedgwick's division once it entered the deadly woodlot. Over the years historians who have written of this action have concentrated on the fact that the division was attacked by strong Confederate forces directly on its left flank, and, being vulnerable to a flank attack, was defeated with heavy casualties and driven from the woods. Palfrey flatly stated that Sedgwick's division was marched into an ambush in the West Woods with its flanks exposed. Walker did not believe that Sedgwick marched into an ambush, but rather that the Confederates had refused the left of their line. Thus, in moving through the West Woods from east to west, Sedgwick was actually marching across the Confederate front "with his flank absolutely unprotected." The Confederates, he said, chose as their point of attack the left flank of Oliver Howard's brigade, and after driving it off, pitched into the flank and rear of Napoleon Dana's and Willis Gorman's brigades. Historian John C. Ropes, in his *The Story of the Civil War*, also credited the Confederates with maneuvering their reinforcements behind the rocky ledges of the West Woods until they

---

[89] Gibbon, *Personal Recollections*, p. 89.

were squarely on Sedgwick's flank, where they suddenly opened fire on the vulnerable Federal regiments.[90]

These descriptions of the Confederate attack on Sedgwick's division are at best gross over-simplifications of a complex and fluid situation. First, both flanks of Sedgwick's division were covered as it entered the West Woods. The right or northern flank passed directly in front of the brigades of Goodrich and Patrick, both of which remained in position on the flank and rear of the division as it continued its advance into the timber. On the opposite flank was the extra-large 125th Pennsylvania, already in position in the woods west of the Dunker Church. This regiment was the body of troops that Sumner had seen entering the woods as he made his initial reconnaissance of the terrain. In his decision to commit Sedgwick into the breach between the Federal forces in the northern and southern ends of the woods, it was Sumner's intent that the division should go in on the right of the Pennsylvanians so that the left flank of the division would be covered. Moreover, on the left-rear of the 125th Pennsylvania were George S. Greene's two brigades, the troops Sumner had seen lying down behind the eastern ridge in quarter-circle formation. It is apparent that Sumner believed that the flanks of Sedgwick's division would be well supported.[91]

As Sedgwick entered and advanced into the West Woods, the Confederate forces there under Jubal Early and Andrew Grigsby were being repositioned to meet the Federal threat at both the northern and southern

---

[90] Palfrey, *The Antietam and Fredericksburg*, p. 86; Walker, *Second Army Corps*, pp. 104-106; John C. Ropes, *The Story of the Civil War: A Concise Account of the War in the United States of America Between 1861 and 1865*, 2 vols. (New York, 1898), 2, pp. 364-365.

[91] *OR* 19, pt. 1, pp. 244-245; Patrick, *Inside Lincoln's Army*, p. 149; Carman, "History of the Antietam Campaign," pp. 26, 51; Sumner, "Antietam Campaign," pp. 10-11; Howard, *Autobiography*, pp. 295-297. That Sumner knew of a body of troops in the West Woods and expected them to cover Sedgwick's left flank is confirmed by both his son's statement that George Greene was on Sedgwick's left, and by Oliver Howard's three references to some of Greene's troops hanging on to a projection of the West Woods. Howard also wrote that he only learned that the division flank was not covered by Greene when Sumner rode up and directed him (Howard) to change the position of his brigade in response to the Confederate attack on Sedgwick's flank. Although both Samuel Sumner and Oliver Howard were wrong in stating that the 125th Pennsylvania was part of Greene's division, they could not have known that at the time and the mistake is inconsequential.

ends of the woodlot. At about the time that Sumner was making his reconnaissance and preparing to order Sedgwick forward from the East Woods, Early was made aware of the presence of Capt. Albert Monroe's battery and the 125th Pennsylvania in the vicinity of the Dunker Church which, as Early tells it, was only 200 yards from his right flank and rear. When the Pennsylvanians moved into the woods, Early decided he would remove his brigade to the southern end of the woods in order to deal with this Federal force, leaving Colonel Grigsby with his small command to deal with Goodrich and Patrick. Early moved his brigade west and then south on the Alfred Poffenberger farm lane, which ran along the western edge of the woods. As Sedgwick's leading brigade under Gorman drove into the West Woods, it came upon Grigsby's right flank, forcing Grigsby to retire out of the woods to the west and to take up a new position just outside of the woods on the Poffenberger Farm, as already described. Gorman, Sedgwick, and Sumner saw nothing of Early's brigade at this point because by the time that they entered the woods, Early had already moved his command to the south.[92]

When Gorman's brigade reached the Poffenberger Farm on the western edge of the woods, it came up against Grigsby's command and the 13th Virginia, supported by Capt. John Pelham's horse artillery a little farther to the north on Hauser's Ridge. The resultant Federal line established as Gorman opened fire marked the farthest advance of Sedgwick's division at Antietam. As the fighting developed, the division was on the right flank of the 125th Pennyslvania, as Sumner had intended, but the connection between the two units was precarious at best. On its march across the open fields Gorman's brigade obliqued to the right, which caused it to overshoot the 125th Pennsylvania's right flank as it passed on to the west side of the woods. Because the Pennsylvanians had only moved about 150 yards into the woods, there was a 300 yard gap between their right flank and Gorman's left. Gorman's left regiment, the 34th New York, should have filled this gap. For reasons that remain obscure, the New Yorkers failed to oblique to

92
    OR 19, pt. 1, p. 970.

the right with the rest of the brigade and thus entered the woods just north of the Dunker Church, coming up in the rear of the 125th Pennsylvania's left flank.[93]

As previously described, Napoleon Dana's brigade followed Gorman's in the advance across the open fields. According to Dana, the regiment on the left of his battle line, the 7th Michigan, received and returned fire to its left front on entering the woods near the southern end of the lower pasture. With the potential for a fight in that direction, Dana took personal charge of the 7th Michigan and the regiment on its immediate right, the 42nd New York. He obliqued them into the woods to the southwest while the remainder of his brigade continued on to catch up with Gorman's regiments.[94]

As the 7th Michigan and the 42nd New York moved to their left front, they filled to some extent the 300 yard gap that existed between the 125th Pennsylvania and the left of Gorman's brigade. Their movement into that area, however, did not establish a solid line of infantry between the two Federal forces. While the left of the 7th Michigan and the right of the 125th Pennsylvania were in close proximity to one another, there is no documentation to show that any coordinated contact was established between them. The same can be said of the connection between 42nd New York and the 15th Massachusetts, the left flank regiment of Gorman's line of battle.[95]

The fighting that caused Dana to break off with two of his regiments was precipitated by three Confederate brigades: Jubal Early's, which had arrived at the southwestern edge of the wood, and Brig. Gen. William Barksdale's and Brig. Gen. Joseph B. Kershaw's of Maj. Gen. Lafayette McLaws' Division. McLaw's brigades were just arriving at the front, but their arrival at the West Woods at this opportune moment was no accident. General Lee had been carefully watching the fighting on his

93
  Ibid., pp. 311, 315-316.
94
  Ibid., p. 320.
95
  Carman, "History of the Antietam Campaign," pp. 31, 39.

left and knew of the precarious situation that existed on that part of the field. As Sumner was making his reconnaissance and Sedgwick's division was entering the East Woods, Lee already had three fresh divisions and a brigade enroute to reinforce his left in and around the West Woods. Sumner, however, could not see the approach of these forces because his view was blocked by both the West Woods and Hauser's Ridge.[96]

By this time, Jubal Early's Brigade had moved far enough south along the western edge of the West Woods to be directly west of the line of the 125th Pennsylvania and almost due south of Gorman's advancing brigade. When Gorman opened fire on Grigsby's force, which was deployed across his front on the Poffenberger farm, Early turned his left regiment, the 31st Virginia, to face north to help hold off Gorman. Early then moved into the woods with the rest of his brigade to engage the 125th Pennsylvania. Early and the Pennsylvanians had just opened fire on one another when Early noticed William Barksdale's and Joseph Kershaw's brigades entering the woods on his right and advancing in a northeasterly direction against the 125th Pennsylvania. Realizing that these two brigades would become mixed with his own regiments if he went forward, Early held his brigade in position, allowing Barksdale's four regiments to pass at an oblique across his front. Barksdale's Brigade marched through a ravine in the woods that lead like a spearhead directly against the unstable connection between the flanks of the 7th Michigan and the 125th Pennsylvania. When Barksdale's regiments came within a short range of the Federals, they unleashed six to eight devastating volleys that broke both the right of the 125th Pennsylvania and the left of the 7th Michigan.[97]

Barksdale's thrust effectively ruptured the line that Sumner hoped could be established by placing Sedgwick's division into the gap

96
    Sears, *Landscape Turned Red*, p. 220.

97
    OR 19, pt 1, pp. 858, 865, 883, 970-971; Lafayette McLaws to Antietam Battlefield Board, December 13, 1894, Ezra Carman Papers, Antietam National Battlefield; Carman, "History of the Antietam Campaign," pp. 31-32, 35.

between Goodrich's and Patrick's brigades in the northern end of the West Woods, and the 125th Pennsylvania and Greene's division in and about the south end of the timber. Barksdale did not achieve this breakthrough by attacking Sedgwick's division on the flank, but by attacking frontally a weak point in the developing line.

The sustained pressure from Barksdale's Brigade forced the 7th Michigan to fall back to the northeast along the line of its earlier advance. As Barksdale followed up his victory over the 7th Michigan, which by this time was in a near rout, his brigade came upon and overwhelmed the 42nd New York, which was still in the process of taking position on the right flank of the 7th Michigan. Both Federal regiments stumbled back into the lower pasture, stampeding through Howard's lines and disrupting his left flank regiments. It was at this point that Gorman called Sumner's attention to the troops streaming through the pasture to the rear.[98]

As Barksdale's assault gathered steam, Kershaw's Brigade swept up against and overlapped the 125th Pennsylvania's left flank, and with the help of Early's brigade, drove it and the 34th New York (Gorman's wayward regiment behind it) out of the woods into the open fields and back toward the East Woods. After Barksdale's brigade had passed Early's front, Early found he could no longer restrain his men and they joined in the pursuit of the Pennsylvanians, coming up on Kershaw's left. After the rout of the 7th Michigan and 42nd New York, Barksdale had his brigade squarely on Howard's left flank and was also pushing into the rear and flank of Dana's brigade. He was soon joined in this attack by Early's brigade which, after helping to drive out the 125th Pennsylvania and the 34th New York, turned back to come up on Barksdale's left and attack the flank and rear of Gorman's brigade. Gorman was also being attacked by this time on the left front by another brigade of McLaws' Division under Brig. Gen. Paul J. Semmes.[99]

---

[98]
   OR 19, pt. 1, pp. 311, 320.

[99]
   Ibid., pp. 858, 883, 971.

With an appreciation of the nature of these Confederate attacks, it is reasonable to conclude that the weaknesses of the formation that Sumner chose for Sedgwick's division contributed directly to its defeat in three ways. First, the lengthy brigade battle lines made it difficult and perhaps impossible for Gorman and his fellow brigadiers to maintain effective control over their brigades. The diminished command control was evident when the 34th New York was allowed to drift away from Gorman's left flank. The New Yorkers' drift was the primary cause of the breach between Gorman's line and the 125th Pennsylvania. Second, Dana had little choice but to give up control of three-fifths of his brigade when he changed the direction of the 7th Michigan and 42nd New York toward the fight developing in front of the 125th Pennsylvania. The deadly consequences of this loss of control became evident when Dana's remaining three regiments closed up on Gorman's line and, at least on the left flank, took casualties because of the close proximity of the two brigades. In the crisis that followed, these regiments lacked unified direction from a senior officer. Finally, the inability to maneuver due to the division's tight brigade-line formation accounts for the quick and complete collapse of Sedgwick's division once Barksdale's attack broke the front line of Federal regiments.

The third criticism of Sumner's generalship at Antietam is that he failed to maintain effective control over the two other divisions of his corps. This charge applies in particular to his handling of William H. French's division. Not only was French not used in conjunction with Sedgwick in the assault on the West Woods, but French put his division into action well south of the West Woods against the sunken farm lane, where it was not in position to help Sedgwick when his division was flanked and driven from the woods.

On this issue Sumner's early critics were somewhat more under-standing than they were regarding his decision to commit Sedgwick to the West Woods or his choice of formation for Sedgwick. Palfrey did not speculate as to whether the misdirection of French's division was accidental or intentional, contenting himself with the comment that "it proved a most unfortunate divergence." Walker concluded that the azimuth of French's advance resulted from directions given by Sumner that sent the division to the left, "too far as it proved." He went on to say that if the two divisions had attacked in tandem toward the West Woods, the disaster that befell Sedgwick's division "would surely have been averted." Ropes believed the question concerning what had happened to Sumner's other two divisions important enough to ask, but he answered it by merely stating that French took his division too far to the southward and Richardson took position on on French's left.[100]

Modern historians have also been more understanding of Sumner's failure to utilize fully all the divisions of his corps than they have of his other decisions. James Murfin suggested that French simply "found himself facing south against D. H. Hill holding forth at the Piper farm" and suggested that no blame could be assessed to either French or Sumner.[101] Stephen Sears noted Sumner's failure to keep track of French and make sure he was following Sedgwick over the open fields beyond the East Woods, but he did not discuss the matter further, at least in critical terms.[102]

As already written, French had positive orders to follow Sedgwick to the front and form immediately on the left of his division once it was fronted and facing to the south. Sumner's plan was that these two II Corps divisions would arrive on the battlefield in a position and formation to either support the attack of the I and XII Corps toward Sharpsburg, or take over that attack entirely should these corps prove to be exhausted. This plan was based entirely on the false intelligence that Sumner had been given by army headquarters, i.e., that all was going well on the Federal right and that Hooker was driving them.[103]

As a result, French moved off from the vicinity of Keedysville on the morning of September 17 directly behind Sedgwick and in the same

100
 Palfrey, *The Antietam and Fredericksburg*, p. 92; Walker, *Second Army Corps*, p. 109; Ropes, *Story of the Civil War*, 2, pp. 367-368.

101
 Murfin, *Gleam of Bayonets*, p. 246.

102
 Sears, *Landscape Turned Red*, pp. 221-222, 237.

103
 Sears, *McClellan*, p. 305.

formation. On the march to the front, however, the two divisions became somewhat separated, probably because French had to wait to cross Antietam Creek behind Sedgwick and because so many of French's regiments were new and had never been in battle. The separation was not of such distance or extent as to cause serious concern. It was, however, sufficient to cause French to lose sight of Sedgwick's division when it entered the East Woods. When French at the head of his division arrived in rear of the East Woods, Sedgwick's division had already moved on and French did not know where it had gone. However, he could see George Greene's XII Corps division lying down at the southern end of the open area below the East Woods. Since much of it was facing to the south, as Sumner had planned for Sedgwick's and French's divisions, French mistook Greene's division for Sedgwick's. Accordingly, French faced his division to the left and moved it south, marching it up on the left of what he believed was Sedgwick's division. In attempting to do so, however, he eventually came up against the Confederate line of battle that Maj. Gen. Daniel Harvey Hill was forming in a sunken farm lane, triggering the fight for what would become known as the Bloody Lane.[104]

When viewed from this perspective, French's mistake in the placement of his division is both understandable and excusable. Sumner, more concerned with Sedgwick's advance over the open area and with learning first hand of the situation in the West Woods, did not personally see or supervise French's movements. At the first opportunity, Sumner dispatched several staff officers to inform French of Sedgwick's position and to communicate to him the plan for the continuation of the advance beyond the West Woods. By the time these staff officers reached French, it was too late to alter his advance against the Confederate center, since his division had already become engaged with the enemy. When Sumner sent orders for French to make an immediate attack in support of Sedgwick, French had already witnessed Federal troops falling back from the West Woods. Still believing that he was on

---

[104]
    OR 19, pt. 1, pp. 323, 327.

Sedgwick's left, French responded to Sumner's call for support by pushing his brigades ahead against D. H. Hill's men in the Sunken Road.[105]

Once the flank attack on Sedgwick's division was discovered, Sumner—because he was with that division—necessarily directed all of his attention and energies to getting the division successfully out of the West Woods and reformed in the vicinity of the North Woods. This meant that for a period of time he was not in a position to direct or even to be aware of the movements and actions of his other two division commanders (French and Richardson). It is important to remember that it was during this period that French fully developed his attack on the Sunken Road. Israel Richardson's division came up on French's left and joined in the assault. All of this was done without specific orders or guidance from Sumner.

At some point after Sedgwick's division completed its withdrawal to the vicinity of the North Woods and control of it had, at least to an extent, been reestablished, Sumner inquired as to the whereabouts of French's and Richardson's divisions. Using the signal station established in the vicinity of the North Woods, Sumner sent a message to army headquarters reporting his situation and asking for reenforcements and for the location of French's division. Sumner soon learned where French and Richardson had gone and once his headquarters was established in the vicinity of the North Woods he was in communications with them. The importance of the fact that Sumner established a headquarters site and from it communicated not only with French and Richardson, but with other commanders and staff officers on that part of the field, should not be overlooked. This action establishes that subsequent to Sedgwick's repulse from the West Woods, Sumner was in control (or regaining

---

[105]
Ibid. The reader should note that Kimball's report was written the day after the battle, and French's on September 20. Both men believed that they had gone into action on Sedgwick's left. What remains a mystery is why the staff officers that Sumner sent to French did not make it clear to him where Sedgwick had gone.

control) of his own corps as well as the other corps operating on the right of the Federal line.[106]

Based on Sumner's apparent lack of control over all three of his divisions, it is not difficult to conclude that his generalship at Antietam was flawed, especially since hindsight demonstrates that the Federals would have enjoyed greater success had he utilized more effectively all three of his powerful infantry divisions. But such a conclusion ignores the fact that Sumner reasonably believed that he needed to commit Sedgwick's division immediately into the Federal breach in the West Woods, as well as the realities of the system of command and control that existed in 1862. Just as brigade commanders could only communicate with their subordinate regimental commanders by personal contact or through orders delivered by a staff officer, protocol dictated that corps commanders communicate with their subordinate division commanders. Moreover, there was no system or established practice whereby regular situation reports were sent from divisional commanders to the corps commander.

Accordingly, corps commanders were expected to be present near enough to the front lines to observe the situation for themselves. Sumner, in following Sedwick's division into the West Woods, placed himself where he could best observe and evaluate a developing and potentially critical situation. It is unfortunate that in doing so he lost control over the movements of his remaining two divisions. Therefore, it cannot be concluded that Sumner, based upon the information he possessed at the time, was remiss in going forward with Sedgwick.[107]

106
    OR 19, pt. 1, pp. 122-123, 134. Again it is odd that Sumner's staff officers had not apprised him of French's location. The only reasonable explanation is that the staff officers sent out to find French had not yet returned to Sumner by the time he sent his message to army headquarters; ibid., pp. 134, 226, 312, 321, 343; Patrick, *Inside Lincoln's Army*, p. 150; Wilson, *Under the Old Flag*, l, p. 112; Smalley, "Antietam," p. 2.

107
    It is interesting to note that both of the corps commanders who preceded Sumner onto the field at Antietam (Joseph Hooker of the I Corps, and Joseph Mansfield of the XII Corps) were also at or near their own front lines and had also lost effective control of their corps. The difference is that both Hooker and Mansfield were wounded (Mansfield mortally), and both lost control of their corps as a result.

Furthermore, Sumner's apparent lack of attention to French and Richardson after the repulse of Sedgwick does not demonstrate an absence of control as much as it underscores his concern with the potential for a renewed Confederate offensive on his right flank. In failing to involve himself in the fight for the sunken farm lane, particlularly Richardson's success in driving the Confederates from that position, Sumner may have lost the opportunity that he had been trying to develop all morning. His concern at that time over a possible Confederate drive against the Federal right is understandable given the activity of the Rebels in that sector. Sumner thereby saw the establishment of a solid defensive line as his first priority and acted accordingly. He should not be faulted for doing so; both Lee and Jackson at that time were considering launching the exact attack against which Sumner was preparing to defend.

The last criticism directed against Sumner concerns his failure, after the repulse of Sedgwick's division from the West Woods, to marshall the available Federal forces on the right for a renewed offensive in accordance with McClellan's original plan of battle. Palfrey, in *The Antietam and Fredericksburg*, raises the issue of a renewed Federal offensive and faults both Sumner and McClellan; the former for not recommending that the offensive be renewed, and the latter for accepting that recommendation at face value. "McClellan. . .made the same mistake which he had made before at Gaines's Mill, and accepted the judgment of his lieutenant instead of deciding for himself." Palfrey makes it clear, however, that he believed a renewed offensive had to involve more than the Federal forces on the right, i.e., the decision and responsibility for not attacking was more McClellan's than Sumner's.[108] Historian Francis Walker is also critical of both Sumner and McClellan for failing to renew the offensive, but he goes to great lengths to describe Sumner's loss of courage at this point in the battle, a dubious assertion at best. Walker described the fortitude he believed Sumner was lacking as

---

[108]
   Palfrey, *The Antietam and Fredericksburg*, pp. 121-122.

"not the courage which would have borne him calmly up a ravine swept by canister. . .but the courage which. . .enables the commander coolly to calculate the chances of success or failure." Walker insisted that had Sumner allowed Franklin to proceed with his attack on the West Woods and supported it with William F. Smith's division of Franklin's VI Corps and French's and Richardson's divisions of the II Corps "it could hardly have failed to succeed." Ropes agreed with Walker's assertion that a renewed attack by the combined forces on the Federal right "could hardly have failed of complete success," and criticized Sumner for not allowing it. George B. Davis, however, who had defended Sumner's decision to commit Sedgwick's division to the West Woods before the Military Historical Society of Massachusetts, believed that the potential success of a renewed assault on the right, even with all of Franklin's corps, "may well be regarded as doubtful."[109]

Of the two modern narrators of the battle, Murfin clearly believed that there was every chance of success in a renewed offensive on the right if Sumner had not "suggested that there was no use to further bloodshed," and if McClellan had not supported him in his evaluation of the tactical situation. Sears agreed with Murfin and placed the blame for the Federal failure to launch another assault squarely on Sumner's shoulders.[110]

Most students of the Battle of Antietam agree that McClellan's handling of the Army of the Potomac with regard to the application of its combat power was extremely poor. At the point in time under discussion, McClellan still had immediately available for a continuation of the offensive—in addition to the rallied units of the I, II, and XII Corps—both Franklin's and Fitz John Porter's corps, both of which were essentially fresh, plus Burnside's IX Corps, which had not yet suffered significant casualties. Furthermore, the situation for the Confederates at and around the sunken farm lane, the center of Lee's line of battle, was

[109]
    Walker, *Second Army Corps*, pp. 117-119; Davis, "The Antietam Campaign," p. 67; Ropes, *Story of the Civil War*, 2, pp. 369-371.

[110]
    Murfin, *Gleam of Bayonets*, p. 264; Sears, *Landscape Turned Red*, pp. 271-273.

beyond desperate. Major General Daniel H. Hill, whose men held the Confederate center, wrote in his official report that "There were no troops near, to hold the center, except a few hundred rallied from various brigades. Affairs looked very critical."[111] It is reasonable to conclude that had McClellan utilized his available manpower in a new and coordinated offensive, he might well have destroyed Lee's army.

The pertinent issue, however, is not what McClellan should have done with the army as a whole, but what Sumner did or did not do regarding a renewal of the Federal offensive with the troops under his control. Four factors are involved in a full consideration of this question: the condition of the Federal forces available and under Sumner's control; the condition and continuing activity of the Confederate forces opposed to them; Sumner's frequently-mentioned state of mind; and the actions that he took as commander of the Federal right.

As the senior officer present on the army's right flank on the afternoon of September 17, Edwin V. Sumner commanded all the Federal units McClellan committed to the right of his line of battle. In terms of territory, the Federal right extended from a point near the Hagerstown Pike (about 1,500 yards north of the North Woods) south and southeast to a point about 300 yards east of the sunken farm lane, where French's and Richardson's divisions had been engaged, a distance of approximately 4,000 yards. This line included the North Woods, the East Woods, and the Mumma and Roulette farms.

In terms of troops, the Federal right flank included the I, II, VI, and XII Corps. Hooker's I Corps had been committed early in the morning and by late afternoon was resting and reorganizing in the vicinity of the North Woods near the Hagerstown Pike. The corps was under the command of Brig. Gen. George G. Meade, who assumed control from Hooker after that officer left the field with a wound. Although Meade, along with other general officers of the I Corps, believed the corps was exhausted, he was able to report to Sumner by mid-afternoon that at least one division, Meade's own under Brig. Gen. Truman Seymour, was "in

111
    OR 19, pt. 1, p. 1024.

readiness to repel an attack. . .and assist in any advance we might make."[112]

The XII Corps had also been committed to battle early in the day, and like the I Corps, it was exhausted and disorganized by the afternoon. In addition, its two divisions were widely separated and not operating under the central control of Brig. Gen. Alpheus Williams, who succeeded to command of the corps when Joseph Mansfield was mortally wounded. Williams' own division, now under the command of Brig. Gen. Samuel W. Crawford, had one brigade (Gordon's) in line of battle just north of the North Woods, with the regiments of its other brigade (Crawford's) scattered about east and northeast of the East Woods. Although George Greene's division (less Goodrich's brigade) was located in the West Woods soon after Sedgwick's repulse, it would be driven back across the open fields in confusion to the East Woods. Greene's men would not be rallied and ready for combat until late in the afternoon. Goodrich's brigade, which had been detached earlier in the day and sent to support the I Corps in the West Woods, was driven from the field in the same attack that drove Sedgwick from the West Woods. It would not rejoin the corps until after dark.[113]

The condition of Sumner's own II Corps has already been discussed. Sedgwick's division, which was reorganizing in the vicinity of the North Woods, had already suffered the highest casualties that any Federal division would experience that day. Both Sedgwick and brigade commander Napoleon Dana were wounded and out of action, leaving Oliver Howard in division command. French's division was bloodied after its assaults on the Sunken Road, but after resting and replenishing its cartridge boxes, it was in the words of its commander, "ready to continue the action."Israel Richardson's division had only recently experienced the elation of driving the Rebels from the Sunken Road, and

---

[112]
    Ibid., p. 270.

[113]
    Ibid., p. 505. It is difficult to determine when Greene's division regained its combat-ready status. According to Greene, he was driven from the West Woods at 1:30 p.m. and ordered back into line in support of Franklin's corps at 5:30 p.m. In that four-hour period he rallied the division and allowed the men "to rest and get water and clean their guns." Ibid., p. 514.

it continued to hold that position. While seeking artillery support for a renewal of the assault deep into the Confederate center, Richardson was cut down with a mortal wound. Command of the division passed to Brig. Gen. John C. Caldwell and then, by order of McClellan, to Brig. Gen. Winfield S. Hancock of Franklin's corps. Hancock found Richardson's division capable of holding its position, but "too weak to make an attack, unless an advance was made on the right."[114]

William Franklin's VI Corps, however, was just arriving on the field. It had not yet been engaged and thus had suffered few if any casualties. It was Franklin's idea to use two brigades of Henry Slocum's division to make an immediate attack against the West Woods. Sumner, however, stopped Franklin's assault before it began: two brigades would not have been a sufficient force for a successful attack.

Whether or not Sumner could have marshaled the bulk of available forces on the Federal right for a successful assault on the West Woods (or into the Confederate center near the Piper Farm) is a question that cannot be definitively answered. The arrival of Franklin's VI Corps formed a strong nucleus around which a new offensive could have been organized. In hindsight, the VI Corps, supported by the divisions of Meade, French, and Richardson, had a strong chance of successfully making a new attack. But that is not how Sumner evaluated the situation and it may not have been how it was reported to him. The I Corps general officers, Ricketts in particular, represented their corps as having suffered severely, and Sumner's presence in the vicinity of the North Woods allowed him to witness firsthand the corps' depleted condition. Even Meade on the following day could not fully endorse using the I Corps in an offensive action.[115] The XII Corps had also suffered severely in the morning hours and was an organizational mess, its divisions widely separated with many of its brigades and regiments fighting independently. Williams believed that his men "were greatly

---

114
    Ibid., pp. 279, 324.

115
    Ibid., pp. 225, 259, 270-271; *Committee on the Conduct of the War*, 1, p. 368; George B. McClellan, *McClellan's Own Story* (New York, 1887), p. 619.

exhausted" and attempted to withdraw them from combat after the II
Corps reached the front. When called on for support as Sedgwick was
being driven from the West Woods, Williams could send only Gordon's
brigade to succor Sumner.[116] The II Corps had fared little better then its
companion corps. Sedgwick's division was knocked out of action in the
West Woods. There is no evidence indicating that Sumner was able to
personally visit with French or Richardson following Sedgwick's
debacle, so in order to evaluate their combat status he had to rely on
reports by staff officers and messengers.

While Sumner probably had a firm grasp of the conditions of the
Federal forces under his control, his immediate focus and his first
priority was the establishment of a coordinated line of defense, for there
was every indication that the Confederates were fully capable of
launching a strong offensive against the Federal right. Sumner's
experience with Sedgwick's division in the West Woods had
demonstrated that Confederate forces there were strong: they had all but
destroyed Sedgwick in a few short minutes. But Sumner did not have the
opportunity to properly gauge Confederate strength because his field of
vision in that vicinity was limited by the smoke and confusion of battle,
as well as by the woods themselves. He was therefore forced to rely on
what he could discern of the Confederate situation from his vantage
points near the North and East Woods. From his own observations, the
evidence was that the enemy possessed the capability of conducting a
successful defense, and probably had the means of launching a strong
offensive.

First of all, Confederate infantry had pursued Sedgwick's division
until sufficient Federal forces were assembled in the vicinity of the
North Woods to stop them and counterattack, driving the Confederates
back into the West Woods. On the left of that counterattack, when
Gordon's brigade of the XII Corps approached the West Woods from the
east with two of its five regiments, it was stopped in its tracks by
Confederate fire before crossing the Hagerstown Pike. As Gordon

---

116
    OR 19, pt. 1, pp. 476-477.

recalled this moment, "So strong was the enemy, that an addition of any force I could command would only have caused further sacrifice, without gain." Under the circumstances, Gordon wisely withdrew his brigade to the East Woods and reported the matter to Williams. On the opposite flank of the counterattack, Lieutenant Colonel Hofmann brought his brigade of the I Corps forward to a position just west of the North Woods, but remained in that precarious location only thirty minutes before withdrawing under the threat of being flanked by Confederate cavalry and "a heavy body of infantry, much larger than my own," he later reported.[117]

After the Federal counterattack, the field on the right remained quiet for some few minutes. The Southerners—at least to Sumner—appeared to be positioning themselves for a renewal of the offensive. When Hancock's brigade (Smith's division, Franklin's VI Corps) arrived on the field and was sent to support batteries covering the open area between the East Woods and the West Woods, Hancock discovered that the Confederates occupied the West Woods in strength with both infantry and artillery. More ominous was the presence of enemy skirmishers, who had advanced almost to the batteries that he was to protect. Confederates also occupied the buildings of the Miller Farm. The situation was so threatening that Hancock felt obliged to send to Sumner for reinforcements.[118]

Shortly after Hancock's arrival on the field, the Southerners made a limited though determined assault from the West Woods onto the Mumma Farm near the center of Sumner's line. Although not intended to break the Federal position, this attack had every appearance of being able to do just that.[119]

117
    Ibid., pp. 236, 477, 495-496.
118
    Ibid., pp. 406-407.
119
    Ibid., pp. 840, 871-872; James Longstreet, *From Manassas to Appomattox* (Secaucus, 1984), pp. 251-252. As previously discussed, this was the two column attack made by the 49th North Carolina from the West Woods, and Cobb's Brigade, together with the 3rd Arkansas and 27th North Carolina regiments under Colonel Cooke, from below the Dunker Church.

Greene's division was summarily driven from the West Woods in great confusion. The victorious Confederate infantry began crossing the southern end of the open area, threatening to drive the right flank of French's division to the east, thereby opening a large breach in the Federal line at the Mumma Farm. Regiments from Richardson's and French's divisions were called over from their positions along and behind the Sunken Road to stop the attack, and two brigades from from William F. Smith's division, which was just arriving on the field in the vicinity of the East Woods, were also thrown in.[120]

Colonel William Irwin's brigade pursued the Rebels as far as the Dunker Church, where two of his regiments were subjected to a severe fire from the West Woods and were forced to seek shelter behind the ridge immediately across from the church. "A severe and unexpected volley from the woods on our right struck full on the Seventy-seventh and Thirty-third New York, which staggered them," Irwin recorded in his report of the fighting. This Confederate attack and the subsequent repulse of Irwin's regiments was another indication that the Confederates still held the woods in considerable strength.[121]

The Confederates continued their show of strength in the vicinity of the West Woods throughout the remainder of the afternoon, even though their forces there were shattered and disorganized. "Sharpshooters from the woods to the right and to the extreme left. . .opened upon us," reported Irwin, who also described being partially enfiladed by a destructive artillery barrage. "Shell, grape, and canister swept from left to right. The practice of the enemy was rapid and very accurate, and in a short time our loss was very heavy, and the dead and wounded encumbered our ranks."[122] Slocum, whose entire division was now posted in the front line in the vicinity of the East Woods recalled that the fire from

---

120
    Smith's two brigades were commanded by Cols. John R. Brooke and William H. Irwin.

121
    Ibid., pp. 278, 290, 402, 408, 409; *Committee on the Conduct of the War*, 1, p. 626; Hitchcock, *War From the Inside*, p. 64; Strother, *A Virginia Yankee*, pp. 110-111.

122
    OR 19, 1, pp. 409-410.

Confederate artillery was heavy until nightfall. "Our infantry, though not actively engaged, were exposed to a heavy artillery fire from the enemy until sundown, and are entitled to great credit for their gallantry under a severe fire, which they were unable to return."[123] In the late afternoon, Confederate infantry was seen massing in the vicinity of the West Woods, and the threatening movement of an enemy infantry column on the left of the troops positioned at the sunken farm lane was also observed. Taken together, there was more than enough Confederate activity to convince Sumner that remaining on the defensive was the proper course of action.[124]

Sumner's state of mind and the effect it had on the outcome of the battle on the Federal right flank has been the subject of debate since before the last gun was fired at Antietam. While his mental state obviously impacted his decision-making abilities, it probably was not the principal reason Sumner remained on the defensive after Sedgwick's defeat, as some historians have suggested or implied. There can be little doubt that Sumner's bloody experience in the West Woods with Sedgwick's division left him to some degree shocked and shaken. Too many witnesses reported Sumner's demoralized demeanor for there to be any doubt as to the influence of Sedgwick's defeat on the general. But this condition was not uncommon for officers who had participated in a bitter battle without the exhilaration of a clear-cut victory. Major Nelson H. Davis, an assistant inspector-general on McClellan's staff, wrote McClellan in 1887 and spoke of seeing Sumner in a demoralized state. Davis also remarked on Burnside being affected by the battle for South Mountain, quoting Burnside as saying that "he could not bear to see his men killed."[125] Sumner was not the only officer that exhibited signs of demoralization. Lieutenant James H. Wilson, the officer of McClellan's

123
    Ibid., p. 382.
124
    Ibid., pp. 226, 279-280, 377, 402, 405.
125
    Nelson H. Davis to George B. McClellan, January 31, 1876, typed transcript in McClellan Papers, Library of Congress, Reel 38, vol. A-95.

staff whom Sumner kept sending back for further clarification of the
orders he carried, remarked that his encounter with Sumner "indicated a
demoralized state of mind." Wilson went on to note, however, that the
whole state of affairs was demoralized and that "the only general whom
I met. . .who sounded a different note was General French."[126]

Although shaken by the morning's reverses, Sumner's actions on the
field on the afternoon of September 17 seem to belie, at least to some
extent, the statements made by eyewitnesses concerning his state of
mind. For example, Sumner was both active and decisive in establishing
a defensive line on the Federal right after the repulse of Sedgwick from
the West Woods. The record is clear that he made decisions with regard
to the placement of brigades and batteries, and those officers who were
with him recognized that he was in command on the Federal right and
exercising his authority. Although remaining on the defensive may not
have been his best option—hindsight reveals the fractured and fragile
state of the Confederate battle line confronting Sumner—it is reasonable
to conclude that the decision was a rational one, based on Sumner's
understanding and appreciation of the battlefield from his perspective of
the fighting. The Federal right did not remain stationary by default
because of a commander who had lost his courage or was so emotionally
distraught that he was paralyzed into inaction.

As a final consideration, there is evidence to the effect that Sumner
hoped to be able to renew the offensive, and that he took steps to prepare
the units under his command for that contingency. Oliver Howard
recalled in an article for the *National Tribune* and again in his
Autobiography that Sumner was planning to renew the offensive on the
right and that he had gone so far as to have his aides carry orders to all of
the corps and division commanders on the right. Howard's contention is
corroborated by the battle report of Capt. William M. Graham, who
commanded Battery K, 1st United States Artillery at the Battle of Antietam. Graham's battery, which was part of the army artillery reserve, was
sent to the support of Richardson's division at about noon. Once in

---

126
   Wilson, *Under the Old Flag*, 1, p. 114.

position, Graham returned the fire of two Confederate rifled batteries but found that they were beyond the range of his smoothbore guns. Graham reported the matter to Richardson who told him "to save the battery as much as possible, in order that it might advance with his division at a signal then expected from Major-General Sumner." Unfortunately, General Richardson received his mortal wound at this time and nothing more is known concerning the planned advance.[127]

With the conclusion of the Maryland Campaign, Lee took his Army of Northern Virginia to a position along Opequon Creek in the northern Shenandoah Valley to rest, refit, and regain its strength. McClellan made little effort to follow Lee into Virginia, contenting himself instead with redeploying his corps along the banks of the Potomac. On September 21, Sumner, still commanding his own II Corps and Williams' XII Corps, was ordered to Harpers Ferry to hold that place until reinforcements could be brought forward.[128]

By that time, however, the long year of campaigning, coupled with the disaster that befell Sedgwick's division at Antietam, had taken its toll on the oldest general in the Army of the Potomac. Early in October he requested a leave of absence from the army for the purpose of gaining a much needed rest. His request was granted and on October 7 Sumner turned command of the II Corps over to Maj. Gen. Darius N. Couch and departed for Syracuse, New York. How long Sumner planned to remain away from the army on leave, or even if he intended to return and resume command of his corps, is unclear. In his request for a leave, he indicated to McClellan that he desired to be reassigned to command a military department. McClellan endorsed Sumner's request to the War Department, recommending that it be complied with if at all possible.

127
   Howard, "Reminiscences," p. 1; *Autobiography*, I, pp. 301-302; *OR* 19, pt. 1, pp. 343-344.
128
   OR 19, pt. 1, pp. 70, 135, pt. 2, p. 343.

On November 7, President Lincoln, frustrated by McClellan's lack of aggressiveness in launching a new campaign, relieved him of command of the Army of the Potomac and appointed Major General Burnside in his stead. Although he did not feel competent for such a high level of responsibility, Burnside set himself immediately to the task of formulating a new plan of campaign. One of his first tasks was the reorganization of the army into three grand divisions of two corps each. At Burnside's request, Sumner returned from his leave of absence and on November 14 assumed command of the right grand division, which consisted of the II and IX Corps.[129]

During the campaign that followed, Sumner's long experience—coupled with his qualities of character, courage, devotion to duty, and loyalty to his commander—made him the most trusted of Burnside's lieutenants. On November 17, when Sumner arrived with his command at Fredericksburg well ahead of the leading elements of Lee's army, he recommended that Burnside make an immediate crossing of the river and seize the town and the heights beyond. Burnside, however, decided against an immediate advance.[130] During the Battle of Fredericksburg on December 13, Burnside gave Sumner responsibility for making the army's secondary attack, which was aimed at seizing the heights beyond the town. Burnside insisted, however, that Sumner himself not cross the Rappahannock with his troops. Rather he was to direct the operation from his headquarters at the Lacy House.[131] Sumner's performance during the Fredericksburg Campaign was not brilliant, but it was competent. He ably directed the operation of his two corps, faithfully carrying out the orders of his commander. His orders for seizing Marye's Heights were specific, and offered little opportunity for maneuver. The attack, therefore, was made frontally and in accordance

[129]
    Ibid., pt. 1, p. 2; pt. 2, p. 400; Walker, *Second Corps*, pp. 128-130; *New York Times*, October 11, 1862, p. 4; *OR* 19, pt. 2, pp. 483-484, 583.

[130]
    OR 21, pp. 85-86; *Committee on the Conduct of the War*, 1, pp. 652, 657.

[131]
    Committee on the Conduct of the War, 1, p. 658.

with the tactical doctrine of the day, which called for columns of assault. It is to his credit that after witnessing the slaughter and failure of that assault he dissuaded Burnside from attempting another on the following morning.[132]

In January 1863, when Burnside asked to be relieved from command of the army, Sumner also requested relief from active field command and again sought assignment to a military department. The War Department granted his request, ordering him to St. Louis to command the Department of Missouri. It was enroute to that assignment while at the home of his son-in-law in Syracuse that "Old Bull" Sumner took ill. He lingered but a short time and died five days later on March 21.[133]

Edwin Vose Sumner will never be counted among the most brilliant of the commanders produced by the Civil War. He was, however, a professional officer whose skill, experience, and leadership abilities helped buoy the Army of the Potomac through its difficult early years. Perhaps he should best be remembered as Francis Walker remembered him at Antietam. According to Walker:

> No one who saw him there, hat in hand, his white hair streaming in the wind, riding abreast of the field officers of the foremost line, close up against the rocky ledges bursting with the deadly flame of Jackson's volleys, could ever fail thereafter to understand the furious thrust with which a column of the Second Corps always struck the enemy, or the splendid intrepidity with which its brigade and division commanders were wont to ride through the thickest of the fight as cavalry was on Parade.[134]

132
    OR 21, pp. 71, 90-91, 94, 184, 219, 222, 457; Ibid., 51, pt. I, p 1025; *Committee on the Conduct of the War*, 1, p. 653.

133
    New York Times, March 22, 1863, pp. 1, 4.

134
    Walker, *Second Army Corps*, p. 13.

Lesley J. Gordon

Lesley Gordon recently graduated from the University of Georgia, Athens, with a Ph.D. in American History. She has contributed numerous articles and bibliographic entries to a variety of publications, including the *Encyclopedia of the Confederacy* (New York, 1993). Her long and deep interest in George Pickett and his wife was the subject of her dissertation, "Days of Darkness and Blood: George and LaSalle Pickett and the American Civil War." She is currently an assistant professor at Murray State University, Murray Kentucky.

The Seeds of Disaster

The Generalship of George E. Pickett
After the Battle of Gettysburg

On July 3, 1863, Gen. Robert E. Lee chose Maj. Gen. George E. Pickett's Virginia division to spearhead an assault on the Union center at the Battle of Gettysburg. Many Americans associate Pickett's name with that dramatic yet suicidal charge upon Cemetery Ridge. Pickett himself bore little responsibility for the charge's failure, aside from following orders to send his division forward against the virtually impregnable Union position. Confident of victory, he watched in disbelief as his men faltered and broke before the formidable power of the Union army deployed along the ridge. Those few deadly hours haunted Pickett for the rest of the war and markedly affected his performance as a general. The ghosts of Gettysburg followed him to his grave.

This essay examines the generalship of George Pickett after the July 1863 Battle of Gettysburg, and concludes with Robert E. Lee's surrender of the Army of Northern Virginia at Appomattox Court House on April 9, 1865. Scholarly treatment of Pickett usually centers on his actions at Gettysburg, with only cursory attention devoted to his activities after July 1863. All too often, Pickett fades from the historical narrative, reemerging at the Battle of Five Forks in April 1865, where he failed to stop the Federals from seizing that vital road junction and turning Lee's right flank. This narrow focus does not allow for a full understanding of Pickett the general. The fascinating chain of events and circumstances that led to (and resulted in) the fiasco at Five Forks must include an examination of Pickett's command of the Department of North Carolina, his failed attack on New Berne, his shaky performance in the Bermuda Hundred Campaign, and his return to the Army of Northern Virginia in May 1864. Included within these events is Pickett's little-known and generally misunderstood role in the execution of twenty-two former members of the North Carolina Home Guard, and his physical breakdown in early May 1864.

When the Civil War began in 1861, George Pickett seemed perfectly suited to take a prominent role in the Southern war effort. He was a member of the elite Virginia gentry, a West Point graduate, and a celebrated Mexican war veteran with twelve years of army service on the frontier.[1] Initially, what Pickett lacked in complexity, penetrating intellect, or even talent, he made up for with zeal and determination. Early in the war this fighting spirit distinguished him as one of the Confederate army's most aggressive brigadiers.[2] His frequent absences, constant complaining, and bungling of even the simplest of orders, however, marked Pickett as an unreliable division leader.[3] After

[1]
    Lesley Jill Gordon, "Before the Storm: The Early Life of George E. Pickett," Honors Thesis, 1987, The College of William and Mary.

[2]
    For examples, see U.S. War Department, *The War of the Rebellion: The Official Records of the Union and Confederate Armies*, 128 vols. (Washington, D.C., 1890-1901), series I, vol. 11, pt. I, pp. 935, 945; pt. 2, p. 758. Hereinafter cited as *OR*. All references are to series I unless otherwise noted.

[3]
    Stories of Pickett's frequent absences from his division to visit LaSalle Corbell are notorious. Moxley Sorrel, *Recollections of a Confederate Staff Officer* (Dayton, 1978), p. 54. Examples of his other poor habits are included in *OR* 5, pp. 991-992, 994; ibid., 25, pt. 2, pp. 852-853; ibid., 27, pt. 3, p. 869.

Gettysburg his performance as a division commander continued its downward spiral.

Pickett's post-Gettysburg status and deteriorating relationship with Lee have often perplexed Civil War historians.[4] Scholars have puzzled over why the Confederate War Department repeatedly bestowed new and important responsibilities upon Pickett when he repeatedly disappointed them. He often seemed overwhelmed with the tasks assigned to him, yet he remained in command until the final days of the war. An exasperated Lee finally removed Pickett just days before the surrender. It was an act long overdue.

Pickett's consistently poor performance after Gettysburg reveals how much that single event affected his military abilities and mental outlook. Although he already showed signs of incompetence prior to July 1863, Gettysburg was a turning point in his Civil War experience. He never recovered from that day when he confidently ordered his division forward, convinced that he would save the day, win the battle, and perhaps even end the war.[5] In the months and years that followed he mulled over the failure of others to support him, negligence that left his men vulnerable and alone. He retained a distorted view of his own ability and other's culpability until the end of his life. His remark to John Mosby about Robert E. Lee in 1870 is as infamous as it is insightful: "He had my division massacred at Gettysburg," Pickett exclaimed, to which Mosby responded, "Well, it made you immortal." [6]

4

   Clifford Dowdey, *Lee's Last Campaign* (Boston, 1960), p. 371; Douglas Southall Freeman, *Lee's Lieutenants: A Study in Command,* 3 vols. (New York, 1944), vol. 3, p. 627.

5

   George E. Pickett to LaSalle Corbell Pickett, July 23, 1863, Arthur Crew Inman Papers, Brown University, Providence, Rhode Island. For a full discussion of Gettysburg and its immediate aftermath, see Lesley Jill Gordon, "'Assumed a Darker Hue:'" C.S.A. Major General George E. Pickett, May 1863-May 1864," M.A. Thesis, University of Georgia, 1991.

6

   John S. Mosby to Eppa Hunton, March 25, 1911, John S. Mosby Papers, Virginia Historical Society, Richmond, Virginia, Mss2m8504; John S. Mosby, *Memoirs of Colonel John S. Mosby*, edited by Charles W. Russell (Boston, 1917), pp. 380-381.

Ironically, despite the immortality Pickett achieved at Gettysburg, his is not the story of either a courageous hero or an innocent victim. George Pickett often displayed poor judgment and disturbing character traits when faced with difficult decisions. Time after time he had opportunities to prove his ability on the battlefield, and failed. The Confederacy could ill afford such serious losses in lives and time.

Pickett's first opportunity to redeem himself on the battlefield came two months after Gettysburg on September 23, 1863, when he received a new assignment as the head of the Department of North Carolina.[7] He established his headquarters at Petersburg, Virginia, and brought his fifteen-year-old bride, LaSalle, to live nearby. The department encompassed southeastern Virginia as well as eastern North Carolina, and by late 1863 Unionists and Confederates had splintered the Tar Heel State into warring factions. Historian Michael Honey contends that North Carolina contained "the sharpest internal opposition to the Confederacy of all the Southern states during the war." Disaffection plagued North Carolina's troops, earning that state the dubious distinction of having the most desertions in the Confederacy. By the fall of 1863, conscription, President Davis' suspension of habeas corpus and freedom of speech, military defeats, and economic hardships took a heavy toll on North Carolina's poor whites. Bands of destitute deserters roamed communities, plundering homes and wreaking havoc, often on their own neighbors. These were trying circumstances for anyone to face. For an embittered and complaining man like Pickett, they were doubly straining. Pickett did not have an easy task ahead of him.[8]

7
   OR 29, pt. 2, p. 746.

8
   The impact of the Civil War on North Carolina communities has been the subject of several recent studies. These include Paul Escott, *Many Excellent People: Power and Privilege in North Carolina, 1850-1900* (Chapel Hill, 1985); Wayne Durrill, *War of Another Kind: A Southern Community in the Great Rebellion* (New York, 1990); and Philip Shaw Paludan, *Victims: A True Story of the Civil War* (Knoxville, 1981); Michael K. Honey, "The War Within the Confederacy: White Unionists of North Carolina," *Prologue: Journal of the National Archives*, vol. 18, no. 6 (Summer 1986), p. 77; Richard Bardolph, "Confederate Dilemma: North Carolina Troops and the Deserter Problem," pts. 1-2, *North Carolina Historical Review*, vol. 66, no. 1-2 (January/April 1989), pp. 61-86;179-210; Honey, "The War Within the Confederacy," p. 77.

Maj. Gen. George E. Pickett
(Generals in Gray)

Soon after assuming his new command, Pickett revealed deep dissatisfaction with efforts to rebuild his broken division. When the possibility arose that the division might go west with James Longstreet's Corps, Pickett protested strongly.[9] Pickett explained to Adjutant and Inspector General Samuel Cooper that plans to reorganize the division had only just begun. Few recruits had been collected, and new officers had little time to learn their new responsibilities. It would take more time and many more men to refill the ranks before it could again become "the crack division it was," related Pickett. "I decidedly would not like to go into action with it," he added.[10]

Although the War Department honored Pickett's request to stay in Virginia, he remained concerned over his division's weak condition. In addition, he began to feel his overall power as department head subverted by what he described as the continual "borrowing" of his brigades. Pickett had faced a similar dilemma in June of 1863 when the War Department ordered him to leave behind two of his five brigades during Lee's raid into Pennsylvania. One of those brigades held back before the Gettysburg Campaign, that of Micah Jenkins, was permanently lost to Pickett when it was assigned to John B. Hood's Division in the fall of 1863.[11]

As the Richmond authorities struggled to meet enemy threats across various portions of the Confederacy, it became apparent that units in Pickett's command were subject to being shifted out of his jurisdiction to aid other departments and districts. Soon after he assumed the reins of departmental command, Pickett was instructed to send Maj. Gen. William H. C. Whiting, the commander of Wilmington, North Carolina, any troops needed to defend that city in case of attack.[12]

[9]
President Davis had requested Pickett's Division join Longstreet to support Braxton Bragg's Army of Tennessee in Georgia. Freeman, *Lee's Lieutenants*, 3, p. 627.

[10]
OR 29, pt. 2, pp. 773-774.

[11]
Ibid., 27, pt. 3, pp. 888, 890; Freeman, *Lee's Lieutenants*, 3, pp. 223-224.

[12]
OR 29, pt. 2, p. 752.

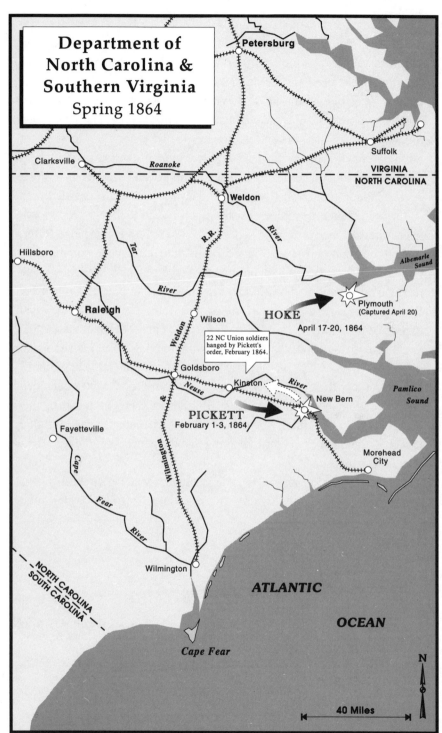

**Department of
North Carolina &
Southern Virginia**
Spring 1864

Petersburg

Clarksville

Roanoke

**VIRGINIA
NORTH CAROLINA**

Suffolk

Weldon

River

R.R.

Hillsboro

Albemarle
Sound

Tar

River

Raleigh

Wilson

HOKE

Plymouth
(Captured April 20)

April 17-20, 1864

Weldon

22 NC Union soldiers
hanged by Pickett's
order, February 1864.

Goldsboro

River

Neuse

Kinston

New Bern

*Pamlico
Sound*

PICKETT
February 1-3, 1864

Fayetteville

&

Cape

Morehead
City

Wilmington

Fear

River

NORTH CAROLINA
SOUTH CAROLINA

ATLANTIC

OCEAN

Cape Fear

N

40 Miles

Mark A. Moore

While poised to assist Whiting, in mid-October Pickett dutifully answered a request to send a brigade to the Department of Southwestern Virginia, a move which further dissipated his strength.[13] In the meantime, he faced distressing reports of possible enemy offensives against Petersburg, Virginia, and Weldon and Kinston, North Carolina, three key points within his jurisdiction.[14] On October 21, he notified Samuel Cooper that, despite assurances to the contrary, "numbers of applications for the return of detailed men on work in the Navy Department, etc., have been sent back disapproved." Secretary of War James Seddon replied that he was "endeavoring to return detailed men as far as the interest of general service will possibly allow." One month later, when notified of a large Federal advance across the Rapidan River, Pickett had but a single brigade under his immediate command.[15] Secretary of War James Seddon ordered Pickett to send a brigade north to Hanover Junction and keep another unit ready to protect Petersburg. Pickett, unaware of the reason for this latest request for troops, expressed his rising level of frustration in a telegram to Richmond: "If I am to take my division into the field, he implored Seddon, I wish to take the whole division, and not a portion of it, as I did at Gettysburg, and I beg of you not to split it up when going into action." Pickett concluded with a parting shot to his superior: "If I am to keep command of this department, do not entirely denude it." Seddon eventually admitted that Pickett's arguments had merit, replying that the general's force was "less than I had supposed."[16]

Pickett had good reason to be concerned about the strength of his command. Federal raids against the towns of Suffolk, Virginia and

13
    Ibid., p. 788.

14
    Ibid., pp. 778, 789-790.

15
    Ibid., p. 798. Major General George G. Meade's November 26 crossing of the Rapidan River with his Army of the Potomac triggered the Mine Run Campaign, which concluded on December 2, 1863 with his recrossing of the Rapidan.

16
    Ibid., pp. 847, 848.

Elizabeth City, North Carolina, commenced in October and continued through the winter.[17] Under orders from Union Maj. Gen. Benjamin "Beast" Butler, Brig. Gen. Edward A. Wild visited plantations to offer freedom to all slaves and Union guns and uniforms to the blacks. One woman from Elizabeth City described Union soldiers as men who looked and behaved "more like deamons [sic] than any thing else," and who threatened to burn and rob her home. "It would make your blood boil to see them rush on your premises throw out your pickets at any door and have your house completely surrounded by them white and black," she declared.[18]

The burning and pillaging of private homes continued into the winter, much to the disgust of Pickett. On December 15, 1863, Col. Joel R. Griffin, commander of a Georgia cavalry unit, sent Pickett the disturbing news that enemy forces south of Suffolk, in Gates County, North Carolina, were destroying property and "committing all kinds of excesses; insulting our ladies in the most tantalizing manner."[19] In addition, Wild's Federals took two female hostages in retaliation for a black soldier held by Confederates. Wild ordered the women shackled with irons and confined "with negro men."[20] An enraged Pickett demanded permission from the War Department to clear slaves out of the northeast region of North Carolina. "Whatever is determined," Pickett urged, "should be carried out at once, as everyday loses so much valuable property to the Confederacy."[21] Pickett deemed the

---

17
    Ibid., pp. 797-798, 818.

18
    John G. Barrett and W. Buck Yearns, eds., *North Carolina Civil War Documentary* (Chapel Hill, 1980), pp. 43, 48.

19
    OR 29, pt. 2, pp. 872-873.

20
    Ibid., p. 847; Frank Moore, *The Rebellion Record: The Diary of American Events with Documents, Narratives, Illustrative Incidents, Poetry, Etc.*, 12 vols. (New York, 1865), vol. 8, pp. 304-305.

21
    OR 29, pt., p. 873.

deteriorating situation an emergency with no time to waste. His frenzied telegram to Richmond reveals his strongly-held view toward blacks and a growing indignation toward the enemy. To Pickett, arming blacks and insulting ladies was inexcusable. He reiterated his complaint to the War Department that his command was too weak to offer protection over such a large area. "Butler's Plan," Pickett warned Richmond on the same day of Colonel Griffin's report, "is to let loose his swarms of blacks upon our ladies and defenseless families, plunder and devastate the country." Butler already threatened Pickett's in-laws' family home in Suffolk. He saw only one recourse to combat such "heathens": "to hang at once everyone captured belonging to the expedition and afterwards anyone caught who belongs to Butler's department." He immediately issued orders to Colonel Griffin that "any one caught in the act (negroes or white men) of burning houses or maltreating women must be hung on the spot, by my order."[22]

The Union raids—or "outrages," as Pickett viewed them—intended to suppress Confederate guerrilla activities in the eastern portions of Virginia and North Carolina, continued unabated.[23] On December 18, Wild captured a man described as "about thirty, a rough stout fellow, [who] was dressed in butternut homespun, and looked the very ideal of a guerrilla." Though this man was actually an enlisted member of the Georgia cavalry, Wild decided to make an example of Pvt. Daniel Bright. Union soldiers left Bright's body hanging from a post, a slip of paper pinned to his back: "This guerrilla hanged by order of Brigadier General Wild. Daniel Bright of Pasquotank County."[24]

Pickett learned of Bright's death the following day and shot off another angry dispatch to Richmond. "I have the honor to report that the enemy have been committing the most brutal outrages upon our loyal citizens in the vicinity of Elizabeth City," he reported. "You will

[22]
  Ibid., 29, pt. 2, p. 874.
[23]
  Moore, *Rebellion Record*, 8, pp. 304-305.
[24]
  Ibid., p. 301.

perceive that they have with their negro troops hung one of our soldiers and manacled ladies, and have taken them off in irons," he continued. The angry general announced his intentions "to spare no one," but feared the enemy too wary to stop. "They, like the Indians," he maintained, "only war on the defenseless. . . .It makes my blood boil to think of these enormities being practiced, and we have no way of arresting them." [25]

Colonel Griffin followed Pickett's instructions to hang anyone caught committing such acts. Within a week after Pickett had issued the order, a group of Unionist citizens from Pasquotank County, North Carolina, notified Federal officials that they had found the hanged body of a black Union soldier with a wooden placard around his neck. The placard read: "Here hangs Private Samuel Jones of Company B, Fifth Ohio Regiment, by order of Major General Pickett in retaliation of [Private Daniel Bright] Company L, Sixty-Second Georgia Regiment, hung December 18, 1863, by order of Brigadier General Wild." [26]

One month after the hanging of Samuel Jones, General Lee ordered Pickett to lead an attack on New Berne, North Carolina, which had fallen into Union hands early in the war when Union Maj. Gen. Ambrose Burnside captured the coastal town with an amphibious assault. On January 20, 1864, Lee sent Pickett detailed instructions explaining his plan to capture the Federal garrison guarding the town. The movement offered Pickett another chance to prove his ability as a field commander. Although he allowed Pickett to "modify [the plan] according to circumstances developed by investigation, and your good judgment," Lee sent Brig. Gen. Robert Hoke with the written orders to "explain" the movement to Pickett. [27]

[25]
    OR 29, pt. 2, p. 882-883.

[26]
    Ibid., series II, 6, p. 846.

[27]
    Robert E. Lee to George E. Pickett, January 20, 1864, Seth Barton Compiled Service Record, National Archives, Washington D.C., Record Group 109.

Lee's strategy called for infantry, cavalry, artillery, and naval units to converge on New Berne and its vicinity in careful coordination. The commander of the Army of Northern Virginia urged the utmost "secrecy, expedition and boldness" in preparation and execution.[28]

By January 30, Pickett had organized an attack force of 13,000 men and 14 cutter ships. Land troops were to assault enemy positions northwest, southwest, and northeast of the the city, while navy vessels under John Taylor Wood moved down the Neuse River to engage and capture or destroy enemy gunboats. If all went as planned, a surprised and surrounded enemy would quickly surrender New Berne to the victorious Confederates. Pickett's offensive got underway during the early morning hours of February 1. Fog and a light rain assisted in masking the movement. For a short while, it seemed the assault might work. Northwest of town, Pickett accompanied Robert Hoke's men as they successfully crossed Batchelder's Creek. Below New Berne, Seth Barton swept over enemy outposts, halting within view of the city's main defenses.

Thereafter, however, the unmistakeable signs of trouble began to appear. The four-pronged land and water attack failed to occur simultaneously, forfeiting the element of surprise the Confederates were relying on to assist them in their assault. Alarmed by the Confederate offensive, Union commanders rushed reinforcements by railroad to bolster defensive positions. Major James Dearing, who was expected to capture Fort Anderson, a stronghold northeast of town, discovered a stronger force than anticipated and halted his advance. Similarly, Seth Barton, positioned outside the city's main defenses, refused to attack as ordered. On the following day, an exasperated Pickett sent an aide armed with orders for Barton to launch his assault against the works in his front. Barton, however, refused to attack on the basis that preliminary reports of Federal strength were woefully inaccurate. Pickett changed his orders and sent Barton to join Hoke's forces across the Trent River,

---

[28]
Ibid. Lee reiterated the need for surprise when he first notified President Davis of the plan, stressing that such an attack be "secretly and suddenly made." *OR* 33, p. 1061.

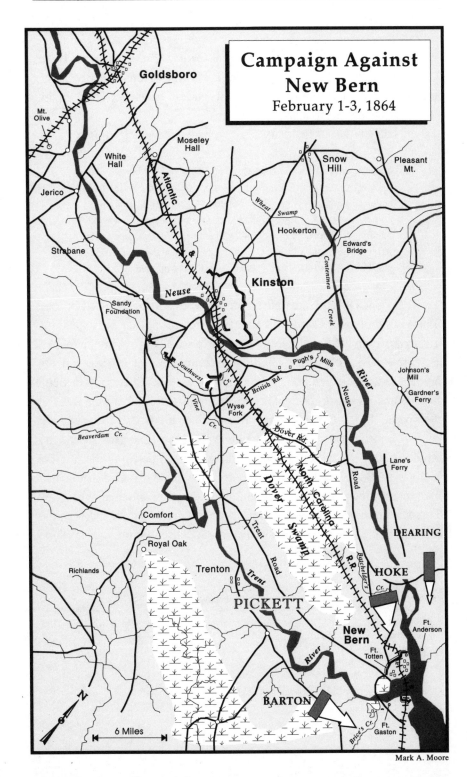

Campaign Against New Bern
February 1-3, 1864

Mark A. Moore

where they would be in a position to move on the city from the northwest. Although Barton, who was nearly 25 miles from Hoke, complied with Pickett's order, he did so without any alacrity in his movements. On February 3, Pickett pulled back, rebuffed in his half-hearted attempt to take New Berne.[29]

Pickett's report of February 3, 1864, belied the attack's failure:

> Made a reconnaissance within a mile and a half of New Berne. . .Met the enemy in force at Batchelder's Creek; wounded about 100 in all; captured 13 officers and 280 prisoners, 14 negroes, 2 rifled pieces and caissons, 300 stands of small arms, 4 ambulances, 3 wagons, 55 animals, a quantity of clothing, camp and garrison equipage and 2 flags. Commander Wood, C.S. Navy, captured and destroyed U.S. gun-boat Underwriter. Our loss, 35 killed and wounded.[30]

President Davis expressed his disappointment to Lee a week later when he wrote that "General Pickett has returned from his expedition unsuccessful in the main object." Lee was also unhappy with the results. He wrote to Robert Hoke: "I regret very much that success did not attend the whole expedition." Lee admitted, however, that "It is difficult in a combined attack to regulate and harmonize on an extreme field all the operations."[31] Pickett seemed ill-suited for a task that required such careful coordination, boldness, and expediency. Lee had repeatedly emphasized the need for swiftness and secrecy in detailing the original battle plan. But Pickett's official report of the battle revealed that he had had reservations from the beginning of the expedition against New Berne. After complaining that there were too many contingencies in the plan, he wrote: "I should have wished more concentration, but still hope

---

29
    Details of the move on New Berne were gathered from *OR* 33, pp. 92-99; Jefferson Davis, *Jefferson Davis, Constitutionalist: His Letters, Papers, and Speeches*, 10 vols., edited by Dunbar (Jackson, 1923), vol. 8, p. 543; B. P. Loyall, "Capture of the Underwriter at New Berne, North Carolina, February 2, 1864," *Southern Historical Society Papers*, 52 vols. (1899), vol. 27, pp. 137, 143; Freeman, *Lee's Lieutenants*, 3, p. 335.

30
    OR 33, p. 1145.

31
    Dunbar, *Jefferson Davis, Constitutionalist*, 6, p. 169; *OR* 33, pp. 1160-1161.

the effect produced by the expedition may prove beneficial." Pickett also blamed Seth Barton, chiding him for his unwillingness to push troops forward and his refusal to cooperate in staging a final "coup de main on the enemy."[32] Pickett concluded, "Had I have had the whole force in hand I have but little doubt that we could have gone in easily, taking the place by surprise."[33] Entrusted with his first real offensive operation as department head, Pickett failed miserably.

Since Gettysburg, George Pickett had felt his authority undermined. This war was quickly evolving into something different than anything he had experienced as a Mexican War hero or frontier army officer. He appeared frustrated by the weakness of his division, the combined failures of Gettysburg and New Berne, and an enemy that preyed on women and interferred with slaves. Soon after his inglorious retreat from New Berne, however, Pickett found an outlet for these months of disappointment.

Not mentioned in either Pickett's cursory report of February 3 or his official report of February 15 was his capture of twenty-two North Carolina soldiers. These men had once worn the colors of the state's home guard, but when threatened with Confederate conscription, opted for Union blue. The United States government refused to view Confederate draft evaders who joined the Union army as deserters. Union officials insisted that the Confederacy treat these men as prisoners of war.[34] Subtle legalities meant little to George Pickett. He had found a

---

[32]
Ibid., 33, p. 94; Barton demanded an investigation to clear his name. Lee endorsed this proposal and a Court of Inquiry assembled in early March to investigate the matter. For reasons that remain obscure, the War Department canceled the special order for the court a few weeks later. During its brief investigation, however, the court did request Lee's orders to Pickett. No other records have surfaced to shed light on the proceedings. Ibid., 33, pp. 92-94, 97-99, 1187; Special Orders Number 54, XXIV, March 5, 1864, Letters Received, Adjutant and Inspector General's Office, Record Group 109, National Archives, Washington, D.C.; W. Gordon McCabe to Walter H. Taylor, March 12, 1864, Barton Compiled Service Records; Freeman, *Lee's Lieutenants*, 3, p. 335, 144n.

[33]
OR 33, p. 94.

[34]
Ella Lonn, *Desertion During the Civil War* (Gloucester, 1966), p. 214; Honey, "The War Within the Confederacy," p. 83; Bardolph, "Confederate Dilemma," pt. 2, pp. 205-206.

scapegoat for frustrations and failures that had been mounting for months. Two weeks after his failed expedition against New Berne, he court-martialed and hanged all twenty-two men for desertion.[35]

Union Maj. Gen. John J. Peck first suspected something was seriously wrong on February 11, when he wrote to Pickett inquiring about a recent article he had seen in a Richmond paper. The newspaper had reported that during the action around New Berne, black troops shot and killed Confederate Col. Henry M. Shaw. The newspaper claimed that incensed Confederates followed, captured, and hung the black soldier who fired the fatal shot. Peck included a copy of President Lincoln's warning to Confederates to make no distinction based on color in the treatment of war prisoners. Lincoln threatened "retaliation upon the enemy's prisoners" by executing Rebel soldiers for every Union soldier killed "in violation of the laws of war." Peck closed his dispatch by writing: "Believing that this atrocity has been perpetrated without your knowledge, and that you will take prompt steps to disavow this violation of the usages of war and to bring the offenders to justice, I shall refrain from executing a rebel soldier until I learn your action in the premises."[36] Although Union officials already knew about the hanging of Private Jones, Peck was giving Pickett the benefit of the doubt about his participation in this criminal act. Before Pickett could reply, however, Peck hurriedly wrote him again about the captured North Carolinians. Peck reminded Pickett of Union policy toward such prisoners of war and asked for special consideration for this specific case.[37]

George Pickett must have enjoyed a chilling laugh. Here was the enemy, the "heathens," asking him to respect the rules of war. On February 16 Pickett sharply denied that he had had any part in the

---

35
    A popular, brief account of the New Berne affair is found in Patricia L. Faust, ed., *The Historical Times Illustrated Encyclopedia of the Civil War* (Harrisburg, 1986), p. 524.

36
    OR 33, pp. 866-867.

37
    Ibid., Series II, 6, pp. 845-846, 858; ibid., 33, p. 867.

hanging of Colonel Shaw's killer. He deemed the story "not only without foundation, but so ridiculous that I should scarcely have supposed it worthy of consideration." In the confusion of a battle, how could anyone single out Shaw's killer, follow and capture him? Nevertheless, Pickett coldly added that if he had caught any black soldier, "I should have caused him to be immediately executed." He indignantly answered Peck's threat of retaliation as expressed in Lincoln's proclamation by stating: "I have in my hands and subject to my orders, captured in the recent operations in this department, some 450 officers and men of the United States Army, and for every man you hang, I will hang 10 of the United States Army."[38]

Pickett on the following day also responded sarcastically to Peck's plea for special consideration for the fifty-three North Carolina prisoners:

General

Your Communication of the 13th instant is at hand. I have the honor to state in reply that you have made a slight mistake in regard to numbers, 325 having fallen into your [our] hands in your [our] hasty retreat from before New Bern; instead of the list of 53 with which you so kindly furnished me, and which will enable me to bring to justice many who have up to this time escaped their just deserts. I herewith return you the names of those who have been tried and convicted by court-martial for desertion from the Confederate service and taken with arms in hand, duly enlisted in the Second North Carolina Infantry, United States Army. They have been duly executed according to law and the custom of war.[39]

Pickett ended his communication with an impertinent and insulting slap: "Extending to you my thanks for your opportune list." He later

<hr>

38
   Ibid., pp. 867-868.

39
   Ibid., p. 868. Brackets added by Pickett.

warned Peck that if he killed any Southern prisoners in retaliation, Pickett would make good his threat of ten Union dead for every one Confederate.[40] Before he received Pickett's communications, Peck had read the disturbing news about the executions in a newspaper that carried an account of the trial and hanging of two of the North Carolinians. The Union commander cautioned Pickett that if he failed to treat the men as prisoners of war, Confederate officers imprisoned at Fort Monroe would suffer the consequences.[41] Pickett ignored Peck's threats and diligently sent copies of all their correspondence to the Confederate War Department.[42] This time, however, he wanted no intervention from Richmond. "The whole of the prisoners captured in this department will be held at my disposal."[43] Pickett wanted complete control over the situation to do as he saw fit with the prisoners.

Details of the execution reveal just how much energy Pickett exerted to confiscate full control over the prisoners' fate. After his retreat from New Berne, Pickett marched the prisoners west to Kinston, where he had them incarcerated in a local jail. He ordered court martial proceedings to commence immediately, and allowed little food or coverings to the men while ignoring pleas for leniency from town officials, relatives, or subordinate army officers. Most of these men resided nearby, and wives came to visit them and provide what little comfort they could offer. Within two weeks of their capture, Pickett decreed three separate hangings of the prisoners in a public square, where they would be surrounded by wives, children, and townspeople. A Confederate army chaplain offered baptism to several of the condemned

40
   George E. Pickett to John J. Peck, February 27, 1864, in United States War Department, Thirty-ninth Congress, 1st Session, House of Representatives, Document No. 98, (Washington, D.C.), p. 9, hereinafter cited as House of Representatives, Document 98.

41
   OR 33, pp. 868-869.

42
   Registers of Letters Received, Adjutant and Inspector General's Office, National Archives, Washington, D.C., Record Group 109.

43
   George E. Pickett to Samuel Cooper, February 26, 1864, House of Representatives, Document No. 98, p. 9.

men, telling them that "they had sinned against their country, and their country would not forgive them but they had also sinned against God, yet God would forgive them if they approached with penitent hearts."[44] After each execution Pickett allowed his soldiers to strip the corpses of all clothing and shoes. According to at least one source, Confederates jeered and taunted widows who attempted to gather their husbands bodies for proper burial. Bodies that went unclaimed were hastily buried in a single grave beneath the gallows.[45]

News of the execution soon reached Peck's superior, Maj. Gen. Benjamin Butler, who wrote directly to the Confederate Commander of Prisoner Exchange. He inquired of Col. Robert Ould if the Confederacy was fully aware of Pickett's disturbing actions and threats toward Union prisoners. Butler sensed the personal anger expressed in Pickett's acts and words and warned Colonel Ould of the larger implications of that behavior. "The question will be whether he [Pickett] shall be permitted to allow his personal feelings to prevail in a matter now in our hands."[46]

Historian Richard Bardolph argues that a comparison of the records of Confederate court-martials kept at the National Archives justifies Butler's concern. Bardolph maintains that most soldiers sentenced to death were eventually spared and that the twenty-two men who died at Kinston "were the luckless exception to general practice." The haste in which Pickett ordered the execution and his denial of clemency made this case, in Bardolph's opinion, "untypical." He points out that desertion from state service was not even a crime in North Carolina.

44
   James O. Hall, "Atonement," *Civil War Times Illustrated*, vol. 29 (August 1980), p. 20.

45
   New York Times, March 11 & 18, 1864; *New Berne North Carolina Times*, March 9, 1864; E. W. Gaines, "Fayette Artillery: The Movement on New Berne Thirty-Three Years Ago," *Southern Historical Society Papers*, 25, pp. 296-297; Chambers, *The Diary of Henry A. Chambers*, p. 175; Walter Harrison, *Pickett's Men: A Fragment of War History* (New York, 1870), pp. 116-119: Hall, "Atonement," pp. 19-21; David Johnston, *Four Years a Soldier* (Princeton, 1887), p. 290; House of Representatives, Document No. 98, pp. 1547, 53-87.

46
   Benjamin F. Butler, *Private and Official Correspondence of General Benjamin Butler During the Period of the Civil War*, 5 vols. (Norwood, 1917), vol. 3, pp. 479-480.

Pickett's anger and frustration overshadowed any notions of discretion. "God damn you, I reckon you will hardly ever go back there again, you damned rascals; I'll have you shot, and all other damned rascals who desert," a soldier heard Pickett yell at two of the prisoners before court martial proceedings even began.[47]

As the clamor over the executions faded, Gen. Braxton Bragg, newly appointed military advisor to President Davis, prepared plans to attack Plymouth, North Carolina. He selected Brig. Gen. Robert Hoke to lead the expedition instead of Pickett, the head of the department.[48] Bragg explained to Pickett that he chose the younger and less experienced officer for the mission merely "so as not to withdraw you from supervision from your whole department at this time." Pickett's lackluster and unsuccessful attempt to wrest New Berne from the Federals, however, was more likely the motivating factor behind Bragg's decision.[49] Why the Confederate high command retained Pickett in the important position as department head is unclear. Perhaps his twenty years of professional army experience and early war record convinced some that he would recover from his setbacks. His close friendship with James Longstreet may have been another factor. Still, there was enough doubt surrounding George Pickett to demote him to spectator as Hoke skillfully seized Plymouth on April 20, 1864.[50]

While Hoke's forces surrounded Plymouth, the Federals began their own spring offensive, one designed to crush the Confederacy by advancing from different directions simultaneously. One of these cooperative efforts entailed a deployment of troops on the south side of the James River as part of Gen. U. S. Grant's overall plan to coordinate

47
    Bardolph, "Confederate Dilemma," pt. 2, pp. 205-209; House of Representatives, Document No. 98, p. 80.

48
    OR 51, pt. 2, pp. 857-858; Herbert Schiller, *The Bermuda Hundred Campaign: Operations on the South Side of the James River, Virginia, May 1864* (Dayton, 1988), p. 18.

49
    OR 51, pt. 2, p. 857.

50
    Hoke's victory won him a major-generalship. Richard N. Current, ed., *Encyclopedia of the Confederacy*, 4 vols. (New York, 1994), vol 2, p. 780.

Federal forces throughout the South.[51] According to Grant's strategy, Benjamin Butler's 30,000 men of the Army of the James would steam up the James River and, while feinting an attack on Petersburg, operate against Richmond from the south. Concurrently, George Meade's Army of the Potomac would cross the Rapidan River in northern Virginia and move south against Lee's army and the Confederate capital. The main objective of the Federal plan was the capture of Richmond while Lee's army was bled into nonexistence.[52]

Pickett had been predicting an enemy assault up the Virginia peninsula toward the vital rail junction at Petersburg since the previous November. Throughout the autumn and winter months he tried unsuccessfully to convince Richmond authorities of his fears. He personally paid visits to the war and naval secretaries, but his pleas fell on deaf ears. The authorities in Richmond simply did not trust George Pickett's judgment on military matters.[53]

On April 13, 1864, Pickett received word at his headquarters in Petersburg of renewed Federal activity in southeastern Virginia. Without a second thought, he passed the report on to Richmond.[54] Most of Pickett's troops had gone with Hoke to Plymouth, leaving Petersburg largely unprotected.[55] Pickett complained to General Bragg and begged that troops be rushed to Petersburg to aid in its defense. Initially, Bragg responded to Pickett's warnings favorably, instructing him: "Your scouts should be very active and vigilant to keep us advised of all movements

51
William Glenn Robertson, *Back Door to Richmond: The Bermuda Hundred Campaign, April-June 1864* (Newark, 1987), pp. 14-16.

52
Ibid., p. 16. Grant's overall plan is described in Ulysses S. Grant, *Personal Memoirs of U. S. Grant*, 2 vols. (New York, 1886), vol. 2, pp. 127-132, 134, 138-141; *OR* 46, pt. 1, pp. 11-21.

53
OR 29, pt. 2, pp. 827, 848, 897; Harrison, *Pickett's Men*, p. 121.

54
OR 51, pt. 2, p. 858.

55
Robertson, *Back Door to Richmond*, pp. 45-46.

about Suffolk and Portsmouth. . . ."[56] Bragg did not realize how literally Pickett would interpret this statement.

Like a dutiful subordinate, Pickett sent word of every report he received from his scouts and Union deserters. Over a twenty-four hour period, this information encompassed eight separate telegrams. Although much of this intelligence was blatantly contradictory or ambiguous, he sent it without bothering to provide his own assessment of its reliability.[57] After the last several months of stress, failure, and anger, he seemed only capable of instant reaction without careful reflection.

Braxton Bragg was not a patient man. After a full day of Pickett's barrage of alarming telegrams, he had had enough. Bragg bluntly advised, "You should keep the enemy closely watched and report his movements frequently, but I must warn you of the evil resulting from exaggerated and unreliable reports." Chastened by Bragg's harsh tone, Pickett explained that he had only followed orders. He hoped that keeping Bragg fully informed, "would enable you to form your own conclusions."[58] Pickett concluded that the Federals were dangerously close and he had no protection. Given his pattern of behavior and subsequent breakdown, it appears that he desperately hoped that someone else might take the situation in hand and tell him what to do.

A few days later, the secretary of war decided to remove Pickett from his predicament. He could no longer allow a distressed and complaining general to remain in charge of so crucial a region. On April 23, 1864, Gen. Pierre G. T. Beauregard officially took charge of the Departments of North Carolina and Cape Fear and soon thereafter renamed them the Departments of North Carolina and Southern Virginia. Beauregard's assumption of command relieved Pickett from

---

[56]
   OR 51,pt. 2, p. 861.

[57]
   Ibid. The record contains several examples of Pickett providing his own views on reports of enemy activity. It is significant that such observations were absent at this critical time. For example, see ibid., 33, p. 1067; ibid., 29, pt. 2, p. 827.

[58]
   Ibid., p. 863, 865.

duty as a department commander, leaving him with the post of district commander of Petersburg. George Pickett's plight had gone from bad to worse. Once the proud leader of a division of battle-hardened veterans, he now led a rag-tag force of regular soldiers, local militia, and civilian volunteers. As district commander he had only 2,000 men under his authority to confront 30,000 well-equipped and confident Yankees heading directly for Petersburg.[59]

The new post did not suit Pickett, who frantically sought a way out by filing a request for a transfer back to Longstreet's Corps with the Army of Northern Virginia, where he could resume command of his old division.[60] Longstreet and Pickett had been friends for many years and unlike Braxton Bragg, "Old Pete" would not scold him or reprimand him for following orders. Moxley Sorrel, a particularly literate and observant staff officer under Longstreet, characterized their relationship as one of father and son. As Sorrel recalled it, "I could always see how he [Longstreet] looked after Pickett, and made us give him things very fully; indeed sometimes stay with him to make sure he did not get astray."[61] Why could he not simply return to that secure place he held only a year earlier? Pickett may have voiced his feelings candidly to his friend, for on May 1, Longstreet wrote directly to Lee and asked that he restore Pickett to field command. This tidy bit of string pulling proved successful, and three days later Pickett received orders to resume command of his division in the Army of Northern Virginia. Pickett, excited by the prospect of once again holding a command in the Army of Northern Virginia, enthusiastically acknowledged his orders to rejoin

59
  Freeman, *Lee's Lieutenants*, 3, p. 451; *OR* 33, p. 1292; Schiller, *The Bermuda Hundred Campaign*, pp. 53, 55-56; Robertson, *Back Door to Richmond*, p. 48; Ibid., pp. 65-66; Alfred Romans, *The Military Operations of General Beauregard in the War Between the States, 1861-1865*, 2 vols. (New York, 1884) vol. 2, p. 542.

60
  George E. Pickett to Samuel Cooper, April 24, 1864, Letters Sent, Adjutant and Inspector General's Office, Record Group 109, National Archives, Washington, D.C.

61
  Sorrel, *Recollections*, p. 54.

his division at Hanover Junction, telegraphing on May 4, "Shall lose no time" in doing so.[62]

Relief would not come so easily to the Virginian. Beauregard, en route for Petersburg had stopped at Weldon, North Carolina, where he wrote to Pickett to inform him that he was ill. Pickett, who was enough of a soldier to feel that it "would have been impossible" to leave Petersburg without a commanding officer under such circumstances, remained in the railroad city.[63] On the day that Pickett decided to remain in Petersburg awaiting Beauregard's arrival, the Federals launched their offensive south of the James River. With each passing hour 30,000 Federals inched their way closer to the Richmond, Petersburg, and the vital railroad connecting the two Southern cities.[64]

Pickett dispatched eight telegrams to Richmond describing Union boats steaming up the James River. The War Department sent no response to these messages. Like the boy who cried wolf too many times, Pickett found his ardent pleas for help ignored, perhaps even derided by the authorities in Richmond. During the early afternoon on May 5, he wrote despairingly, "I have telegraphed you four times this morning and received no answer. Please answer this." His tide of complaints, pleas, and warnings continued flowing northward into the capital.[65] By 3:00 p.m. that afternoon, Pickett's nerves were almost shattered. Although he had orders to report to a command he had craved to rejoin for some time, his sense of duty left him mired in the path of a large Federal army without a contingent of soldiers capable of stopping or even slowing the Union juggernaut. He sent another telegram, for there was little else he could do: "I have sent you numerous telegrams this morning and fail to obtain an answer. The emergency is so great that

---

62
  OR 36, pt. 2, pp. 940, 950.

63
  George E. Pickett to Samuel Cooper, May 17, 1864, Letters Received, Adjutant and Inspector General s Office, Record Group 109, National Archives, Washington, D.C.

64
  Schiller, *The Bermuda Hundred Campaign*, p. 59; Robertson, *Back Door to Richmond*, p. 66.

65
  OR 36, pt. 2, pp. 951, 955-956.

I sent a courier by train to say that the enemy in force are coming up the river. You had better send troops." Bragg scribbled the word "seen" across Pickett's telegram and filed it. Before the day came to an end Pickett hurried another appeal for help to the War Department. Again nothing but silence was received from Richmond and no signs of reinforcements were in sight. According to historian Douglas Southall Freeman, the night of May 5 was, "in a word, a black night for George Pickett."[66]

May 6 brought help in the form of Maj. Gen. D. H. Hill, an experienced infantry officer who had recently volunteered to serve on Beauregard's staff. According to Special Order No. 3, "Gen'l Hill is specially charged with communicating to Maj-Gen'l Pickett the views of the commanding General."[67] Beauregard tried to ease Pickett's anxiety by expressing his full confidence in Hill to "aid you in the discharge of your onerous duties in the present emergency." The judgment that Pickett lacked military acumen seemed pervasive. Herbert Schiller, who has written extensively on this campaign, notes that "Beauregard, like Bragg seemed to have little confidence in Pickett's abilities."[68] On May 7, Secretary of War James Seddon confessed to General Bragg that he, too, felt "some distrust of Pickett's adequacy to the load upon him." Seddon hoped Beauregard might soon relieve Pickett and take control of the situation at Petersburg.[69]

The next several days passed quickly for the Confederates. Pickett rushed his few troops to the crucial railroad junction near Petersburg, scraped together a group of mounted and armed civilians for a makeshift

---

66
   Ibid., p. 958; Freeman, *Lee's Lieutenants*, 3, p. 456.

67
   Hill lacked an official assignment. Special Orders No. 3, May 6, 1864, Department of North Carolina, Confederate States Army, 1861-1865, Record Group 109, National Archives, Washington, D.C.

68
   OR 36, pt. 2, p. 965; Schiller, *The Bermuda Hundred Campaign*, p. 74.

69
   James Seddon to Braxton Bragg, May 7, 1864, Braxton Bragg Papers, Duke University.

cavalry screen, and ran locomotive cars in and out of town to give the appearance of arriving reinforcements. Reportedly, Pickett personally rode along the lines perhaps hoping that by rallying the men's spirit, his own anxieties might lessen. With a total of only 1,400 men, Pickett braced for the arrival of Butler's army. Throughout he continued to bombard Richmond with frenzied descriptions of the enemy's imminent approach.[70]

It was only a matter of time before the load upon Pickett became unbearable. After twelve months of increasing tension and stress—the bitterness of Gettysburg, the disappointment of New Berne, the anger of Kinston—Pickett's system could take no more. On May 9, he sent orders to attack and then mindlessly canceled them. Mentally and physically exhausted, Pickett collapsed the following day and crawled into a bed for some rest. Seven days later he would describe himself as being "far from well," and "confined to my bed."[71] Word of Pickett's illness spread quickly. Confederate Chief of Ordnance, Josiah Gorgas, recorded in his diary, "Pickett is very dissipated, it is asserted."[72] Beauregard, who had finally arrived at Petersburg on May 11, wrote Bragg: "Major General Pickett reported himself sick yesterday evening. He has been confined to his room since."[73] Ironically, Pickett's meager forces managed to protect Petersburg from the Federals until reinforcements arrived. Out of sheer desperation, Pickett took control and succeeded in his task of defending Petersburg. Two recent studies of the campaign applaud Pickett for his "heroic exertions" as "the man who. . .saved Petersburg for the

---

[70]
Robertson, *Back Door to Richmond*, pp. 66-67; Schiller, *The Bermuda Hundred Campaign*, p. 78; *OR* 36, pt. 2, pp. 964-965.

[71]
Clifford Dowdey, *Lee's Last Campaign*, p. 238; Robertson, *Back Door to Richmond*, p. 112; George E. Pickett to Samuel Cooper, May 17, 1864, Letters Received, Adjutant and Inspector General's Office, Confederate States Army, National Archives, Washington, D.C., Record Group 109.

[72]
Josiah Gorgas, *The Civil War Diary of General Josiah Gorgas*, edited by Frank Vandiver (University, 1947), p. 100.

[73]
OR 51, pt. 2, p. 920.

Confederacy."[74] The irony of the situation did not escape historian Clifford Dowdey, who described the situation as "one of the curious twists of the war." According to Dowdey, "Pickett is remembered for a charge that failed in a glory-seeking hour, and unknown for his key part in saving Richmond by unheroic actions performed in a bureaucratic chaos which shook his nerves beyond the breaking point."[75] A member of Pickett's command told his wife, "General Pickett deserves much credit for having successfully defended with a very small force the town till [sic] the arrival of reinforcements." At that time, however, Pickett may not have had any sense of this accomplishment. As soon as he was able, he left for Hanover Junction and by May 19, was in command of his division with the Army of Northern Virginia.[76]

The 1864 division that greeted Pickett on his arrival was markedly smaller than the one he had commanded at Gettysburg. After the disaster in Pennsylvania, his three brigades had spent the winter rebuilding their broken ranks. By mid-May 1864, the division totaled only about 5,000 men, including recovered wounded, returned prisoners, and a few conscripts.[77]

The First Corps had changed as well. Pickett's trusted friend and mentor, James Longstreet, was absent from command due to a near-fatal wound he had suffered on May 6 in the Battle of the Wilderness. Command of the First Corps devolved upon South Carolinian Richard Heron Anderson, an experienced but uninspiring division commander.

74
    Schiller, *The Bermuda Hundred Campaign*, p. 165; Robertson, *Back Door to Richmond*, p. 128.

75
    Dowdey, *Lee's Last Campaign*, p. 233.

76
    H. A. Carrington to Charlotte Elizabeth Carrington, May 12, 1864, Carrington Family Papers, Virginia Historical Society, Richmond, Virginia; Braxton Bragg to George E. Pickett, May 19, 1864, Letters Sent, Adjutant and Inspector General's Office, National Archives, Washington, D.C., Record Group 109.

77
    Dowdey, *Lee's Last Campaign*, pp. 231, 247; Edward Porter Alexander, *Military Memoirs of a Confederate* (New York, 1907), p. 530.

The enemy that Pickett had led his division against in 1862-1863 had also changed. In the past, Union commanders had retreated to reorganize their wounded armies after each round of battle. Unlike his predecessors, however, the aggressive Ulysses Grant viewed the war as a single battlefield and no longer based Union strategy solely on the capture of Richmond. Instead, he sought to destroy the Confederate armies piece by piece. This strategy dictated that George Meade's Army of the Potomac lock itself in almost daily combat with Lee's forces in order to weaken and eventually break Lee's ability to wage successful battle.[78] As Pickett traveled north from Petersburg to resume field command, Grant was again preparing his army to destroy Lee's force swiftly and decisively.

Temporarily assigned to A. P. Hill's Third Corps, Pickett reported to Hill near the North Anna River on May 22 and soon thereafter resumed his penchant for complaining to Lee.[79] He pointed to contradictory orders and bemoaned instructions that "had to be corrected." Lee may have responded to this line of inquiry by questioning Pickett's whereabouts and health, for Pickett penned a letter claiming: "I considered myself as much with my division as to have gone as contemplated, as to have been anywhere on the road, the division going as it is in detachments." He closed with a testy assurance: "Had it been intended for me to stop at Hanover Junction, or any other point with the Division and such instructions, given me, I would have carried them out."[80]

Six days later he was back with Longstreet's [Anderson's] First Corps. The next day, he dispatched three couriers and two staff officers to corps headquarters demanding rations for his brigades. "The men are calling loudly for bread," he claimed, "We must get something or the

78
    Thomas J. Howe, *The Petersburg Campaign: Wasted Valor June 15-18, 1864* (Lynchburg, 1988), pp. 1-3.

79
    Freeman, *Lee's Lieutenants*, 3, p. 497.

80
    George E. Pickett to Robert E. Lee, May 21, 1864, typescript copy in George E. Pickett Papers, Virginia Historical Society, Richmond, Virginia.

division will be worse than useless."[81] During the next several weeks Pickett's Division moved from Hanover Junction north of Richmond to Bermuda Hundred, a large neck of land between the Appomattox and James rivers about 15 miles south of the Southern capital.[82]

As the spring turned to summer and casualties mounted in both armies, Pickett's men were, perhaps by design, kept out of the most intensive engagements. Portions of the division were often shifted to support various points north of Richmond and outside of Petersburg.[83] The division essentially served as the army's mobile reserve under Lee's direct command.[84] Despite the strain of life in the field, morale was initially high, despite (or because of) the lack of battle action. Pickett's brother-in-law and staff member, Blair Burwell, wrote his wife on May 26, 1864, that the entire army remained confident: "Genl Lee's army is in fine condition & full of enthusiasm & only awaits the opportunity to crush Grant when they get a fair chance at him."[85]

One of the division's few opportunities to prove its renewed fighting capacity came on June 17, when it was ordered to assault captured fortifications along the Howlett Line south of the Clay house. Another division under Maj. Gen. Charles Field was also slated for participation in the attack. Confederate engineers, however, realized just as the assault was to begin that they could seal off Union-held Battery—Pickett's objective—by constructing additional lines around the threatening emplacement. Although Field received the message repealing the attack

81
    OR 36, pt. 1, p. 1058; ibid., 3, pp. 843-844.

82
    Freeman, *Lee's Lieutenants*, 3, p. 532.

83
    Robert T. Bell, *11th Virginia Infantry* (Lynchburg, 1985), p. 52; "Official Diary of First Corps, Army of Northern Virginia While Commanded by General Richard H. Anderson, from May 7-Oct 10, 1864," *Southern Historical Society Papers*, vol. 7 (1879), pp. 491-494; 503-504.

84
    Freeman, *Lee's Lieutenants*, 3, p. 627.

85
    Blair Burwell to Jenny Pickett Burwell, May 26, 1864, Burwell Papers, Special Collections, Swem Library, College of William and Mary, 39.1 B95, folder 1.

order, the cancellation came too late for Pickett's men, who rushed forward to recapture the lines. Many of Field's soldiers joined in the attack, which successfully carried the works with but little loss of life. I have "never seen anything done so handsomely," wrote Eppa Hunton, one of Pickett's brigadiers. "We drove the enemy past Beauregard's abandoned works, and in their own line, and turned our works upon them."[86]

Lee congratulated the unit by writing corps commander Anderson: "General I take great pleasure in presenting you my congratulations upon the conduct of the men in your corps. I believe they will carry anything they are put against." Lee added, "We tried very hard to stop Pickett's men from capturing the breastworks of the Enemy but could not do it." Pickett's brother, Charles, proudly remembered this dispatch as "one of the highest compliments Gen'l Lee ever paid to a command." Lee's biographer Douglas Southall Freeman also paid the Virginian a high compliment by writing that "Pickett's men advanced as if the hill at Mrs. Clay's Farm were another Cemetery Ridge."[87] In August, a portion of Pickett's Division again had the chance to pursue the enemy while occupying trenches near Fussell's Mill. "Don't fire," several soldiers shouted across the battlefield, "we're Pickett's Division," hoping the name would instill fear in their foe.[88] His men remained full of vigor and fight after the many months that had passed following their disastrous charge at Gettysburg. By mid-June, Pickett's brigades settled into the trenches on the Howlett Line northeast of Petersburg. Pickett's wife, not always a reliable source, recalled, "there was no lack of social diversions. In a small way we had our dances, our conversaziones and musicales, quite like the gay world that had never

86
     Howe, *The Petersburg Campaign*, pp. 79-80; Eppa Hunton, *Autobiography* (Richmond, 1933), p. 114.

87
     Robert E. Lee to R. H. Anderson, June 17, 1864, reproduced in La Salle Corbell Pickett, *Pickett and His Men* (Atlanta, 1899), p. 350; Charles Pickett to Henry T. Owen, October 14, 1881, Owen Papers, Virginia Historical Society, Richmond, Virginia, Mss1OW25a97; Freeman, *Lee's Lieutenants*, 3, p. 532.

88
     Bell, *11th Virginia Infantry*, p. 52.

known anything about war except from the pages of books and the columns of newspapers. True we did not feast."[89] Although lacking ample provisions, Pickett's men made the most of the dull routine. A private in the 18th Virginia described "the dull monotony of camp life" on Bermuda Hundred. "We have nothing around us to engage our attention," he complained, "other than the discharge of the regular routine of military duty."[90] With his division stretched out over a three-mile front, Pickett occasionally ordered attacks on the enemy line to straighten his own lines or feel for weaknesses in his opponent's. Daily existence became a test in patience and durability, as shelling by artillery and rifle fire from enemy sharpshooters took their toll on the men in the trenches.[91]

Pickett and his men essentially remained in the Bermuda Hundred lines until March 1865. Despite his earlier protest against splitting his division, Pickett's brigades were occasionally shifted to other fronts during the winter and early spring as circumstances demanded. There is little in the available public and private record to lend insight into Pickett's generalship during these long months of siege warfare. It is apparent, however, that a cloud of uncertainty continued to linger as to whether he was a reliable field commander. Even though he was the army's senior major general, he was not entrusted by Lee with any independent command following his shaky performance at Bermuda Hundred in May 1864. In June, Lee moved his headquarters to Drewry's Bluff to supervise the occupation of the Bermuda Hundred line and,

---

[89]
Pickett, *Pickett and His Men*, p. 357.

[90]
James Barrow is quoted from James Robertson, *18th Virginia Infantry* (Lynchburg, 1984), p. 31.

[91]
Pickett, *Pickett and His Men*, pp. 364-365. See John E. Divine, *8th Virginia Infantry* (Lynchburg, 1984), p. 31, for details on a failed attack that took placed on August 25, 1864. A typical day on the line is described by George E. Pickett in a letter to Walter H. Taylor, August 28, 1864, Venable Papers, Southern Historical Collection, University of North Carolina, Chapel Hill, North Carolina.

quite possibly, to supervise the division's actions.[92] For at least a short time, Pickett would be under the watchful eye of Lee.

Desertion, which continued to plague Pickett's Division during the ensuing fall and winter of 1864, was a disturbing problem for the entire Confederate Army. The number of men leaving Pickett's ranks, however, can justifiably be described as staggering. Many of these soldiers were conscripts who searched for any opportunity to leave the ranks, while others answered desperate pleas from loved ones by simply returning home. Others had just grown tired of the stagnancy of siege and trench warfare. In November of 1864, Assistant-Adjutant and Inspector-General Walter Harrison informed Pickett of men "straggling to the rear of the line for several miles and committing depredations." The problem was so serious that Harrison sent out patrols, using up a "number of the more active and efficient men" in the process. From March 9-18, 1865, over 500 men deserted from Pickett's Division.[93]

There were a few bright spots during this time. In November 1864, Harrison reported that James Kemper's Brigade, which was under the command of Col. William R. Terry, was "in the best condition I have ever seen it," with clean camps and sufficient food, clothing, weapons and horses.[94] Unfortunately, this single favorable report did not speak for the division as a whole, nor did it address the abilities of its leader.

On January 19, 1865, Lee wrote to Longstreet, who had recovered sufficiently from his crippling Wilderness wound to return to command

---

92
   Harrison, *Pickett's Men*, p. 66, 135; *OR* 46, pt. 2, pp. 1008, 1014, 1308, 1312-1313; Edwin Bearss and Chris S. Calkins, *The Battle of Five Forks*, (Lynchburg, 1985) pp. 10; 20-21; Freeman, *Lee's Lieutenants*, 3, p. 627; Howe, *The Petersburg Campaign*, p. 73.

93
   OR 46, pt. 2, pp. 1265; 1292-1293; Divine, *8th Virginia Infantry*, p. 31; Walter Harrison to George E. Pickett, November 14, 1864, Fairfax Papers, Virginia Historical Society, Richmond, Virginia, MssLFl613al 1; *OR* 46, pt. 3, pp. 1332, 1353. Pickett's Division was inspected on February 28, 1865, and reported 5,967 men "present for duty," 8,073 men and officers "aggregate present," and 6,151 men "present effective for duty." Ibid., p. 388. See also, Douglas Southall Freeman, *R. E. Lee: A Biography*, 4 vols. (New York, 1935), vol. 4, pp. 25-26, who estimates that the division numbered about 5,000 men.

94
   Confederate Inspection Book #171, January 1, 1863-January 31, 1865, pp. 4, 8, 9, 11, Southern Historical Collection, University of North Carolina, Chapel Hill, North Carolina.

his corps, of his deep dissatisfaction with the conditions existing in Pickett's Division. In one brigade, Lee chided, "the articles of war were seldom read, accommodations for the sick bad, and religious exercises neglected." He labeled another brigade as "unsoldierly & unmilitary, lax in discipline & loose in military instruction." Lee suggested that Pickett and his officers were not "sufficiently attentive to the men," and "not informed as to their condition." Lee warned Longstreet that "unless the division and brigade commanders are careful and energetic, nothing can be accomplished." As a subordinate (and as a friend) Pickett was Longstreet's responsibility. Lee, in an unusually strong statement, directed Longsteet to do all in his power to correct the evils in Pickett's division. [95]

As the spring months of 1865 approached, Grant finalized his plans to drive Lee from his entrenchments before Richmond and Petersburg. The responsibility of turning Lee's extended right flank fell to Maj. Gen. Philip Sheridan's veteran Federal cavalry, which Grant dispatched to tear up the Southside Railroad in a move designed to turn Lee's flank and cut the logistical lifeline to the Southern army.[96] Sheridan was joined in this effort by infantry from the II and V Corps. On March 30, the cavalry commander had his troopers at Dinwiddie Courthouse with the infantry nearby.[97] To meet this threat, Lee ordered three of Pickett's four brigades to move for the extreme right of the Confederate line, which Pickett's men reached by daybreak on March 30 after a tiresome march through mud and pouring rain. Pickett, joined by his cousin, Maj. Gen. Henry Heth, together with Richard Anderson, met with Lee on the

[95]
Robert E. Lee to James Longstreet, January 19, 1863, Fairfax Papers, Virginia Historical Society, Richmond, Virginia, Mss1F1613a2.

[96]
OR 46, pt. 3, p. 325.

[97]
Freeman, *Lee*, 4, p. 22.

morning of March 30 in what one observer described as "a considerable *pow-wow* [emphasis in original]."[98]

Lee unveiled his plan to his subordinates to send a combined force of cavalry, artillery, and infantry, some 19,000 men, to oppose the enemy's movement. Longstreet, the originator of this plan, believed "that such a force, in proper hands, will be able to frustrate [the] object of [the] enemy."[99]

Surprisingly, Lee selected George Pickett to lead the mission. The existing records reveal some disagreement between Longstreet and Lee as to whether Pickett's Division could be spared for the offensive, but, at least formally, Longstreet did not give any preference as to who should lead the special task force.[100] Lee's reasons for choosing Pickett as the leader of such an important movement are unclear. Perhaps Longstreet suggested his old friend to Lee and against his better judgment, Lee agreed. The record is silent as to this issue.

Pickett was ordered to take his command, which consisted of three of his brigades, an additional two brigades from Maj. Gen. Bushrod R. Johnson's Division, and six guns from Col. William J. Pegram's artillery, to Five Forks, an important road junction beyond Lee's right flank south of Hatcher's Run. Cavalry from Thomas Rosser, W. H. F. Rooney Lee, and Fitzhugh Lee were to join Pickett there. Together, with Pickett as overall commander, the combined force would advance southeast toward Dinwiddie Courthouse and assail Sheridan's Federals. According to Douglas Southall Freeman, "It was an order in the old spirit of the Army-to disdain odds and attack." The odds were indeed long. Pickett's

---

[98]
    Harrison, *Pickett's Men*, pp. 135-136. According to Harrison, ibid., p. 135, the brigades of Montgomery Corse and William Terry were ordered from their Swift Creek positions to join George Steuart's Brigade, which was already in the trenches west of Petersburg. Eppa Hunton's Brigade was operating with Longstreet north of the James River. Pickett's post-Appomattox report of the Battle of Five Forks, dated April 10, 1865, in Pickett, *Pickett and His Men*, p. 393, should also be consulted.

[99]
    OR 46, pt. 3, p. 1357.

[100]
    Ibid., p. 1360; Bearss and Calkins, *The Battle of Five Forks*, p. 13.

19,000 men, which composed almost one-third of Lee's army, faced some 50,000 Federals.[101]

Earlier in the war Pickett would have eagerly welcomed such an assignment. He was zealous and aggressive as both a brigadier and division commander, rarely concerned with odds or danger. His confidence at Gettysburg was at its height, despite the apparent risk his men faced in charging across an open field into the very teeth of a strongly-positioned enemy. Only when he perceived himself unsupported and alone on the battlefield did his certainty shatter. The New Berne expedition proved a fiasco. His desperate actions at Bermuda Hundred were successful almost by accident. The chronic desertion problems that plagued his division, combined with poor inspection reports, further weaken his record as a commander. His physical health was not good, and he continued to suffer following his collapse in May of 1864. As late as March 20, 1865, his brother Charles reported that "Genl Pickett is in Richmond sick."[102] Pickett's chief surgeon, M. M. Lewis, notified corps headquarters the next day that Pickett had been "quite sick for several days with disease of the bowels and is still too unwell for duty."[103]

Although George Pickett could not have known it, this critical expedition was his final opportunity to prove his worth and competence as a general. He had been a soldier for twenty years and knew no other life. In the past he had faced great personal grief and loneliness, but always found direction and a sense of purpose in battle.[104] Now more than ever, he—and the Army of Northern Virginia—needed a victory. At

---

[101]
Faust, *Encyclopedia*, p. 261.

[102]
Charles Pickett to Osmun Latrobe, March 30, 1865, Robert E. Lee's Headquarters Papers, Virginia Historical Society, Richmond, Virginia, Mss3L515a. Hereinafter cited as Lee's Headquarter's Papers.

[103]
M. M. Lewis to Osmun Latrobe, March 31, 1865, Lee's Headquarter's Papers.

[104]
Gordon, "Before the Storm," pp. 17-77, 109-111.

noon on March 30, Pickett set out for Five Forks with his five brigades
of infantry and single artillery battery. "The march," Pickett explained
later, "was necessarily slow, on account of the continual skirmishing
with the enemy's cavalry, both in front and flank."[105] Captain W.
Gordon McCabe, Col. Willie Pegram's adjutant, disagreed with Pickett's
assessment. Frustrated at the delay McCabe confided to his diary that
"General Pickett, instead of pushing on, stopped, formed a regiment in
line of battle, and awaited some attack." Rather than post skirmishers on
his flanks, McCabe continued, Pickett wasted "much valuable time."[106]
The movement had only just begun and already a veteran officer found
Pickett's handling of his command questionable.

A cold rain continued to fall as the Confederates marched west
along the White Oak Road. By 4:30 p.m. Pickett reached Five Forks.
Only Fitz Lee's cavalry had reached him and Pickett deemed his men
"in much need of rest, having been marching nearly continuously for
eighteen hours." He decided to wait until morning before striking the
enemy cavalry concentrated around Dinwiddie Courthouse, five miles
south of Five Forks. By driving the Federals from Dinwiddie, Pickett
would protect the Southside Raiload and halt Grant's latest offensive and
threat against Lee's extreme right flank.[107] At daylight Pickett
determined that the Federal cavalry, reinforced by infantry, held a strong
position on the Dinwiddie Courthouse Road, just outside town. He
advanced south from Five Forks along Scott Road, turning southeast at
Ford Station Road toward Dinwiddie. Around 2:00 p.m., he readied his
troops to cross Chamberlain's Bed, a small stream, in a two-pronged
attack on Sheridan's west (left) flank. Coordination failed, however,
when Fitz Lee's Confederate cavalry moved out toward Fitzgerald's
Ford before the infantry was ready. Mounted and dismounted troopers

---

105
     Pickett's Report of Five Forks, in Pickett, *Pickett and His Men*, p. 394.

106
     McCabe's journal is quoted in Armistead Churchill Gordon, *Memories and Memorials of
William Gordon McCabe*, 2 vols. (Richmond, 1925), vol. 1, p. 163.

107
     Freeman, *Lee's Lieutenants*, 3, pp. 657-659; Pickett's Report of Five Forks, in Pickett, *Pickett
and His Men*, p. 394.

fought stubbornly on opposite sides of the creek bank. The Federals initially yielded to the weight of the Confederate assault, but a Federal counterattack pushed the Southerners back over the ford. Meanwhile, Confederate infantry waded across Danse's Ford farther north on Chamberlain's Bed. Montgomery Corse's Brigade stormed enemy outposts, soon followed by Pickett's remaining troops. Federals hurriedly prepared a line of battle to meet the Confederate flank attack. Spirited fighting raged through the afternoon, with Sheridan's troopers only grudgingly giving ground. By sunset on March 31, Pickett had successfully wrested the initiative from Sheridan and had driven him back to Dinwiddie Courthouse. "This engagement was quite a spirited one," Pickett wrote in his report, "the men and officers behaving most admirably."[108]

Pickett halted the advance with the onset of darkness. Veterans were surprised at the order, as many could still see the Federals in retreat.[109] Pickett later admitted that "half an hour more of daylight and we would have gotten to the Court-House." He argued in his report that his halt was premised on the realization that Federal infantry was rapidly reinforcing Sheridan.[110] At 4:00 a.m. on April 1, Pickett pulled back to Five Forks, where he believed he could better protect the Confederate right flank and the vital Southside Railroad two miles in his rear. The enemy, Pickett reported, "was. . .pressing upon our rear in force."[111]

Lee was not pleased with Pickett's decision. A telegram from Pickett's commanding officer, which appears only in LaSalle Corbell Pickett's often suspect *Pickett and His Men*, urged Pickett to "Hold Five

108
    Bearss and Calkins, *The Battle of Five Forks*, pp. 36-47; Freeman, *Lee*, 4, p. 35; Pickett's Report of Five Forks, in Pickett, *Pickett and His Men*, p. 395.

109
    J. Risque Hutter, "The Eleventh at Five Forks Fight," *Southern Historical Society Papers*, 35 (1907), p. 359.

110
    Pickett's Report of Five Forks, in Pickett, *Pickett and His Men*, p. 395.

111
    Ibid., p. 395; Freeman, *Lee's Lieutenants*, 3, p. 660.

Forks at all Hazards. Protect the road to Ford's Depot and prevent Union forces from striking the South-side Railroad. Regret exceedingly your forced withdrawal, and your inability to hold the advantage you had gained."[112] Pickett later claimed that he assumed Lee would rush reinforcements to aid him in this task. In his report he alleged that he informed "the general commanding of the state of affairs, that the enemy was trying to get in between the main army and my command, and asking that a diversion be made or I would be isolated."[113]

No acknowledgement from Lee exists to support Pickett's assumption that reinforcements were imminent. In fact, Lee notified Secretary of War John C. Breckenridge on April 1 of Pickett's predicament at Five Forks without mentioning the need of support, nor did he indicate that Pickett had even asked for it.[114] After the fiasco that subsequently occurred at Five Forks, Pickett looked for others to blame, unwilling to admit any mistakes on his own part. Just like Gettysburg, he convinced himself that he and his men had been left alone to the slaughter.

Pickett's carelessness is evident in the hasty deployment of his troops. He posted only a small cavalry force to cover a gap of some three miles between himself and the main Confederate siege line, which exposed his left flank to a turning movement. Rooney Lee's cavalry division was posted to cover his right flank, and in between he entrenched his infantry along the White Oak Road. Harrison described the men "throwing up a temporary breastwork. Pine trees were felled, a ditch dug, and the earth thrown up behind the logs."[115] At that point in

---

112
    Pickett, *Pickett and His Men*, p. 386. Freeman, in *Lee's Lieutenants*, 3, p. 66, notes that although there is no copy of this telegram in the *Official Records*, "there is no reason to question its authenticity. It has verisimilitude." Walter Harrison presents a slightly different version, with Lee telegraphing Pickett to "hold Five Forks at all hazards and to prevent if possible, the enemy from striking the Southside Railroad." Harrison, *Pickett's Men*, p. 138.

113
    Pickett's Report of Five Forks, in Pickett, *Pickett and His Men*, p. 395.

114
    OR 46, pt. 1, pp. 1263-1264; Freeman, *Lee's Lieutenants*, 3, p. 662n.

115
    Harrison, *Pickett's Men*, pp. 138-139.

the vital preparations to meet Sheridan's men, Pickett lost all sense of the importance of his responsibilities and left the field. Sometime between noon and 1:00 p.m., he and Fitz Lee departed from the front lines to attend a shad bake hosted by cavalry commander Tom Rosser. This luncheon interlude was held somewhere north of Hatcher's Run at least one mile in the rear of White Oak Road. Several officers did not even know that Pickett had left the front.[116] While he ate fish and perhaps drank whiskey—Douglas Southall Freeman suggests that the officers drank whiskey or brandy, but were not intoxicated—Pickett ignored repeated reports of the advance of the enemy.[117]

Pickett's official report on Five Forks makes no mention of either the shad bake or his whereabouts on the afternoon of April 1. In fact, the shad bake did not become public knowledge until 1886, when Tom Rosser first told of the luncheon in an article in the *Philadelphia Weekly Times.*[118]

Pickett acknowledged in his report that he received word that the enemy had "pushed steadily from the Court-House and commenced extending to our left." Pickett claimed he ordered Fitz Lee to assess the position of his cavalry, and if necessary, "cover the ground at once." The Virginian attempted to place the blame for the ensuing debacle on Fitz Lee by writing that he [Pickett] "supposed it had been done, when, suddenly the enemy in heavy infantry column appeared on our left front,

116
     Letter of Thomas L. Rosser in the *Philadelphia Weekly Times,* April 5, 1895; C. Irvine Walker, *The Life of Lieutenant General Richard Heron Anderson of the Confederate States Army* (Charleston, 1917), pp. 225-226; Freeman, *Lee's Lieutenants,* 3, pp. 667-668. According to Munford, one of his staff officers could not locate Pickett. Thomas Munford, "Unpublished Sketch of Five Forks," in Walker, *Richard Heron Anderson,* p. 227.

117
     Thomas L. Rosser to James Longstreet, October 22, 1892, in personal collection of Matt Masters; Rosser Letter, *Philadelphia Weekly Times,* April 5, 1895: Freeman, *Lee's Lieutenants,* 3, p. 668.

118
     Freeman, *Lee,* 4, p. 40n; Freeman, *Lee's Lieutenants,* 3, p. 668n.

and the attack which had, up to that time been confined principally to our front towards the Court-House now became general."[119]

Cavalryman Fitz Lee, upon whom Pickett's accusation fell, saw the situation differently:

> When we moved towards Five Forks, hearing nothing. . .of the infantry's move which we heard of the night before, I thought that the movements. . .for the time being, were suspended, and we were not expecting any attack that afternoon, so far as I know. . . .Our throwing up works and taking position were simply general matters of military precaution.[120]

Based on Fitz Lee's words and Pickett's actions, it is apparent that neither anticipated any serious enemy attack, despite Pickett's insistence that he demanded reinforcements and diversions on his command's behalf. Even when he received word that an enemy attack was in progress, Pickett refused to believe it was a serious attempt to break his lines. Rosser damned Pickett's generalship by stating that "One would have thought that he would have been on the alert in the presence of the enemy he had so recently [been] fighting."[121] Pickett's later claim that he assumed reinforcements were on their way was a shoddy attempt to cover his own misjudgment.

While Pickett enjoyed shad (and perhaps whiskey), the Federals were massing for a powerful offensive. Union cavalry had explored Pickett's position and had been engaging in intermittent skirmishing throughout the morning. By the afternoon of April 1, Sheridan began assembling Governeur K. Warren's infantry corps to storm Pickett's vulnerable left flank. Simultaneous to Warren's attack, George Custer's

---

119
  Pickett's Report of Five Forks, in Pickett, *Pickett and His Men*, p. 395. The Federal attack was launched about 4:00 p.m., which means that Pickett, Rosser, and Fitz Lee had been lunching on shad for three hours. It may have been even longer, since Munford claimed the trio had been attending the shad bake for four hours. Walker, *Richard Heron Anderson*, p. 226.

120
  Freeman, *Lee's Lieutenants*, 3, p. 664.

121
  Philadelphia Weekly Times, April 5, 1895.

cavalry was to feint toward Pickett's right flank, followed by a frontal assault by another division of Federals. Sheridan hoped that by hurling his entire command upon Pickett's lines, he would drive the Confederates west and isolate them from the rest of Lee's army, where they would be in a position to be destroyed piecemeal. Such a victory would expose the Southside Railroad to destruction.[122]

The army's senior major general and on this day commander of almost one-third of Lee's army, finally realized the seriousness of the situation when he witnessed the capture of two couriers he had just dispatched to the front. As a line of Federals came swarming through the woods, Pickett bolted for his horse and raced across the stream toward Five Forks. Hunched forward on the animal, he was forced to run a gauntlet of enemy infantry fire to reach his own lines. One of Rooney Lee's staff officers tried to stop the harried general to deliver a message, but Pickett barked at the young officer "not to talk to him," and rapidly rode on.[123]

Pickett arrived at the front in time to witness his men locked in a stubborn battle with Sheridan's Federals. "Charge after charge of the enemy was repulsed," Pickett later reported, "but they still kept pouring up division after division, and pressing around our left."[124] He attempted, as he had at Bermuda Hundred, to rally the men on his own accord. "I depend upon your regiment to save the day," he exhorted Col. Charles C. Howeree of the 7th Virginia Infantry.[125] It was far too late for anyone to play savior, however, for by this time the battle had already

---

[122]
    Bearss and Calkins, *The Battle of Five Forks*, pp. 83-84, 86, 90.

[123]
    Testimony of Fitz Lee in Warren Court of Inquiry, in "Five Forks," John Daniel Papers, University of Virginia, Charlottesville, Virginia, Box 22; Freeman, *Lee's Lieutenants*, 3, p. 669; Munford, "Unpublished Sketch," in Walker, *Richard Heron Anderson*, p. 227; Frank Robertson, "Memoirs," Bulletin of the Washington County Historical Society (1986), pp. 18-19.

[124]
    Pickett's Report of Five Forks, in Pickett, *Pickett and His Men*, p. 395.

[125]
    Johnston, *Four Years a Soldier*, p. 390.

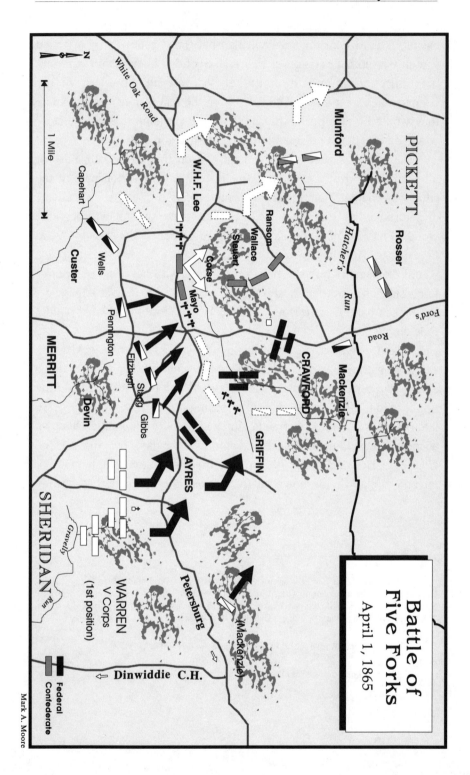

Battle of
Five Forks
April 1, 1865

Mark A. Moore

Federal
Confederate

been lost. Sheridan's men had initially swarmed across White Oak Road too far east of Pickett's main line to make contact. After some confusion, Sheridan reorganized and reoriented his attacking columns. Pickett arrived on the scene as the enemy overlapped the left portion of his line and began rolling up his flank. He desperately tried to form a new battle line, but by that point the enemy's strength was simply overwhelming and his units were in chaos. Union cavalry blocked Ford's Road, Pickett's route of retreat north toward Hatcher's Run. Large numbers of Pickett's soldiers panicked and ran in the face of the overwhelming numbers confronting them, while others merely surrendered in helplessness. One colonel recalled that "each private could see for himself the odds against him."[127]

By nightfall the enemy had turned Pickett's left flank and crushed Lee's right. Sheridan's victory was devastating to both Pickett's contingent and Lee's Army of Northern Virginia, as the success resulted in the capture over 4,000 men, together with four artillery pieces and 11 flags. Pickett was cut off from Lee's army and the Southside Raiload was soon severed by the Federals. Grant had flanked Lee and cut his last viable logistical line. The heavy widespread attacks against the Army of Northern Virginia that followed forced Lee to abandon the Richmond-Petersburg front, a position held by the Confederates since June of 1864. Could Pickett have prevented this catastrophe had he been at the front when the Federal attack began? Although speculative, it is doubtful given the strength of the opposition his men faced that his personal presence would have turned the tide of battle on April 1. As the general in command of the Confederate forces at Five Forks, however, it was his responsibility to be with his men at the front. He had been entrusted by Lee to hold the position "at all costs," yet he was not accessible to his subordinates at several critical stages prior to and during the opening phases of the battle.

127
George K. Griggs, "The Thirty-Eighth Virginia (Steuart's Brigade) at Battle of Five Forks," *Southern Historical Society Papers*, 16, p. 231.

Douglas Southall Freeman, who offers perhaps the most thoughtful discussion of Five Forks, concludes that Fitz Lee and Pickett "cherished the general belief of the Army—a belief which had helped to create high morale—that the commanding General somehow would contrive to achieve the 'impossible,' even though, in this case, the line was stretched to the breaking point."[127] Freeman defends their decision to attend the shad bake because of their "overconfidence. . .lack of understanding" of the military situation, and downright hunger.[128]

Freeman's explanation of Pickett's behavior at Five Forks is far too charitable. Even if the odds were against him, as the senior major general commanding on the field, Pickett acted irresponsibly at Five Forks. His performance at Five Forks, however, was not inconsistent with his past actions. Two years earlier Pickett habitually left his division to visit his lover. He had repeatedly held a distorted view of his responsibilities and the threats (real and imagined) he had faced in the past. In the immediate aftermath of Gettysburg he was so consumed with his own grief that he wandered aimlessly about the field, sobbing openly about the defeat of his division.[129]

As the war progressed he proved unwilling to admit error or take responsibility for his actions. At Gettysburg and New Berne, Pickett lashed out at others for his own mistakes. Five Forks was no different. In his report he reproached Lee for failing to send reinforcements and criticized him for choosing Five Forks rather than a position behind Hatcher's Run. Pickett even blamed his lunch partner, Fitz Lee, for failing to protect his left flank. This variety of unproductive and unprofessional complaining may well have comprised the bulk of his infamous "lost" report from Gettysburg, which purportedly castigated his fellow officers for the defeat of July 3. Five Forks was the beginning of the end for George Pickett and his men. A lieutenant colonel spotted

---

127
   Freeman, *Lee's Lieutenants*, 3, p. 665.

128
   Ibid., pp. 665-666.

129
   Gordon, "'Assumed a Darker Hue,'" pp. 31-33.

Pickett after the battle and described him as "hopeless, demoralized and prostrated. He did not look like Pickett, but like an old and broken man."[130]

Following Pickett's defeat, Lee evacuated his lines at Petersburg and Richmond and marched west toward Amelia Courthouse, where badly needed supplies were supposedly waiting. Pickett, with the remainder of his command, was ordered to report to Lt. Gen. Richard Anderson enroute to that location. On April 4, tired and hungry Confederates discovered that no supply trains were waiting for them as anticipated.

Lee then moved his army southwest to Rice Station to obtain supplies via the railroad from Lynchburg. He planned to continue moving west and south to get around the pursuing Federals and eventually join forces with Joseph E. Johnston's army in North Carolina. The odds against the success of such a move were long. Grant, in close pursuit, hurried to block Lee's retreat, which was becoming more desperate by the day. On April 6 at Sayler's Creek, Sheridan's cavalry interrupted Lee's march and forced a confrontation with a segment of his army. The few survivors of Pickett's proud division, perhaps numbering some 2,000 men, weak with hunger and exhausted from lack of sleep, experienced battle—and another resounding defeat—for the last time.[131] Brigadier General Henry Wise attested to the fiasco at Sayler's Creek when he described the pathetic nature of the fighting there: "We had hardly formed and begun to move in his rear before Pickett's whole command stampeded. . ." After numerous examples of incompetence on the field, Lee finally relieved Pickett of command during the final days of the war. Pickett, however, for reasons that remain obscure, did not

---

130
    Pickett's Report of Five Forks, in Pickett, *Pickett and His Men*, p. 395; Freeman, *Lee*, 4, p. 40n; Gordon, "'Assumed a Darker Hue,'" p. 34; Theophilus G. Barham, from typescript at Fredericksburg and Spotsylvania National Military Park, Virginia.

131
    Robertson estimates that Pickett had about 2,000 men left by April 6, 1865. Robertson, *18th Virginia Infantry*, p. 33; Harrison is in general agreement, putting the number at 2,200. Harrison, *Pickett's Men*, p. 153; William R. Aylett, Pickett's Division, Virginia Historical Society, Richmond, Virginia, Mss1 Ay445a2123.

leave the army's ranks. Freeman ponders the possibility of whether Pickett even received the order. If he received such an order, his emotional fatigue could have perhaps caused him to ignore it and remain with his command. The sketchy nature of the records from this phase of the war make it impossible to definitively determine the issue.[132]

Regardless of whether or not he received the order removing him from command, George Pickett remained with the pathetic remnants of his division until the bitter end. On April 9, 1865, his division, which numbered only slightly more than 1,000 officers and men, surrendered at Appomattox Court House. Of that number, only 60 soldiers actually surrendered weapons. Pickett signed his soldiers' paroles with the words, "Maj. Genl. Comdg.," possibly unaware that such was no longer the case. One of Lee's aides remembered the general spotting Pickett a few days before the surrender and asking bitterly "Is that man still with this army?"[133]

Through it all James Longstreet remained true to his old army friend. It is more likely than not that Pickett's close relationship with Longstreet kept him in active service despite Lee's growing distrust. In an introduction to one of LaSalle Pickett's many eulogies to her husband, Longstreet even argued that Five Forks was Pickett's "greatest battle." He described Pickett's dubious performance as "masterful and skillful," adding that if Pickett had been allowed to exercise his own plans and operations "there might have been no Appomattox." Sounding much like Pickett himself, Longstreet reasoned that "despite the disparity of overwhelming numbers a brilliant victory would have been his, if reinforcements which he had every reason to expect had opportunely reached him. . ." According to Old Pete, "it was cruel to

132
        Henry Wise, "The Career of Wise's Brigade," *Southern Historical Society Papers*, 25, p. 18; Freeman, *Lee*, 4, p. 112.

133
        OR 46, pt. 1, p. 1277; Freeman, *Lee's Lieutenants*, 3, p. 750. Harrison estimated divisional strength at 800. Harrison, *Pickett's Men*, pp. 66-67; Signed paroled prisoner's pass for T. P. Wallace, April 10, 1865, Armistead-Blanton-Wallace Papers, Virginia Historical Society, Richmond, Virginia, Mss1 Ar554C33; Mosby, *Memoirs*, p. 381; Freeman quotes another version in *Lee*, 4, p. 112.

leave that brilliant and heroic leader and his spartan band to the same hard straits they so nobly met at Gettysburg."[134] George Pickett could not have agreed more.

* * *

Pickett lived for ten years after the war's end, but his life was one of continual misery and at times, outright fear. In March 1865 the Federal government launched an investigation into the hangings at Kinston. For several months he, his wife, and their infant son, lived in hiding in Canada while friends and family tried to procure a pardon for the general. The court of inquiry convened to hear the matter went to great lengths to determine whether the Confederate Army denied the dead men rights guaranteed by military law to prisoners of war, and if so, who was to blame. The court also paid close attention to the correspondence between Peck and Pickett. Judge Advocate Joseph Holt ruled that Pickett's letters revealed an "imperious and vaunting temper," that indicated "his readiness to commit this or any kindred atrocity. . . ."[135] Several witnesses accused Pickett of being solely responsible for the hangings, including several former Confederate officers who indicated that Pickett was the highest ranking officer with the authority to order such an action. "All tend to show," concluded Judge Advocate Holt, "that he was in responsibile command, and furnishes evidence upon which it" is believed charges can be sustained against him. On December 30, 1865, Holt recommended that Pickett be immediately arrested. Ironically, only the intervention of Ulysses Grant saved him from an indictment on war crimes.

Sometime in 1866 he returned to his native Virginia to try farming and for a time, sell insurance. Pickett failed miserably at both. Postwar

[134]
Pickett, *Pickett and His Men*, pp. xii-xiii.

[135]
Bardolph, "Confederate Dilemma," pt. 2, p. 207; House of Representatives, Document No. 98, p. 53.

life was dismal for the once flamboyant general. He confided to a friend in 1869 that he hoped "there might be something in the future for us." That future, whatever it held, would not include writing about his wartime experiences, for Pickett never wrote publicly about the war—despite his many prominent roles and the resentment he nursed against Lee. George Pickett did not regain his health or his peace of mind. He died at the age of fifty in July 1875, with his obituary citing his failed charge at Gettysburg as his most brilliant moment.[136]

136
     Ibid., pp. 53-55, 74, 75, 77. A thorough discussion of this can be found in Gordon, "'Assumed A Darker Hue,'" pp. 70-78; George E. Pickett to Henry Coalter Cabell, March 4, 1869, Cabell Papers, Virginia Historical Society, Richmond, Virginia, Mss1C118a; *Richmond Dispatch*, July 31, 1875.

Steven E. Woodworth

Series Editor Steve Woodworth has published widely on the American Civil War in general and command-related issues in particular, and is the author of *Jefferson Davis and His Generals: The Failure of Confederate Command in the West* (Kansas, 1990), which won the Fletcher Pratt Award for best Civil War book of the year. Another volume, entitled *Davis and Lee at War* (Kansas, 1995), explores similar themes in the Eastern Theater. Professor Woodworth teaches history at Toccoa Falls College in Toccoa Falls, Georgia.

On Smaller Fields

General P. G. T. Beauregard
and the Bermuda Hundred Campaign

Of all the events in the colorful Civil War service of Confederate general Pierre Gustave Toutant Beauregard, none does him such credit, in the popular mind at least, as his defense of the vulnerable "back door" of Richmond south of the James River in May and June 1864. The Confederate Creole is particularly celebrated for the Bermuda Hundred Campaign, a series of actions that shoved Federal Maj. Gen. Ben Butler and his substantial army into a pocket formed by a bend of the James River, where it languished "as completely shut off from further operations directly against Richmond as if it had been in a bottle strongly corked."[1] Here at last, claim the Louisiana general's defenders, is a demonstration of the battlefield genius obscured by various circumstances—or worse, Confederate President Jefferson Davis' malignity—in Virginia in 1861 and Mississippi the following year. The success of the Bermuda Hundred Campaign is presented as proof that

---

[1]
U.S.War Department, *The War of the Rebellion: The Official Records of the Union and Confederate Armies*, 128 vols. (Washington, D.C., 1890-1901), vol. 46, pt. 1, p. 19. All references are to series I unless otherwise noted.

Beauregard was a capable and practical field commander who might have accomplished far greater things for the Confederacy had Davis not conceived a dislike for him.[2]

Pierre Gustave Toutant Beauregard's long journey to the May 1864 battlefield on the south bank of the James River began in Charleston, South Carolina. The Palmetto State was the scene of his initial taste of Civil War glory, when Fort Sumter surrendered under the weight of his bombardment during the first April of the war. The crucial port city had more recently been the scene of his most effective wartime service, where he directed the successful Confederate resistance to a months-long Union effort to capture the city. Though his military reputation was in a measure refurbished by his solid defensive performance, Beauregard grew tired of static service in what he considered a backwater of the war. As was often the case when Beauregard was unhappy, he began to complain increasingly of his chronic throat ailment. He was on the point of prescribing for himself another of his therapeutic vacations at his favorite spa at Bladon Springs, Alabama, when a dispatch arrived from Richmond that changed his mind.[3]

General Braxton Bragg, President Davis' chief military advisor, telegraphed to ask if Beauregard felt up to assuming a command in southern Virginia. The Old Dominion State was the place of action, glory, and widespread recognition, and the Creole had an ear keenly tuned for public acclaim. Throat ailment forgotten, Beauregard quickly replied that he was ready to travel north. The following day, April 15,

---

[2]
 The concept of Beauregard as an unused military asset crops up repeatedly in Civil War literature. See Bruce Catton, *Never Call Retreat* (New York, 1965), pp. 333-334; Archer Jones, *Civil War Command & Strategy* (New York, 1992), pp. 121-122; Charles P. Roland, *An American Iliad: The Story of the Civil War* (Lexington, 1991), pp. 112, 182; William G. Robertson, *Back Door to Richmond: The Bermuda Hundred Campaign, April-June, 1864* (Newark, 1987), p. 253. Historian T. Harry Williams makes a similar claim for Beauregard, but in connection with his defense of Petersburg against Ulysses S. Grant's forces later that same year, as opposed to the action at Bermuda Hundred. T. Harry Williams, *P. G. T. Beauregard: Napoleon in Gray* (Baton Rouge, 1955), p. 235.

[3]
 Williams, *Beauregard*, p. 207; Alfred Roman, *The Military Operations of General Beauregard in the War Between the States, 1861-1865*, 2 vols. (New York, 1884), vol. 2, p. 193.

Gen. Pierre G. T. Beauregard
(*Generals in Gray*)

1864, the wire from Richmond carried a terse message from Adjutant and Inspector General Samuel Cooper: "Repair with the least delay practicable to Weldon, N.C., where instructions will be sent to you."[4]

Several reasons lay behind the summons. Command arrangements in North Carolina and southside Virginia were diverse and confusing. Command of the sector immediately south of the Richmond district was entrusted to the weak-minded Maj. Gen. George Pickett, an adequate brigade commander whose promotion to major general was owing mostly to the favoritism of his mentor, Lt. Gen. James Longstreet. Without Longstreet's overbearing personal presence, and faced with a task more complicated than leading a division on a battlefield, Pickett was even more inadequate than usual. Bragg—who with Davis' approval was giving considerable attention to the southern Virginia and North Carolina region—had felt that someone with more ability was needed. Also, Robert E. Lee had written the president to suggest that Beauregard and some of his troops around Charleston be moved northward to cover the southern approaches of Richmond.[5]

So it was that Beauregard moved a good deal closer to the scene of his glory earlier in the conflict. He officially assumed command of the Department of North Carolina and Cape Fear, as well as that part of Virginia lying south of the James and Appomattox Rivers, on April 23, and promptly thereafter renamed his enlarged sphere of command the Department of North Carolina and Southern Virginia. The situation he found upon his arrival was little to his liking. For Beauregard, concentration of forces, always and for every purpose, was the ultimate distillation of military wisdom. Confederate units in his new department, however, were sprawled across the countryside from the Carolina coast to the Virginia piedmont.[6] Their eclectic errands included not only the securing of Richmond's inland approaches, but also the gathering of

4
   OR 33, p. 1283.

5
   Williams, *Beauregard*, p. 208; Judith L. Hallock, *Braxton Bragg and Confederate Defeat, Volume II* (Tuscaloosa, 1991), pp. 182-183; *OR* 33, pp. 1282-1283; Clifford Dowdey and Louis H. Manarin, eds., *The Wartime Papers of R. E. Lee* (New York, 1961), p. 699.

6
   Roberston, *Back Door to Richmond*, pp. 47-50.

supplies and (as the authorities in Richmond devoutly hoped), the dislodging of the Federals who had early in the war established enclaves on the tarheel state's long and intricate shoreline. A success had recently been scored at Plymouth, North Carolina, and Richmond hoped for similar results at New Berne. The policy made good sense during the winter's lull on the major fighting fronts, but Beauregard had no use for it. "It occasioned an untimely division of some of the most available troops in my new command," he later complained, "rendering their immediate concentration at any threatened point very difficult, if not impossible."[7] Despite his perennial penchant for complaint, Beauregard was correct. Ulysses S. Grant was within a fortnight of launching the largest and best coordinated set of offensive thrusts yet aimed at the Confederacy. As Northern preparations became increasingly obvious, Southern enthusiasm waned for sideshows like New Berne.

Already doubtful about the enterprise but under orders to supervise its execution, Beauregard remained as aloof as possible from the New Berne expedition.[8] The troops marched off toward their objective May 2, but the operation was still in its preliminary stages two days later when a wire arrived from Davis: "Unless New Berne can be captured by coup-de-main," the president instructed, "the attempt must be abandoned, and the troops returned with all possible dispatch to unite in operations in N[orthern] Virginia. There is not an hour to lose. Had the expedition not started, I would say it should not go."[9]

Grant's grand coordinated offensive, which had opened that very day, lay behind this sudden change in Richmond's policy. While Maj. Gen. George G. Meade's Army of the Potomac advanced across the Rapidan River against Lee's Army of Northern Virginia, Union forces led by cock-eyed Massachusetts politician-turned-general Benjamin F.

7
    P. G. T. Beauregard, "The Defense of Drewry's Bluff," in Robert U. Johnson and Clarence C. Buel, eds., *Battles and Leaders of the Civil War*, 4 vols. (New York, 1884-1889), vol. 4, p. 195.

8
    Robertson, *Back Door to Richmond*, p. 53.

9
    OR 51, pt. 2, p. 886; Dunbar Rowland (ed.), *Jefferson Davis, Constitutionalist: His Letters, Papers, and Speeches*, 10 vols. (Jackson, 1923), vol. 6, pp. 246-247.

Butler were preparing to move up the James River toward the Confederate capital.[10] Though Lee's army had not yet collided with Meade's, the Army of Northern Virginia's commander was convinced that the enemy's main thrust was aimed at him, and he was demonstrating in his dispatches to the president that he could, at times, be as much of an advocate of concentration of force as Beauregard. "I regret that there is to be any further delay in concentrating our. . .troops," Lee wrote. "I fully appreciate the advantages of capturing New Berne, but they will not compensate us for a disaster in [Virginia]."[11]

Sensitive as always to Lee's urgings, Davis immediately besought Beauregard for troops. The Creole, responding promptly and decisively, ordered the forces comprising Maj. Gen. Robert Hoke's Division, to disengage and move north for Richmond with "utmost dispatch."[12] Other units were soon on their way to Lee's front, both from North Carolina and southern Virginia as well as from Charleston, where the Federal threat was correctly judged to have diminished as Union troops departed for Virginia.[13] Among the units moving north were two brigades from George Pickett's Division, with Pickett himself accompanying them. Service south of the Appomattox River had been a distasteful exile for the Virginian, and he was eager to rejoin Lee, Longstreet, and a war he at least believed he understood.[14]

Amidst all the tension of an impending collision of the major armies in northern Virginia, no one seems to have remembered the threat posed by the Federals debarking down on the James River. Though Davis had mentioned in a dispatch to Lee on May 4 that "the enemy's forces from S[outh] C[arolina] and Florida are no doubt on the Peninsula,"

10
   OR 51, pt. 2, p. 887.

11
   Douglas Southall Freeman and Grady McWhiney, eds., *Lee's Dispatches: Unpublished Letters of General Robert E. Lee, C. S. A., to Jefferson Davis. . .1862-1865* (New York, 1957), pp. 169-174.

12
   OR 51, pt. 2, p. 889.

13
   Ibid., p. 887.

14
   Rowland, *Jefferson Davis*, 6, p. 247.

Confederate units moving up from the southern coastline were slated for transport through the Richmond area and on to Lee's army.[15]

That same day, the eve of the combined Federal offensive, Beauregard wrote a friend that he saw "no prospect now, of active operations in this Dept."[16] This amazing lapse in Confederate planning was not the result of poor intelligence information but rather of hesitance at the highest level of command. At the moment Davis had better information than Beauregard, but characteristically he was simply passing the raw data on to Lee and naively trusting that general somehow to know what was best to be done in the situation. Even as Butler's troops were landing and establishing their beachhead at Bermuda Hundred, the neck of land at the confluence of the James and the Appomattox Rivers, Davis was reporting the Union concentration to Lee on May 5, concluding, "With these facts and your previous knowledge, you can estimate the condition of things here and decide how far your own movements should be influenced thereby."[17] Lee could do nothing of the sort. That morning he had hurled his divisions against Meade's army in the tangled thickets of the Wilderness, and it was 11:00 p.m. before he could so much as pause to scribble a few lines to the War Department, briefly describing the day's carnage.[18] Lee's attention was fully occupied on his front. On the subject of other units he remained silent, no doubt hoping the Richmond authorities would send him whatever troops they could spare. For the moment no military response was made to Butler's landing.

This was a potentially fatal oversight. A Federal army at Bermuda Hundred would possess several strategic alternatives, all of them disastrous for the South. Most significant, a body of troops could either march up the James to take Richmond from the rear, or move up the

15
  Ibid.

16
  Robertson, *Back Door to Richmond*, p. 54.

17
  Rowland, *Jefferson Davis*, 6, pp. 247-248.

18
  OR 36, pt. 2, p. 951.

Appomattox, seize the vital rail junction at Petersburg, and cut off
Richmond's—and Lee's—supply conduit from the Deep South. A third
possibility involved a lunge for the Richmond & Petersburg Railroad, a
vulnerable single line of track connecting the Confederate capital and
Petersburg. Federal success in any of these movements or a combination
of them would amount to the same thing: an end to Confederate hopes of
independence.

The first high-ranking Confederate officer to begin to grasp what
the Federals were about was the hapless Pickett. Not yet having left
Petersburg to join his brigades in northern Virginia, Pickett could hardly
have helped but notice the oncoming Union juggernaut, for he stood
almost directly in its path and less than a dozen miles away. Beauregard
had already given him permission to communicate directly with
Richmond if the need arose, and Pickett frantically began to bombard
both Richmond and Beauregard with pleas for troops and instructions.[19]

Beauregard in turn sent a string of messages to Braxton Bragg in
Richmond, requesting that Pickett be allowed to keep the small force he
had already at Petersburg and to stop other units passing through the
town on their way from the southern coast to join Lee on the Rapidan.
Davis took a direct interest in these matters, and while allowing that
Pickett could keep the token forces then in Petersburg, insisted that the
reinforcements bound for Lee must not be diverted. Beauregard's
protests got the order at least partially rescinded, allowing one brigade to
be halted at Petersburg for the defense of that point. He urged Pickett to
do the best he could and ordered him to remain in command in the
threatened city until the situation stabilized.[20] At the same time, while
assuring Bragg that "all possible will be done," Beauregard declined to
go personally to the scene of action, pleading lamely that he was "too
unwell to go to Petersburg tonight," but promising to "do so tomorrow
evening, or next day."[21] Richmond authorities—and Pickett—would

19
      Robertson, *Back Door to Richmond*, pp. 66-69.

20
      OR 51, pt. 2, pp. 890-891; ibid., p. 890; Robertson, *Back Door to Richmond*, pp. 65-69;
Beauregard, "Defense," p. 196.

21
      OR 51, pt. 2, p. 890.

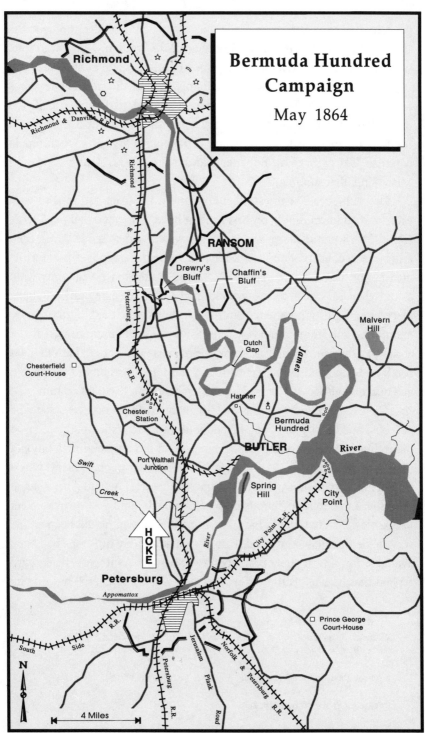

Bermuda Hundred Campaign

May 1864

Richmond

Richmond & Danville R.R.

Richmond

Petersburg

RANSOM

Drewry's Bluff

Chaffin's Bluff

Malvern Hill

Dutch Gap

James

Chesterfield Court-House

R.R.

Chester Station

Hatcher

Bermuda Hundred

BUTLER

River

Swift

Creek

Port Walthall Junction

Spring Hill

City Point

City Point R.R.

River

HOKE

Petersburg

Appomattox

Prince George Court-House

South Side R.R.

Jerusalem Plank Road

Petersburg R.R.

Norfolk & Petersburg R.R.

N

4 Miles

Mark A. Moore

have to content themselves with that assurance. For the moment the Creole remained in his secure headquarters in Weldon, North Carolina, well away from the arena in which crucial decisions had to be made.

This was vintage Beauregard. Simply put, he did not handle stress well. Often when the military situation looked particularly bad, his mysterious throat ailment would flare up, allowing him a convenient excuse to decline to take command or responsibility. This occurred in western Tennessee in February and March 1862, and again in Mississippi that summer.[22]

On each occasion the strategic picture in his front had looked very grim, and an uncharitable observer might have concluded that the Creole feared lest some disaster occur on his watch and mar his reputation. After the second of these occasions Davis had perceptively taken the measure of the man when he wrote, "There are those who can only walk a log when it is near to the ground, and I fear [Beauregard] has been placed too high for his mental strength, as he does not exhibit the ability manifested on smaller fields."[23] As Butler's Federals appeared to be about to advance through the almost nonexistent Confederate defenses south of Richmond, Beauregard found the lonely heights of command and decision altogether too giddy, and his health, at least, failed him.

There can be no denying that Beauregard had good reason to be nervous, and that by this time he had a far more realistic appreciation of the military situation south of the James than did anyone in Richmond, Davis not excepted. On May 6, the Confederate president wired Beauregard to express the hope that the general would "be able at Petersburg to direct operations both before and behind you, so as to meet necessities."[24] That would have been fine if Beauregard had been on his way to the threatened city and if any substantial body of troops had been available for him to direct either before or behind. As it was, Beauregard replied that he was "still confined to [his] tent by sickness" but that he

22
     Williams, *Beauregard*, p. 118; *OR* 7, pp. 895-896, 912; 10, pt. 2, pp. 297, 302, 327; Grady McWhiney, *Braxton Bragg and Confederate Defeat* (New York, 1969), p. 205.

23
     Jefferson Davis to Varina Davis, June 13, 1862, The Museum of the Confederacy.

24
     Rowland, *Jefferson Davis*, 6, p. 248.

hoped to be able to set out for Petersburg in another day or so. Meanwhile, he was "concentrating as rapidly as possible all available troops."[25] The troops were indeed on the way from all over Beauregard's department and South Carolina. As his dispatches and Pickett's almost frantic, well-nigh hourly telegraphic pleadings made their impact, Davis and Bragg began to grasp the gravity of the Bermuda Hundred situation.[26] Authorization finally arrived to retain troops at Petersburg, and by May 6, it was Adjutant and Inspector General Samuel Cooper, on behalf of Davis, who was urging Beauregard to hasten "forward by rail the troops ordered from the south to Petersburg, which is much threatened."[27]

Fortunately for the South, the Confederate high command had recognized the danger to Petersburg in time to shore up its defenses. The first brigade to halt there in its northward movement was able to baffle a pair of halfhearted probes by Butler toward the vital railroad between Richmond and Petersburg on May 6 and 7.[28] Still, the Federal threat remained and in Richmond anxieties continued to grow. On May 6, Beauregard, still in Weldon, sent duplicate messages to Cooper, Bragg, and Secretary of War James A. Seddon, asking if he were authorized "to control to best advantage I may think proper all troops now in this department or arriving?"[29] It was natural for a commander to want to be sure of the extent of his authority, but from Richmond it may have appeared that the temperamental Creole was refusing to move to Petersburg and carry out his duty unless he were promised a free hand.

25
  OR 51, pt. 2, p. 894.

26
  Robertson, *Back Door to Richmond*, pp. 75-76.

27
  OR 36, pt. 2, p. 964.

28
  Beauregard, "Defense," p. 196; Johnson Hagood, *Memoirs of the War of Secession* (Columbia, 1910), pp. 219-227; Charles M. Cummings, *Yankee Quaker Confederate General: The Curious Career of Bushrod Rust Johnson* (Rutherford, 1971), pp. 282-283. The apportionment of Federal blame among Butler and his various subordinates for not acting more decisively in their operations is beyond the scope of this article.

29
  OR 36, pt. 2, pp. 963-964.

However this may have appeared to Davis, the Southern president was quickly losing patience with Beauregard. He wanted troops brought up from the south more quickly, and he wanted "a prompt and earnest attack" against Butler's Federals.[30]

Davis saw clearly that the Union movement represented a serious threat to Richmond. By this time he had also learned that the Federals were commanded by Benjamin "Beast" Butler, whose administration of occupied New Orleans earlier in the war had drawn from Davis a proclamation that he was to be hanged upon capture.[31] For Davis, the prospect of carrying out his decree, coupled with his desire to safeguard Richmond and Petersburg, provided strong incentive for a quick and decisive attack. He wrote in a note to Bragg on May 8 stating that "if General Beauregard's health disqualifies him for field operations, it would be well to order [Maj. Gen. Robert F.] Hoke to proceed in advance of his troops and take command of the forces in front of Petersburg." In an off hand comment that told much about what the Richmond authorities thought of George Pickett, Davis concluded, "For the defensive operations of that point General Pickett will be enough."[32]

Bragg communicated Davis' advice to Beauregard, along with the president's suggestion that the railroad through Danville, Virginia, might be used to move troops more quickly into Petersburg.[33] The Creole responded with a stream of dispatches in which he promised that troops would "be pushed through as fast as possible," although he considered the president's suggested alternate route as impractical.[34] As for going to Petersburg himself, this was something he seemed always on the verge

30
    Ibid., 51, pt. 2, p. 902.

31
    Dick Nolan, *Benjamin Franklin Butler: The Damnedest Yankee* (Novato, CA, 1991), p. 223.

32
    OR 51, pt. 2, p. 902.

33
    Evidence that Bragg did indeed forward this information to Beauregard is demonstrated by that general's reply, one of at least three dispatches he sent Bragg on May 8, in which he assured him that he would leave that night by the first train, although he dismissed Davis' observation, claiming that the "Danville route [is] too long for troops." *OR* 51, pt. 2, p. 904.

34
    Ibid.

of doing. First he wrote, "I hope to leave today for Petersburg, where prompt and energetic measures will be adopted." Then he would "leave here tonight by the first train." This was postponed to "will leave here at 11 p.m. for Petersburg," which in turn finally gave way to an admission that he "should have started today for Petersburg," but a nuisance raid by some northern cavalry had prompted him to postpone his going until morning. At that time, he insisted, "I shall run through and assume command as desired." In case the president might still be in a mood to take the general's poor health as an occasion to relieve him of command, Beauregard hastened to add the assurance, "The water has improved my health."[35]

All this proved to be sufficient to save Beauregard from removal, but he was not quick to forgive Davis for coming so close thus to committing, for a second time in the war, such an unpardonable sin. Long after the war he wrote of this period, "Rapid as were the movements of our troops. . .their celerity failed to satisfy or reassure the War Department, whose trepidation grew hourly more intense, and whose orders, telegrams, and suggestions became as harassing as they were numerous."[36] Harassing or not, they did finally have the effect of budging Beauregard from his secure seat on the sidelines of the conflict at Weldon. By May 9 he reached Raleigh and telegraphed Richmond that he would proceed from there by way of Danville to Petersburg, where he finally arrived the next day.[37]

By that time, the flow of the campaign had shifted and Petersburg was no longer the focal point of Butler's Federals. Acting on his understanding of Grant's grand plan of campaign, and in response to information he was receiving from north of the James, Butler shifted his attention from Petersburg to the southern approaches of Richmond itself. Skirmishing with troops of the Richmond garrison slowed Butler's

[35]
   Ibid., pp. 903-904.
[36]
   Beauregard, "Defense," p. 196.
[37]
   Ibid.; *OR* 51, pt. 2, pp. 906, 915.

advance to a timid creep, but Richmond's garrison commander, Maj. Gen. Robert Ransom, realized that he did not have nearly enough troops on hand to stop a resolute Federal advance.[38] The Richmond authorities knew it too. At 10:00 p.m. on the evening of May 9, Bragg telegraphed Hoke, then assumed by the War Department to be at Petersburg, to advance with his "whole force" to join Ransom in the defense of Richmond. In fact, Hoke, along with his division moving up from North Carolina, did not arrive in Petersburg until 1:30 p.m. the following day, five and a half hours after Beauregard. At this point, some confusion arose as to whether the order to Hoke was still in effect, and if so, what was meant by his "whole force." Did Bragg mean just his division, or all the troops at Petersburg? Beauregard sent an inquiry to Richmond for clarification, proceeding with his own plans in the meantime.[39]

As it turned out, the issue was moot. On May 10, Ransom met elements of Butler's command just east of Chester Station, a small village south of Richmond. After inconclusive fighting, Ransom withdrew north into the fortifications around Drewry's Bluff, a Confederate strong point on the south bank of the James just below the city. The defensive bulwark at Drewry's Bluff had saved the Confederate capital in early 1862 by turning back a determined Union naval assault up the James River. Now, however, the position was threatened by Butler's ground troops, and defending it were Ransom's few, thin brigades. Davis and his advisors waited anxiously throughout May 10 for news of Ransom's action with Butler.[40]

As the day passed, they became aware of an additional danger. Union Maj. Gen. Philip Sheridan, with two divisions of Union cavalry, had detached himself from Meade's army and was moving to destroy a key bridge on the Virginia Central Railroad at Beaver Dam Station. The loss of the bridge would seriously threaten the supply lines to Lee's hard-pressed army. With Ransom's Richmond garrison occupied south

38
    Robertson, *Back Door to Richmond*, p. 128.
39
    OR 51, pt. 2, p. 915; Robertson, *Back Door to Richmond*, pp. 122-123.
40
    Rowland, *Jefferson Davis*, 6, p. 249; *OR* 36, pt. 2, p. 986.

of the James with Butler, Sheridan's troopers also posed a serious threat to the capital itself. At 3:30 p.m. Bragg wired Petersburg urging Beauregard to attack. "Let us know when you will be ready, that Ransom may cooperate. Every hour is now very important."[41] Bragg spelled out the danger more fully in a later communication: "We are seriously threatened here from above," he explained. "You should make a heavy demonstration and change to attack, if practicable, at an early hour in the morning."[42] In response, Beauregard telegraphed that night to promise that he would be ready for offensive operations the following evening.[43]

That was not good enough. Twenty minutes after midnight on the morning of May 11, Bragg fired off an order for Beauregard to send Hoke, along with all available field forces at Petersburg, directly north up the turnpike for Drewry's Bluff to join Ransom—even if they had to cut their way through Butler's command to do so.[44] Beauregard responded, pleading for more time to get things organized before going over to the offensive.[45]

Receiving no reply, Beauregard had enough sense of the frustration in Richmond to realize this was an order that had best be carried out. He accordingly obeyed the order and the troops prepared to move out. As daylight crept up the broad tidal rivers of eastern Virginia, Beauregard sent Bragg an upbeat message. "My forces are being united. . .You may then rely on my hearty co-operation in defense of Richmond." He then added cryptically, however, "Appearances here this morning are that the enemy is about withdrawing from this point to reenforce elsewhere. I

41
  Noah Andre Trudeau, Bloody Roads South: The Wilderness to Cold Harbor, May-June 1864 (Boston, 1989), p. 162-163; *OR* 51, pt. 2, p. 916.

42
  Alfred Roman, *Military Operations*, 2, p. 554.

43
  Ibid., 51, pt. 2, p. 915.

44
  Robertson, *Back Door to Richmond*, p. 140-142; *OR* 51, pt. 2, p. 920.

45
  OR 51, pt. 2, p. 920.

will try to strike him a severe blow before he leaves."[46] This, in fact, was a mistake. What Beauregard was perceiving was merely Butler's shift toward Richmond. In that city, Bragg and the rest of the circle around the president could hardly have known what to make of the statement, but it must have been good at last to hear Beauregard speaking of striking "a severe blow" to the enemy.

At 7:00 a.m. further encouraging word came from the Creole. "Offensive movement against enemy has commenced," he grandly proclaimed. "General Hoke's division in the advance supported by Pickett's division." He concluded the short telegram by stating "Give necessary orders to General Ransom," meaning that Ransom should be ordered to cooperate with him from Drewry's Bluff. This information from Beauregard was not exactly true either. The previous evening, Pickett, having fretted himself into a state of nervous prostration during his few days of responsibility for Petersburg, relinquished his duties and took to his bed.[47]

From Richmond's perspective, at any rate, Beauregard appeared to be proceeding as ordered. In a dispatch to Ransom through Bragg, however, Beauregard began to speak of "a forced reconnaissance" by Hoke and Pickett. His men would attack Butler "should [the] opportunity be favorable." He was proposing an attack—not toward Richmond and the threatened lines at Drewry's Bluff—but instead toward Bermuda Hundred. He even planned to send some of his men through Petersburg and around the south side of the Appomattox to attack City Point, across the wide confluence of the James and Appomattox Rivers from Bermuda Hundred.[48] Beauregard was moving his troops 60 degrees in the wrong direction, and he was planning to straddle them across a broad tidal river controlled by enemy warships.

Consternation reigned in the War Department at this shocking proposal. "Division of your forces is earnestly objected to," Seddon

46
    Ibid., p. 921.
47
    Ibid., p. 920.
48
    Ibid., pp. 919, 921.

hurriedly replied. "It is decidedly preferred that you carry out the instructions given last night, and endeavor to unite all forces."[49] At 12:45 p.m. Beauregard's reply was equivocal. "My division of force is only temporary to meet present emergency." He asked the secretary to "state [his] objections," and insisted, "I am carrying into effect to best of ability instructions received." The Creole concluded his message with a vague assurance—which was not very reassuring under the circumstances—that "the movement is now in progress."[50]

Shortly thereafter, Beauregard received a dispatch from Seddon that had crossed his in transit. "This city is in hot danger," the secretary raged.

> It should be defended with all our resources to the sacrifice of minor considerations. You are relied on to use every effort to unite all your forces at the earliest practicable time with the troops in our defenses, and then together either fight the enemy in the field or defend the intrenchments.[51]

When Seddon received the general's reply, he fired back a message of stinging rebuke:

> Your two telegrams of this date are received. They pain and surprise. I do not feel this to be an appropriate time to reply fully to them. I may do that hereafter. At present I have only to say, that while your past services, patriotism, and reputation are fully appreciated, you are on those accounts only the more relied on and expected to use every effort in your power with all your forces to carry out the instructions of the Department and accomplish the junction of all our forces to fight the enemy or defend the capital.[52]

49
  Ibid., 36, pt. 2, p. 991.

50
  Ibid., p. 992.

51
  Ibid., 36, p. 986; Roman, *Military Operations*, 2, p. 554.

52
  OR 36, pt. 2, p. 992.

Beauregard took offense at Seddon's reprimand and replied with a longer dispatch, defending his actions and motives and pointing out that he had passed up a sick leave to take this assignment. "I am ready and willing to serve the cause to the utter sacrifice of [my] health, but if my course be not approved by the War Department I wish to be relieved at once."

To Davis, who was monitoring the correspondence, this exchange must have looked very familiar. Beauregard was in his usual form, spinning complex and unrealistic plans, indulging in melodramatic self-promotion, and taking offense at any suggestion of an authority above himself. Indeed, that Beauregard was worked up to a higher than usual pitch of strategic pipedreaming was evidenced by the fact that this plan abandoned even his cherished principle of concentration of force. Another aspect of the general's behavior might have put Davis in mind, unpleasantly, of the Creole's behavior at Shiloh: Beauregard had not gone forward with his troops. This became apparent for the first time to those in Richmond when Davis intervened in the process at 2:15 p.m. The distressed president dashed off a quick dispatch addressed simply to the "Commanding Officer, Petersburg." He inquired "What forces have you today to unite with General Ransom?". . . .When did General Beauregard leave?"[53]

The answer of course was that Beauregard had not left at all, and the general himself replied to the queries. "I have not yet left here," he wrote, "my presence being still absolutely necessary." He would go, he promised, "immediately after arrival of two last brigades—hourly expected from Weldon." He further informed Davis that he had canceled the movement on Bermuda Hundred in response to Seddon's rebuke, but that shortly thereafter, "the order to make forced reconnaissance was approved by General Bragg, and is now being executed." What, Beauregard wanted to know, did Davis think of all this?[54]

Without waiting for an answer, which apparently never came, Beauregard telegraphed Bragg a few minutes later, complaining of

[53]
Rowland, *Jefferson Davis*, 6, p. 250.
[54]
OR 5l, pt. 2, p. 920.

Seddon's interference and concluding, "I must insist on receiving orders only from one source, and that from the general commanding."[55]

By this time, however, Beauregard's fitful gestures toward Bermuda Hundred had come to nothing after all. Hoke and his two divisions had proceeded directly up the turnpike without incident, and by 5:00 p.m., easily made contact with Ransom.[56] Beauregard seemed to reconcile himself to this turn of events, and the temporary storm between him and the secretary of war apparently blew over.

It was fortunate for the Confederacy that Hoke arrived when he did. That day Maj. Gen. Jeb Stuart's Confederate cavalry had clashed with Sheridan's troopers north of Richmond at Yellow Tavern. Stuart fell mortally wounded in the action, and the Federal horsemen were just a few miles outside the city. Davis and his advisors felt compelled to pull most of Ransom's Division off the southern front to hold back Sheridan, a move made possible by Hoke's timely arrival. For the moment, Richmond was again secure. After briefly threatening the city, Sheridan retired to Butler's base on the James River. The authorities in Richmond, however, had worries enough, as the news from all fronts was disheartening. On May 12, Lee's army was nearly broken in two at the Bloody Angle at Spotsylvania, where hours of desperate fighting were needed to repair the rupture in the line. Twenty cannon and thousands of men were lost in the fighting. Lee, who had been asking for reinforcements to replace his heavy losses, also needed men to protect his flow of supplies from raiding Union cavalry.[57] The only reasonable source for these reinforcements were the troops concentrated in the Richmond-Petersburg area. Butler, however, had yet to be decisively dealt with, and he still posed a considerable threat to both Richmond and the vital rail junction at Petersburg.

---

[55]
Ibid.

[56]
Robertson, *Back Door to Richmond*, p. 142; Hagood, *Memoirs*, pp. 231-232.

[57]
OR 36, pt. 2, p. 988.

On May 11 and 12, Beauregard had promised Ransom, Seddon, and
Davis that he would leave for Drewry's Bluff on the 12th, probably by
noon.[58] When he finally left Petersburg, it was 24 hours later on May
13. In Petersburg he left two brigades of troops along with Maj. Gen.
William Henry Chase Whiting, who had left his post at Wilmington,
North Carolina, to travel to Petersburg merely to consult with
Beauregard. Instead, Beauregard asked him to stay and command the
city in his absence. By the time the Creole left for Drewy's Bluff with a
small escort, pushing through to Richmond's southern defenses was a
daring enough undertaking by any standard. The Federals controlled the
turnpike, and Beauregard had to take a roundabout route that finally
brought him into Confederate lines south of the James at 3:00 a.m. on
May 14. Upon his arrival, he learned that Hoke, with the small force left
him after troops were shifted north to counter Sheridan, had spent the
day stubbornly skirmishing with Butler's men. Though he still held
Drewry's Bluff, he had been forced back from the outer fortifications
into the intermediate defensive lines.[59]

Beauregard discussed the situation with staff officers on the scene
for about an hour before turning to his favorite military occupation: the
manufacture of grandiose and far-fetched strategic plans. His new
scheme called for Lee to fall back more than forty miles to the outer, or
even intermediate, defensive works around Richmond, at the same time
detaching 10,000 men to reinforce Beauregard. This addition to his
force, plus the 5,000 troops of Ransom's Richmond garrison, would
bring Beauregard's numbers to 25,000 or 30,000 men, perhaps more.
With these he would assail Butler's right flank, aiming to pry the Union
army away from the James River and its base at Bermuda Hundred.
Simultaneously, proposed the Creole, Whiting would move up from
Petersburg with 4,000 men and strike the rear of the Union position.
Beauregard believed that his plan would "insure his [Butler's]
unconditional surrender." That accomplished, Beauregard would turn

---

[58] *OR* 51, pt. 2, p. 927; Robertson, *Back Door to Richmond*, p. 142.

[59] Robertson, *Back Door to Richmond*, pp. 146-149; Hagood, *Memoirs*, p. 232.

north with 25,000 men, attack the left flank of Grant's army while Lee assaulted it in front, and thus win the war.[60]

Beauregard later admitted having formed this scheme "hurriedly," and he was no more inclined to lose time in getting it approved. He dispatched a galloping staff officer for Richmond to see Davis and gain his blessing for the plan—a program that had yet to be set down in writing. When the aide arrived in Richmond, it was still exceedingly early in the morning. Davis had not been well and his aides were reluctant to disturb him with such a hasty plan. Instead, the officer gave his message to Bragg, who decided to ride down to Drewry's Bluff and talk to Beauregard about the matter. There, Beauregard presented his case in impassioned terms and urged Bragg to order its immediate execution on his own responsibility. Bragg was not about to do anything of the sort. He was polite but noncommittal, and he harbored a number of serious reservations about the plan, though he did not share these with Beauregard. Indeed, so anxious was Bragg to be pleasant, that Beauregard later claimed Bragg had fully agreed with the plan. The best the Creole could get from Bragg in concrete terms was a promise to put the matter to the president as soon as possible.[61]

Beauregard decided to follow up his discussion with Bragg with a written proposal of his plan, and its details were set down on paper for the first time in a dispatch that morning. To his written version he added a flourish or two—the undoing of Butler should be the work of, at most, two days, once Beauregard received the reinforcements he sought. The destruction of Butler would provide such a windfall of supplies that for "a few days" the Confederates could proceed in blissful unconcern to all considerations of logistics.[62] The hours passed, however, with no

60
    Beauregard, "Defense," pp. 198-199; Douglas Southall Freeman, *Lee's Lieutenants: A Study in Command*, 3 vols. (New York, 1944), vol. 3, pp. 478-479; Robertson, *Back Door to Richmond*, pp. 149-150; Henry A. Wise, "The Career of Wise's Brigade, 1861-5," *Southern Historical Society Papers*, 52 vols. (1897), vol. 25, p. 10.

61
    Beauregard, "Defense," pp. 197-198; Ibid., pp. 197-199; Freeman, *Lee's Lieutenants*, 3, pp. 479-480.

62
    OR 36, pt. 2, p. 1024.

instructions from Richmond as to whether his plan would be adopted. Finally, about mid-afternoon, Beauregard's suspense was ended, not by the arrival of an answer from Davis, but by the arrival of Davis himself.

Beauregard endeavored to convince the president of the merits of his operation, but it was no use. Davis was too much of a realist to be drawn into approval of such a bizarre and unrealistic scheme. The president pointed out the obvious problems involved in having Lee make such a precipitate retreat on Richmond. He also objected to Beauregard's plan to have Whiting move from the opposite side of the enemy and yet coordinate his movements with those of Beauregard. With the state of communications as they were in the nineteenth century, such coordination was all but impossible and Davis knew it. Instead, he suggested that Whiting and his men make a night march, skirting Butler's positions by way of the Chesterfield Road, and joining Beauregard "by or soon after daylight" on Sunday, May 15. After a day of rest they would be ready to join in an assault at dawn on the morning of Monday, May 16.[63]

The general, of course, was not happy with this at all. Whiting's movement was, as Beauregard later put it, "a salient feature of my plan."[64] Hoping to block the president's objections, he lamely complained that it would be terribly difficult to get "a courier who knew the route and could certainly deliver the order to General Whiting." Unfortunately for Beauregard, he chose a most unfortunate excuse, for just at that moment a courier rode up, having come from Whiting by way of the Chesterfield Road.[65] Thus checkmated, Beauregard, as he put it in a postwar account that dripped with bitterness, "reluctantly yielded to" the president's objections.[66] He still had a trick or two up his sleeve, though. In agreeing to the president's plan, Beauregard "said the

[63]
    Beauregard, "Defense," p. 199; Jefferson Davis, *The Rise and Fall of the Confederate Government*, 2 vols. (New York, 1881), vol. 2, pp. 511-513.

[64]
    Beauregard, "Defense," p. 200.

[65]
    Davis, *Rise and Fall*, 2, p. 512.

[66]
    Beauregard, "Defense," p. 200.

order [to Whiting] would have to be drawn with a great deal of care, and that he would prepare it as soon as he could." That seemed to satisfy Davis, who then returned to Richmond, no doubt to Beauregard's immense gratification.[67]

With the president gone, Beauregard sat down to prepare "with a great deal of care" his instructions to Whiting. Flagrantly ignoring Davis' orders, he directed Whiting to depart from Petersburg not at nightfall on Saturday, May 14, but at dawn on Monday, May 16.[68] This directive, of course, would result in a two-day delay in opening the battle—unless Whiting were to revert to his original role of leading an independent force to fall against the rear of Butler's army while Beauregard was engaged in front. Clearly, Beauregard never for a moment intended to comply with Davis' orders regarding Whiting.

Beauregard's true intent gradually began to dawn on Davis and Bragg the next day. On Sunday morning, May 15, Davis had Bragg send dispatches to both Whiting and Beauregard. He urged the former to "join [Beauregard] at the earliest moment with his whole force," while informing the latter officer that "It is hoped you may receive [Whiting] in time to attack tomorrow. . . .Time is all important to us, as the enemy gains more by delay than we possibly can. Sheridan's cavalry, with re-enforcements, will again threaten the city very soon, which is almost stripped of troops to aid you."[69] That this last statement was true, Beauregard had good reason to know, for even then the troops of Ransom's Division—the only force available to protect the capital from Sheridan—were filing into reserve positions just to the rear of his lines at Bermuda Hundred.[70] It was 4:00 p.m. before Beauregard replied. "I have already sent General Whiting his instructions to cooperate with me,

67
   Davis, *Rise and Fall*, 2, pp. 512-513.

68
   Robertson, *Back Door to Richmond*, p. 153.

69
   OR 51, pt. 2, p. 934.

70
   Ibid., p. 930. The dispatch from Beauregard to Davis is labeled as having been sent on May 14, but it is most likely misdated.

the Creole haughtily informed Bragg. "Please telegraph him to follow them," he continued. "Yours may conflict with mine." By this point in the war it is doubtful that any manner of insubordination could have shocked Braxton Bragg, but this gross demonstration probably came as close as anything. One can almost hear the sputter in his reply. "My dispatches of this morning to you and General Whiting were by direction of the President and after his conference with you."[71]

Since May 15 was a Sunday, Davis and Bragg were probably not in close contact for much of the day. At any rate, it seems likely that after ordering Bragg to send the dispatches to Whiting and Beauregard that morning, Davis did not talk with him again until at least evening. The president was learning of Beauregard's perfidy by other means. Sometime before noon, a staff officer stopped by Davis' residence with another oral message from Beauregard. The general had now decided, the officer related, "to order Whiting to move by the direct road from Petersburg, instead of by the Chesterfield route." This, of course, was a return to Beauregard's original plan of launching Whiting against the Federal rear, and Davis objected as he had before. In reply, the officer "said General Beauregard had directed him to explain to me [Davis] that upon a further examination he found his force sufficient; that his operations, therefore, did not depend upon making a junction with Whiting."[72] Twenty-four hours before, Beauregard had claimed that Whiting must approach the enemy rear because the plan could not go on without him. Now the Creole was claiming that Whiting was free to approach the enemy rear precisely because his force was not essential to the plan. The contrary claims, one coming close on the heels of the other, made little sense and as events would eventually prove, the latter contention was untrue.

That Sunday evening, Beauregard took time out from his preparations for battle to complete the job of deception he had begun on his superiors. In response to Bragg's indignant protest, he wired blandly that a "change of plan of operations since [the] President was here

71
    Ibid., p. 934.
72
    Davis, *Rise and Fall*, 2, pp. 512-513; Beauregard, "Defense," p. 200.

necessitated a corresponding change in Whiting's instructions, which I have ordered accordingly."[73] The president would require more verbal camouflage than Bragg, and consequently Beauregard prepared one of his lengthier dispatches of the campaign. He now claimed that "it was found [Whiting] would require two days to reach here." Since the battle could obviously not be delayed that long with any degree of safety, Beauregard had "ordered Major-General Whiting to co-operate with all his forces by attacking the enemy in rear" while the forces at Bermuda Hundred attacked head-on the next morning.[74] That, after all, had been Beauregard's original plan.

Robert Ransom's four-brigade division, holding the Confederate left flank near the James River, was to lead off the attack. They went in "at the first glimpse of daylight," as Ransom recalled it, hindered by trees the Federals had felled in their front as well as by wire entanglements "interwoven among the trees" in front of the Union lines. The half light of dawn and a dense fog aided them in their approach to the enemy position. Butler had planned to threaten the opposite end of the Confederate line along the axis of the Richmond Turnpike. As a consequence he expected little trouble on his own right flank. Between that flank and the James River, Butler mistakenly left a substantial gap covered by nothing but cavalry—which promptly de-camped for the rear when Ransom's infantrymen emerged from the mist. Just to the left of the skedaddling troopers was the rightmost Federal brigade under Brig. Gen. Charles A. Heckman, a tough, battle-seasoned outfit composed of one New Jersey and three Massachusetts regiments. Caught by surprise while boiling their morning coffee, the Jerseymen and Bay Staters nonetheless stood their ground, hurling back the frontal assaults of Archibald Gracie's and Seth Barton's Rebel brigades.

Meanwhile William R. Terry, another of Ransom's brigadiers, was guiding his Virginia brigade—which was but a shadow of what it had been when James L. Kemper led it up the slopes of Cemetery Ridge ten

---

73
  OR 51, pt. 2, p. 934.

74
  Ibid., p. 1077.

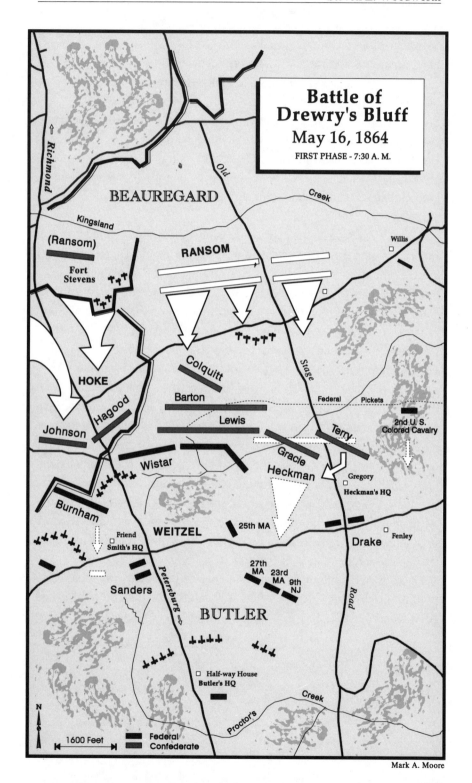

Battle of
Drewry's Bluff
May 16, 1864

FIRST PHASE - 7:30 A. M.

Mark A. Moore

months before—around the exposed right flank of Heckman's hard-fighting Federals. The fog masked Terry's movement, allowing his men to fall on the exposed flank and rear of the Federal battle line. No troops could stand up to the terrifying crossfire that resulted, and the collapse that followed triggered a chain reaction that soon had the entire Federal right rolling backward while Ransom's brigades surged forward in pursuit. The Federal commanders actually had more men on the ground than did Ransom, but in the dense mist they could not effectively concentrate them against the hard-charging Confederates, who were sweeping down their line from the right, rolling it up like a blanket. Before they could stabilize their position they had lost three quarters of a mile of ground and an impressive collection of guns, flags, and prisoners—including Brigadier General Heckman.[75]

By this time, however, Ransom's attack was beginning to unravel. Fog, wire, and abatis had snagged and torn the fabric of the division's organization, and the shock and casualties of combat had shredded it still more. On top of that, Ransom's soldiers were reaching for the last few rounds in their now alarmingly light cartridge boxes. The assaulting brigades desperately needed a pause to catch their breath, restore their alignment, and refill their cartridge boxes. Hoping to retain the initiative and preserve the momentum of the assault, Ransom asked Beauregard for the use of a large brigade from the general reserve. Beauregard, who was concerned about the state of affairs on the army's right flank, where things were not going nearly as well, refused Ransom's request. As a result, Ransom's attack stalled before the weakened Federals. Delays were also encountered in attempting to resupply ammunition to the men at the front. Ransom once again renewed his request for additional troops, but Beauregard deemed he could spare him only a couple of weak regiments, which Ransom was forced to commit almost immediately to blunt a Federal counterstroke that nearly caved in the junction between his division and Robert Hoke's troops on his right. When

---

[75] Charles T. Loehr, "Battle of Drewry's Bluff," *Southern Historical Society Papers*, 19 (1891), pp. 100-111.

ammunition finally arrived and the division moved forward again, it advanced only a short distance to, or just beyond, the line of the old breastworks from which Hoke had been driven several days before. There, further delay occurred as it became necessary to correct the alignment of two of Ransom's brigades. Riding off to report the delay to Beauregard before continuing the advance, Ransom found his superior only a few hundred yards away. To his surprise, Beauregard seemed almost relieved. "It is as well," he responded. "I am hard pressed on the right, and we may have to withdraw to the breastworks, and most of our force come to the right." Beauregard went on to explain to the stunned officer, "I fear my flank may be turned."[76]

Things were not as bad as that, but the right wing of Beauregard's army had not been very successful. Hoke's Division had attacked the left front of Butler's army from their entrenchments, and the direct assault exacted a correspondingly high price. The proverbial "fog of war" had been compounded by the literal fog that morning, to say nothing of woods, abatis, and wire entanglements. Attempting to wheel to the right too soon, before Ransom's brigades had rolled the enemy's line back that far, Hoke exposed his left flank to the Union counterattack that had forced the commitment of Ransom's scant reserves. Another Union counterattack had torn at the division's (and the army's) right flank. Though the Confederates had held on this part of the field, it was this event that prompted the concern Beauregard expressed to Ransom regarding his right flank.[77]

The army had not been fought to a standstill, but it was clear that further advance, if any, would come at the cost of substantial losses. This

---

[76]
Varina Howell Davis, *Jefferson Davis: Ex-President of the Confederate States of America, A Memoir by His Wife*, 2 vols. (New York, 1890), vol. 2, pp. 509-514. The intensity of the confusion on the field that morning is borne out by the fact that Johnson Hagood, commanding the left brigade of Hoke's Division, later denied having received any help at all from Ransom. Hagood, *Memoirs*, pp. 244-246. It is therefore reasonable to conclude that Ransom was fighting Federals on his right, where he presumed Hagood to be, while Hagood was fighting Federals on his left, where he presumed Ransom to be, with neither perceiving the actions of the other. This would imply that the Federals had before them a gap that offered a remarkable opportunity to ruin Beauregard's army. That they did not exploit it is probably a factor both of poor visibility and a reflection of the timid mindset of Butler and his lieutenants.

[77]
OR 36, pt. 2, pp. 236-238, 253-254; Cummings, *Yankee Quaker Confederate General*, p. 285.

was all the more true because of the equally obvious fact that Butler's army simply was not going to be pried loose from the James River and cut off from its base of operations—at least, not by Confederate troops advancing from Drewry's Bluff. But what of Whiting, and the column he was supposed to be leading from Petersburg against the Federal rear? As his frontal attack against Butler sputtered out, Beauregard pinned his hopes increasingly on the aspect of his battle plan that he had for the previous two days been assuring the president was inconsequential. All would now hinge on Whiting's timely and forceful arrival.[78]

In Richmond the president and his advisors anxiously awaited news of the battle. At 8:30 a.m. Beauregard had sent word to say that all was proceeding well. Ransom had turned the enemy right and was driving them. "I think," Beauregard stated reassuringly, "I can rely on Whiting's support. Distant firing now heard in direction of Petersburg."[79] A 9:45 a.m. dispatch told of Ransom's delay to replenish ammunition. "When he comes up," expounded a confident Beauregard, "I will push the enemy. . . .I hope soon to make a junction with Whiting." The situation, as far as Davis was concerned, was still encouraging.[80]

Later that morning, a dispatch announced that Hoke had driven the enemy back, "capturing several siege field pieces and many prisoners." It was, Beauregard assured his superiors, "a brilliant success." Conspicuous in its absence was the issue of Whiting, of whom Beauregard said nothing at all. At 1:15 p.m., he wrote that there was "no material change since last dispatch." Beauregard's troops were stationary with the enemy still before them. For the first time the general related something of the damaged condition of his army—"some of the brigades are much cut up"—but he stated hopefully that he was "preparing for a combined attack." That could only mean an assault in concert with the forces moving up from Petersburg, but of them

---

78
  Robertson, *Back Door to Richmond*, p. 194.

79
  OR 36, pt. 2, pp. 196-197.

80
  Ibid., p. 197.

Beauregard only related ominously, "I hear nothing yet of Whiting's movements."[81] That was about as much as the patience of Jefferson Davis could endure. Always eager to take to the battlefield whenever possible, he had his horse saddled and set off for Drewry's Bluff. About midafternoon he rode up and joined Beauregard near the point where the turnpike for Petersburg crossed the Confederate front lines. His presence would probably have been acutely embarrassing to Beauregard in any case. It was made infinitely more so, however, by the fact that the Creole's entire plan of battle was about to founder on precisely the rocks Davis had foreseen and ordered him to steer clear of. Together, silent for the most part, they waited for the sound of firing to the south that would tell them that Whiting had finally moved up and engaged the enemy. The afternoon wore on. Then, from the direction of Petersburg, came the boom of a cannon. "Ah!" said Davis with a smile, "at last!" But after the solitary shot, silence stole down again, and with the passing minutes it became clear that no push was yet being made from the south.[82]

At 5:45 p.m. Beauregard sent word to Bragg back in Richmond that he was still hoping for that "combined attack," but that he had "nothing positive as to position of Whiting save the knowledge that he was at Port Walthall Station [between Petersburg and Drewry's Bluff] this morning at 10 o'clock."[83] As Beauregard's troops waited in formation, prepared to renew the assault, hope of a complete victory on this day faded with the waning light of evening. By 9:30 p.m., Beauregard finally gave up on Whiting. "The approach of darkness," he wired Bragg, "made it imprudent to execute this evening the plan set forth in my dispatch of 5:45 p.m." Although he still hoped to carry out the design at daylight next morning, in conjunction with Whiting, to whom he had been sending dispatches all day urging haste and aggressiveness in joining the concentration against Butler, all was for naught.[84] At 4:00 p.m. that

81
   Ibid.
82
   V. H. Davis, *Jefferson Davis*, 2, p. 520.
83
   OR 36, pt. 2, p. 198.
84
   Ibid.

afternoon, the Federals had begun withdrawing to their base on Bermuda Hundred, and the following morning found Butler and his army well along toward barricading themselves into the peninsula. There, his communications would be secure and no amount of Confederate troops Beauregard was remotely likely to gather would possibly be able to dislodge them.[85]

Why had Whiting failed? What went through the mind of William Henry Chase Whiting on May 16, 1864, is one of the Civil War's enduring command and leadership mysteries. Whiting the general was a puzzle; alternatingly brilliant, temperamental, and unstable. Despite his record-setting academic achievements at West Point, his wartime career is marked by more failure than success. No failure, however, seemed as inexplicable as his simple refusal to make more than the most halfhearted of efforts at moving toward Drewry's Bluff to assist Beauregard in his desperate attempt to crush Butler. A brief and belated advance had stopped at Port Wathall Junction before hurrying back to Petersburg without any discernible reason. Whiting's contemporaries were at a loss to explain his behavior. Some believed it was the result of drunkeness, for Whiting had given himself increasingly to drink during his sojourn at Wilmington. On May 16, one of his brigade commanders observed him mounting a horse with great difficulty and concluded that strong drink was the source of his distress. Still others believed Whiting to have been under the influence of narcotics.[86] Confederate Postmaster General John H. Reagan, who, like Davis, had ridden out to the lines that afternoon to see the action, claimed Whiting later wrote a letter to Davis admitting to intoxication at the time of the battle.[87] If Reagan's improbable claim is to be believed, the letter has since disappeared. Publicly at least, Whiting denied having taken anything stronger than

85
   Robertson, *Back Door to Richmond*, p. 206.

86
   Ibid., pp. 209-215; Freeman, *Lee's Lieutenants*, 3, p. 492; Wise, "The Career of Wise's Brigade," pp. 10-11.

87
   John H. Reagan, *Memoirs, With Special Reference to Secession and the Civil War*, (New York, 1906), p. 191.

coffee during the entire episode. Instead, he claimed his failure was the result of extreme exhaustion and prolonged lack of sleep.[88] Modern historians have tended to accept Whiting's own explanation and suggest that his anxiety may have compounded the problem.[89]

The specific cause of Whiting's failure, however, is largely beside the point. Beauregard's decision to base his plan of battle on the convergence of two separate columns of troops—divided from each other by the enemy's force—created so many possibilities for problems that the chances of one or another of them actually occurring were high to the point of near-certainty. For a general preparing his battle plans, it was not as significant what would go wrong as it was to realize that something almost undoubtedly would go awry. In Beauregard's case, when the unexpected occurred, it was serious enough to destroy the effectiveness of the entire operation. Davis had recognized this and had ordered Beauregard to eliminate from his plan the ill-conceived idea of having Whiting's forces approach the battlefield separately. Beauregard disobeyed this order, and the result was as Davis had foreseen. A malfunction in the plan had ruined the effectiveness of the attack. The specific malfunction was probably a failure of nerve on the part of Whiting, but Beauregard's plan was preprogrammed for failure.

Conclusion

The most striking thing about all of Beauregard's behavior during the campaign is the remarkable continuity with his performances throughout the war: Beauregard at Bermuda Hundred was virtually indistinguishable from the Beauregard of 1861-1862. He did not transcend himself or reveal talents previously obscured by Davis' enmity or unfavorable circumstances. His talents and his failings were as they had been since his arrival on the Manassas line some three years before. In the early days of the crisis he had shown a remarkable

---

[88] Freeman, *Lee's Lieutenants*, 3, p. 493.

[89] Robertson, *Back Door to Richmond*, p. 216n; Freeman, *Lee's Lieutenants*, 3, p. 493.

slowness about going in person to the threatened points; he did not arrive in Petersburg until May 10, by which time the focus of the Union advance had shifted from that point to Drewry's Bluff. Again, he did not depart for the new scene of action until May 13, when it was almost too late to affect the outcome. This reluctance to be in the thick of the campaign did not spring from any lack of physical courage. Beauregard had displayed much of that on the field of First Manassas. Even at Drewry's Bluff, he had stood under enemy artillery fire almost to the point of recklessness. Rather, the delays seem to point to Beauregard's reluctance to take responsibility and make vital decisions. As had been the case in the Western Theater in 1862, the Creole had plenty of courage but not quite enough nerve. In that, he was anything but alone among Civil War officers.

On the other hand, Beauregard had displayed considerable strategic insight in recognizing—well before the Richmond authorities had done so—that the Federals were making a major effort on the south side of the James. Along with Pickett, who from his fortuitous position at Petersburg could hardly have thought otherwise, he may indeed have helped to save Petersburg—and thus Richmond—by his insistent messages calling for the diversion of troops to that sector. Yet, the Creole's worst enemies had never accused him of a lack of strategic ability or mental acuteness. Davis himself had merely suggested, two years earlier, that Beauregard was unable to use his great mental gifts to advantage when placed in a position of extreme responsibility. In this way also, Beauregard in the Bermuda Hundred Campaign had proved true to his earlier form.

His various plans for dealing with Benjamin Butler had shown a characteristic mixture of brilliance with almost absurd flights of fancy. Just as before First Manassas, he had prepared to open his campaign by suggesting to his superiors in Richmond a grandiose and unrealistic scheme for shuffling armies about the country—heedless of issues of transportation and supply—while his enemies inertly stood by to be defeated in detail. Beauregard simply could not resist the temptation to let his overactive imagination run away with him. His plans were elaborate to the point of being unwieldly and unrealistic. This was equally true of his final plan for the battle of Drewry's Bluff. The failure of his unrealistic scheme to unite his and Whiting's forces on the field of battle, from opposite sides of the enemy, had extinguished the last hopes of a decisive Confederate victory south of Richmond. Here too, as in his battle plans for Manassas and Shiloh, Beauregard displayed a characteristic trait that accompanied him throughout the war.

Of course, Butler's army did end up "tightly corked" in the "bottle" formed by the curving loops of the James and Appomattox Rivers at Bermuda Hundred, and Grant was understandably disgusted with Butler's equally inept performance. Still, the Union Army of the James remained intact, dangerous and uncomfortably close to Richmond. Though Beauregard might eventually establish the shortest and most fortified lines he could across the neck of the peninsula, keeping Butler's troops corked would require several thousand southern soldiers that the Confederacy could well have used elsewhere. When Grant finally stole a march on Lee in mid-June, 1864, and crossed the James River for Petersburg, the logistical bases at Bermuda Hundred and City Point, just across the river, were of some considerable value to him. On the whole, Beauregard's failure to win the decisive victory Butler's incompetence offered him cost the Confederacy significantly. Such success as Beauregard did achieve in bottling Butler up at Bermuda Hundred was more the result of Yankee miscues than Rebel tactical or strategic genius.

Thus Beauregard was not, after all, the flawless hero of Petersburg and savior of Richmond, not exactly, anyway. He was, as he had always been, complicated, frustrating, and paradoxical, a general of many excellent parts but unsatisfactory as a whole. As Jefferson Davis rode back to the Confederate White House through the gathering darkness of the evening of May 16, 1864, he might have had much to contemplate in disappointment, but likely very little in surprise. The Louisiana general of Napoleonic pretensions had performed throughout the Bermuda Hundred Campaign precisely as his previous record had given cause to expect.

INDEX

Other Civil War titles available from
Savas Woodbury Publishers

The Campaign for Atlanta & Sherman's March to the Sea, vols. 1-2, edited by Theodore P. Savas and David A. Woodbury. Fifteen essays in a landmark series covering a broad range of topics on the pivotal 1864 campaigns. Three fold-out maps in text and two over-size, 3-color campaign maps in front pocket. 6x9, cloth, d.j., photos, index. 496pp., ISBN 1-882810-26-0 Price: $42.50.

"...a refreshing must for those who dare to reassess these epic campaigns, the leaders, and the challenges posed in the Empire State of the Confederacy more than 130 years ago."
— *Blue & Gray Magazine*

Abraham Lincoln, Contemporary: An American Legacy, edited by Frank J. Williams and William D. Pederson. Original, thought-provoking essays on various aspects of the Lincoln presidency by some of the nation's leading Lincoln scholars. 6x9, cloth, d.j., photos, index, 236pp. Price: $24.95.

Last Stand in the Carolinas: the Battle of Bentonville, March 19-21, 1865, by Mark L. Bradley. A definitive examination of the military events that culminated in the bloody fighting at Bentonville, North Carolina, between the veteran campaigners of William T. Sherman and Gen. Joseph E. Johnston's motley Confederate army. 6x9, hardcover, d.j., photos, 36 maps, index, 471pp. Price: $32.95.

"...Bradley has researched and written a *tour de force*....there has long been a need for a quality history focusing on the Battle of Bentonville." —Edwin C. Bearss, former Chief Historian of the National Park Service

The Red River Campaign, edited by Theodore P. Savas and David A. Woodbury. This special, stand-alone issue of *Civil War Regiments* journal contains five in-depth essays on aspects of the critical, but overlooked 1864 campaign in Louisiana. Introduction by Edwin C. Bearss, Assistant to the Director, Military Sites, National Park Service. 6x9, softcover, photos, maps, index, 157pp. Price: $12.00 ppd.

Blood on the Rappahannock: The Battle of Fredericksburg, edited by Theodore P. Savas and David Woodbury. This special issue of *Civil War Regiments* journal (vol. 4, no. 4), is an inciteful collection of original essays by Park Service historians and others, highlighted by unpublished diary material, all centered on the Dec. 13, 1862 battle. Essays include the death of CSA Gen. Thomas Cobb, the Pennsylvania Reserves, artillery action on the Confederate right, street fighting in Fredericksburg, and an unpublished memoir by a member of the Irish Brigade. 6x9, softcover, photos, maps, index, 156pp. $12.00 ppd.

Civil War Regiments: A Journal of the American Civil War, edited by Theodore P. Savas and David A. Woodbury. Published quarterly by Regimental Studies, Inc., *CWR* is the only fully-footnoted, non-partisan Civil War periodical available which showcases in-depth articles on military events in all theaters of the war. Each 120+ page softbound book contains meticulously researched articles by leading scholars in the field, original maps tailored for each essay, and comprehensive book reviews of current Civil War titles. 6x9, 120+ pages, photos, maps, index. Subscriptions: $27.00/year (4 books) ppd.

Coming in 1995/1996

Capital Navy: Confederate Naval Operations on the James River, by John Coski. This major new study by a staff historian at the Museum of the Confederacy in Richmond is the first book-length account examining the critical role played by the makeshift Southern navy on the James River. Hardcover, d.j., photos, maps, index, approx. 253pp. 6x9.

The Last Rays of Departing Hope: The Wilmington Campaign, by Chris Fonvielle. A compelling account of the complicated series of Federal combined operations designed to capture one of the most important cities in the Confederacy. Inquire as to availability.

Cleburne's Guard: Granbury's Texas Brigade, by Danny Sessums. The first comprehensive study of Confederate Brig. Gen. Hiram Bronson Granbury and his famous Texas Brigade, with appendices, rosters, and detailed tactical maps. Inquire as to availability.

The Battle of Carthage, July 5, 1861, by David C. Hinze. The only full-length study of this early war engagement in Missouri. Includes modern "guided tour" of sites associated with the battle. Inquire as to availability.

The Campaign for Atlanta & Sherman's March to the Sea, vol. 3: The Death Roster, compiled by William E. Erquitt. A unique military and genealogical reference work containing the names and original burial sites of over 3,000 Federal soldiers. Inquire as to availability.

The Battle of Secessionville, by Patrick Brennan. Brennan's work on Secessionville marks the first in-depth study of that June 16, 1862 battle near Charleston—the definitive examination of an overlooked Federal repulse. Inquire as to availability.

Savas Woodbury Publishers

1475 S. Bascom Avenue, Ste. 204, Campbell, CA 95008, (800) 848-6585

Call or write for a free catalog

Please add $3.00 shipping and handling for the first book, and $1.50 for each additional book